Principles of
Artificial Intelligence
and Expert Systems
Development

Principles of Artificial Intelligence and Expert Systems Development

David W. Rolston

ESL, Inc., a subsidiary of TRW, Inc.,
Sunnyvale, California

McGraw-Hill Book Company

New York   St. Louis   San Francisco   Auckland
Bogotá   Hamburg   London   Madrid   Mexico
Milan   Montreal   New Delhi   Panama
Paris   São Paulo   Singapore
Sydney   Tokyo   Toronto

Library of Congress Cataloging-in-Publication Data

Rolston, David W.
    Principles of artificial intelligence and expert
systems development.

    Bibliography: p.
    Includes index.
    1. Expert systems (Computer science)   2. Artificial
intelligence.   3. Computer software—Development.
I. Title.
QA76.76.E95R65   1988   006.3   87-22645
ISBN 0-07-053614-7

    4 5 6 7 8 9 0   DOC/DOC   9 9 8 7 6 5 4 3 2 1

ISBN   0-07-053614-7

*The editors for this book were Theron R. Shreve and Galen H.
Fleck, the designer was Naomi Auerbach, and the production
supervisor was Richard A. Ausburn. It was set in Century
Schoolbook by Techna Type, Inc.*

Printed and bound by R. R. Donnelley & Sons Company.

To Vicki, Amy, LeAnne, and Chad

Contents

Preface

The goal of this book is to provide computer science professionals and students with a readable and understandable introduction to the concepts and techniques of expert systems (ESs) and the underlying artificial intelligence (AI) technology.

The presentation style is pragmatic and development-oriented. It is geared to developers who want to know how to build an ES rather than philosophers who are attempting to answer (admittedly interesting) can-computer-really-think questions. Throughout the book specific fundamental principles of AI and ES development are extracted and explicitly presented, thus allowing the reader to gain a solid introductory understanding as rapidly as possible.

The development of this book is based on the assumption that the reader has a solid background in computer science (gained through study and/or practice) but not in AI. As a result, the first five chapters provide an introduction to AI; they focus on concepts that are especially important as ES foundations. The AI section is intended to provide the reader with an understanding of the essence of what constitutes an AI approach, along with an understanding of the components of an AI system.

Chapters 6 to 11 describe the application of AI concepts within the domain of ES. Each of these chapters focuses on one aspect of ES development—knowledge acquisition and deals with uncertainty, system organization, explanation, resolution (as an example of formal inference), and the development process itself. The scope of this presentation is broad: As many alternative views as possible are presented, and no one approach is advocated. The objective is to familiarize the reader with the collection of camps that comprise the ES community.

Chapter 12 is a detailed description of an actual implementation that has been very successfully and routinely applied to solve real-world problems. It is intended to illustrate how the material presented in the preceding chapters relates to real-world development. The direct application of theoretical principles is described, and the need for compromise is demonstrated.

Although this book is development-oriented, it is not intended as a detailed implementation guide. Detailed language discussions are not presented both to keep the book of manageable size and to avoid cluttering an understanding of significant concepts with relatively insignificant side issues. Moreover, because the world of languages and tools is constantly changing and evolving, today's valid description is tomorrow's antiquation. Brief overviews of Lisp, Prolog, and development tools are, however, presented for readers who have not been introduced to those areas. The overviews allow the reader to develop at least a feel for the subjects.

Although this book is primarily intended for computer science professionals, it can also be very useful as a primary reference in an AI/ES undergraduate course or as a supplementary reference in a graduate course. References to the literature are included throughout the book to allow the reader to pursue each area in much greater depth.

Above all else, this book is intended to allow the person who has become intrigued with the ideas of AI and ES to break into those worlds as quickly as possible. It is a book for beginning serious work in the areas.

David W. Rolston

An Introduction to Expert Systems

This chapter provides a very basic overview of expert systems and introduces fundamental concepts. It briefly introduces many terms, each of which is explained in greater detail in later chapters. Readers who have previously been exposed to expert systems may wish to begin with Chap. 2.

Expert systems (ESs) are used to perform a variety of extremely complicated tasks that in the past could be performed by only a limited number of highly trained human experts. Through the application of *artificial intelligence* (AI) techniques, ESs capture the basic knowledge that allows a human to act as an expert when dealing with complicated problems.

Perhaps the most intriguing and powerful characteristic of ESs, and that which distinguishes them from more traditional computer applications, is their capability to deal with challenging real-world problems through the application of processes that reflect human judgment and intuition.

ESs are being used in a wide variety of applications including diagnosis, planning, forecasting, design, interpretation, control, status monitoring, and instruction. In the future, as new hardware architectures that directly support ES execution are developed and AI technology matures, it is reasonable to expect the development of systems that asymptotically approach expert human behavior in many areas.

Development of such systems will allow us not only to provide very powerful technical capabilities but also to further nurture our own understanding of human thought processes.

1.1 Definition of an Expert System

An ES is a computer application that solves complicated problems that would otherwise require extensive human expertise. To do so, it simulates the human reasoning process by applying specific *knowledge* and *inferences.*

Internally, an ideal ES can be characterized as including the following:

- Extensive specific knowledge from the *domain* of interest
- Application of *search* techniques
- Support for *heuristic* analysis
- Capacity to infer new knowledge from existing knowledge
- *Symbolic* processing
- An ability to explain its own reasoning

TABLE 1.1 Early Expert Systems

System	Date	Author	Subject
Dendral	1965	Stanford	Infers information about chemical structures
Macsyma	1965	MIT	Performs complex mathematical analysis
Hearsay	1965	Carnegie-Mellon	Natural-language interpretation for subset language
Age	1973	Stanford	Expert-system-generation tool
Mycin	1972	Stanford	Diagnosis of blood disease
Teiresias	1972	Stanford	Knowledge transformation tool
Prospector	1972	Stanford Res. Inst.	Mineral exploration and identification tool
Rosie	1978	Rand	Expert-system-building tool
OPS5	1974	Carnegie-Mellon	Expert-system-building tool
R1	1978	Carnegie-Mellon	Configurator for DEC computer equipment
Caduceus	1975	Univ. of Pittsburgh	Diagnostic tool for internal medicine

1.2   History of Expert System Development

The technology represented by current ESs is an outgrowth of AI techniques that have been the subject of intensive research since the late 1950s. Related research began in the area of languages to support symbolic reasoning. The programming language IPL, the first symbolic, list-processing language, was used extensively in early AI implementations. Lisp, currently one of the most popular languages for artificial intelligence, was developed by John McCarthy in 1958.

Research specific to ESs actually began in the middle 1960s. Several systems were developed between 1965 and 1970; most of them were very limited in scope and were directed toward games or highly academic, idealized subjects. Table 1.1 presents several systems that are of particular interest, primarily because they form much of the technical and historical base of ES technology. Although ES development is still relatively new, there are currently many ESs in use by a wide variety of organizations for many different applications [Buchanan, 1986; Waterman, 1986].

1.3   Analysis of Expert Problem Solving

There are individuals who have summarized their view of expert behavior by stating that an expert is someone who "carries a briefcase and is more than 50 miles from home." If, however, we are to simulate the process that a human expert uses to solve a complex problem, we must first establish a clear understanding of the process.

Consider, for example, an airline pilot's response to a warning light that indicates an impending electrical failure. For discussion purposes, assume that the pilot must decide whether to execute an emergency landing, shut down one engine, or ignore the warning entirely. In addition, assume the following events occur:

The pilot quickly formulates a plan which is as follows:

- Attempt to verify the warning light.
- If the warning is invalid, make a note in the log and continue normal flight, ignoring the warning.
- If the warning is valid and only one engine is involved, shut down the offending engine.
- If the warning is valid and more than one engine is involved, execute an emergency landing.

The pilot begins to execute this plan by attempting to verify the warning light. The verification process consists in observing the general condition of the airplane, checking the flight instruments, and asking the flight attendants to report any unusual conditions. Upon checking the flight instruments, the pilot notes that the attitude indicator shows level flight and the vertical speed indicator indicates that the airplane is dropping at 4000 ft/min. The pilot, noting that the instruments with the conflicting readings are driven electrically and observing the cabin lights flicker, concludes that the warning is valid.

The pilot then attempts to determine whether the problem can be isolated to the electrical generation system in a single engine. He or she attempts to make this determination by executing a series of diagnostic tests by using the on-board flight computer. The results of the test are inconclusive. Five tests indicate that only one engine is involved, and one test indicates a general-system failure. The pilot is also concerned about the general reliability of the test results in light of the fact that the questionable electrical system also powers the computer that executes the tests.

The pilot concludes that an emergency landing should be initiated, based on the general principle that it is better to attempt an emergency landing in a controlled condition than to continue flying in an unknown condition.

It can also be observed that the pilot must attempt to approach an objective (i.e., avoiding passenger inconvenience) while maintaining several constraints (e.g., passenger safety). In addition, it is significant that the pilot has to perform the task very quickly.

1.4   Role of Knowledge in Expert Systems

The pilot in the above example displayed two distinct forms of expertise. First, he or she understood the basic procedure for approaching a problem. This is a rather general form of expertise that is common across many domains. The same basic problem-solving techniques would probably have been employed by a ship's captain faced with a similar situation. Early research in AI focused heavily on scrutinizing this aspect of expert behavior. The second form of expertise applied by the pilot was *domain-specific knowledge*. This form of expertise permeates the pilot's entire response.

The significance of specific knowledge can be further illustrated by considering the contrast between the pilot's observation of the instrument readings and the nonpilot's typical response to the cockpit of a major airliner. Most nonpilots, even if very intelligent, view such an area as a morass of instruments, gauges, and controls.

A ship's captain's understanding of airplane instruments probably would not be significantly greater than that of an individual who possessed no expert abilities. That is in spite of the fact that the captain may spend considerable time at sea engaged in expert activities, many of which are very similar to the pilot's activities.

This observation yields a principle that is very fundamental to the design of expert systems. It was elucidated as long ago as 1547, when Francis Bacon wrote, "knowledge is power."

PRINCIPLE 1.1: An expert's power derives from extensive domain-specific knowledge rather than from an understanding of generic expert behavior.

The impact of ESs accelerated rapidly when recognition of Principle 1.1 began to influence research in the late 1970s. The principle is now widely accepted as foundational.

1.5 Analysis of Knowledge

There are many components of the knowledge that is the source of an expert's ability to perform. They may be viewed generally as:

- *Facts.* Statements that relate some element of truth regarding the subject domain. For example:
  Milk is white.
  Ceramic tile adhesive will not stick to concrete that is less than 2 months old.
  A Boeing 747 will fly safely on three engines.

- *Procedural rules.* Well-defined, invariant rules that describe fundamental sequences of events and relations relative to the domain. For example:
  Always check the traffic before attempting to merge onto the freeway.
  If the attitude indicator shows level flight, the vertical speed indicator should read zero.

- *Heuristic rules.* General rules in the form of hunches or rules of thumb that suggest procedures to be followed when invariant procedural rules are not available. These are approximate and have generally been gathered by an expert through years of experience. For example:
  If a chain saw appears to be OK but still will not start, loosen the tension on the chain.
  It is better to attempt an emergency landing under controlled conditions than to fly in an unknown condition.

The presence of heuristics contributes greatly to the *power* and *flexibility* of ESs and tends to distinguish ESs from more traditional software.

In addition to these specific forms of knowledge, an expert also has a *general conceptual model* of the subject domain and an *overall scheme* for finding a solution. These "global views" form a basic framework for the expert's application of detailed knowledge.

1.6 Architecture of Expert Systems

ESs use a wide variety of specific system architectures, primarily because one architecture will be more applicable than another for a given application. Extensive research is currently in progress to investigate various aspects of ES architectures, and considerable debate remains.

In spite of significant differences, most of the architectures have several general components in common. Figure 1.1 shows a general architecture with the typical components. The following sections provide further details regarding each of the components from Fig. 1.1.

User

The user of an expert system can be operating in any of several modes:

- *Tester.*   User attempts to verify the validity of the system's behavior.
- *Tutor.*   User provides additional knowledge to the system or modifies knowledge already present in the system.
- *Pupil.*   User seeks to rapidly develop personal expertise relative to the subject domain by extracting organized, distilled knowledge from the system.
- *Customer.*   User applies the system's expertise to a specific real task.

The recognition of the above roles is in contrast to the more typical recognition of only one role (the customer) for traditional software systems.

User interface facility

The *user interface facility* must accept information from the user and translate it into a form acceptable to the remainder of the system or accept information from the system and convert it to a form that can be understood by the user.

Ideally, this facility consists of a *natural-language-processing system* that accepts and returns information in essentially the same form as that accepted or provided by a human expert. While there are no systems today that duplicate natural-language capabilities, there are several that have demonstrated impressive results through the use of restricted language subsets.

User interface facilities for ESs are often designed to recognize the mode in which the user is operating, the level of the user's expertise,

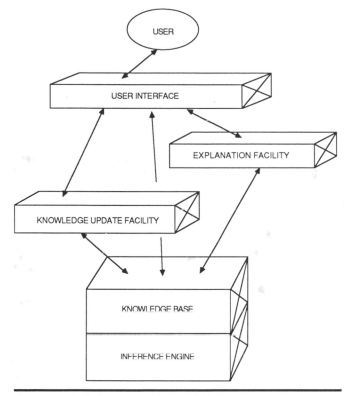

Figure 1.1 Typical expert system architecture.

and the nature of the transaction. Even though natural-language dialog is not yet fully feasible, the communications with an ES should be as natural as possible in light of the fact that the system is attempting to substitute for human behavior.

Knowledge storage and generation system

The *knowledge storage and generation system* consists of a *knowledge base* and an *inference engine*. It is the heart of an ES. It is the function of this system to safestore expert knowledge, to retrieve knowledge from storage, and to infer new knowledge when it is required.

Knowledge base. The knowledge base represents a storehouse of the *knowledge primitives* (i.e., basic facts, procedural rules, and heuristics) available to the system. As described in Principle 1.1, the knowledge stored in the base establishes the system's capability to act as an expert.

In general, knowledge is stored in the form of facts and rules, but the specific schemes used for storing the information vary greatly. The design of this *knowledge representation scheme* impacts the design of the inference engine, the knowledge updating process, the explanation process, and the overall efficiency of the system.

PRINCIPLE 1.2: The selection of the knowledge representation scheme is one of the most critical decisions in ES design.

Knowledge engineering. *Knowledge engineering* is the process of acquiring specific-domain knowledge and building it into the knowledge base. Figure 1.2 illustrates this process as it typically occurs. Although knowledge can be secured from a variety of sources, including documentation and existing computer information systems, most of it must be elicited from human experts. The knowledge provided by the expert will generally be in a form that is oriented toward the subject domain.

A *knowledge engineer* (KE) is the person who *acquires* the knowledge from the domain expert and transports it to the knowledge base. Because the ES requires that knowledge in the knowledge base be stored in accordance with the system's knowledge representation convention, the KE must *transform* the representation of the knowledge as a part of the transportation process.

To acquire the necessary knowledge, the KE must first establish an overall understanding of the domain, form a mental dictionary of the domain's essential vocabulary and jargon, and develop a fundamental understanding of the key concepts. He or she must then distill succinct knowledge from the information provided by the expert.

The knowledge acquisition function is frequently the most difficult aspect of ES development. This is due primarily to the fact that the process requires extended human communications between the domain expert and the KE and, therefore, suffers from the associated problems.

As a result, the knowledge acquisition process is not well understood and is not well defined. If the ES development process were itself viewed

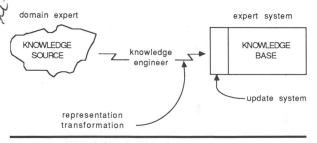

Figure 1.2   Knowledge engineering.

as an expert domain, the knowledge associated with the knowledge acquisition process would be considered heuristic.

Inference engine.   ESs must, by their nature, deal flexibly with varying situations. The capability to respond to varying situations depends on an ability to infer new knowledge from existing knowledge. As a simple example of an inference, consider the following two basic facts:

1. All animals breathe oxygen.
2. All dogs are animals.

A new fact, "All dogs breathe oxygen," can be inferred from those two facts. To respond to a given situation, an ES must apply appropriate knowledge. For example, in the airplane illustration described earlier, the pilot must apply the fact that a Boeing 747 will fly safely on three engines. Applying the appropriate knowledge implies that the required knowledge was either located as existing knowledge in the knowledge base or was inferred from existing knowledge.

PRINCIPLE 1.3: The process of searching for appropriate knowledge and from it inferring new knowledge is a key element of expert system processing.

Of course, it would have been entirely valid to store the "All dogs breathe oxygen" fact directly in the knowledge base rather than requiring that it be inferred from the knowledge primitives during execution.

One of the greatest difficulties involved in operating from primitives is the fact that even a few individual elements (i.e., primitives) can be combined into a very large number of unique combinations. The number of possibilities from a large set of elements quickly becomes astronomical. This problem is known as *combinatorial explosion*. To overcome the problem, most ESs rely on the use of *compiled knowledge*—high-level knowledge that has been generated in a "background mode" through years of experience—rather than attempt to actually operate from primitives.

The *inference engine* is the software system that locates knowledge and infers new knowledge from the base knowledge. The engine's *inference paradigm* is the search strategy that is used to develop required knowledge. Many different paradigms are used in an ES, but most are based on one of two fundamental concepts: *backward chaining*, which is a top-down reasoning process that starts from the desired goals and works backward toward requisite conditions, or *forward chaining*, which is a bottom-up reasoning process that starts with known conditions and works toward the desired goal.

PRINCIPLE 1.4: The selection of the inference paradigm, with consideration for combinatorial explosion, strongly influences the overall performance of an ES.

Knowledge update

Presumably, the knowledge base is an accurate reflection of the domain at the time the system is placed in service. Unfortunately, knowledge in many complex domains is constantly expanding and changing and the knowledge base must be modified correspondingly. The *knowledge update facility* is used to perform such updates. This process can take one of three basic forms, as described below.

The first form is *manual knowledge update*. In this case the update is performed by a KE who interprets information provided by a domain expert and updates the knowledge base by using a limited knowledge update system.

In the second form, which represents the state of the art in ESs, the domain expert enters the revised knowledge directly, without a knowledge engineer's mediation. The knowledge update system in this case must be much more sophisticated.

In the third form, *machine learning,* new knowledge is generated automatically by the system and is based on generalizations drawn from past experience. The system, in effect, learns from experience and so, ideally, is self-updating. This process, which is still in a conceptual state, is the subject of much research. The ability to learn is an important component of intelligence, and fully providing this capability would greatly enhance the power of an ES.

PRINCIPLE 1.5: In an ideal ES the inference engine would never need modification.

Ideally, all enhancements of the knowledge system are implemented by expanding the knowledge base. It is, however, rarely possible to ensure complete independence of the knowledge base and the inference engine.

Explanation system

Beyond simply reaching a conclusion when faced with a complex problem, an expert is also capable of explaining, to some extent, the reasoning that led to the conclusion. An ES should be designed to provide a similar capability. This is an important facility that is generally missing from traditional computer systems.

The explanation typically consists of an identification of the steps in the reasoning process and a justification for each step. Providing the capability to communicate this information is, in essence, a subset of the natural-language-processing problem. The system must access a record of the knowledge that was used in processing, based on the representation scheme of the knowledge base, and translate it into a form that is palatable to the user.

PRINCIPLE 1.6: The credibility afforded an ES depends on the ES's ability to explain its own reasoning process.

A human expert may also be capable of explaining reasoning in a form that is tailored to the listener's level of expertise. An airline pilot might, for example, explain to the passengers that, "The flight was terminated prematurely due to technical difficulties." To another pilot the equivalent explanation might be, "I got a T-37 [warning light] that looked like the inboard port fan [engine]. I couldn't plug it [shut down], so I went in [landed]."

To provide discriminating levels of explanation, the system must recognize the user's level of expertise and understand how to tailor the explanation to match. The explanation facility in many current systems is limited to simply listing the rules that were employed during execution.

1.7 Programming Languages for Expert Systems

In general, expert systems programming focuses on issues of inference and heuristic search and depends heavily on the manipulation of *symbols:* strings of characters (i.e., "names") that are freely used to represent any possible element from the domain.

The programming languages Lisp and Prolog are by far the most common languages used in ES development, although more conventional languages—especially C—are coming into more common use. Lisp is conceptually a *functional language;* every statement in the language is a description of a function. Prolog is conceptually a *logic language;* every statement in the language is an expression in a formal logic syntax.

Symbolic processing is important in ESs because the knowledge primitives in a knowledge base, and the relationships between the knowledge primitives, are stored by using symbolic representations. It is useful if programming languages for ES can deal freely with "things" without being concerned with the composition of those things.

The relative merits of Lisp vs. Prolog vs. other candidate languages are a source of continuing debate. Although the basis of these arguments is sometimes traditional and geographical rather than technical, it is certainly true that each language is more suitable to certain applications than the others. In addition, the languages that are most popular (i.e., Lisp) are strongly supported by established software development tools.

As the rate of ES development increases, and as new hardware architectures develop, it is probable that new symbolic languages will grow in popularity. Considerable research is also being directed toward the development of languages that combine functional (e.g., Lisp) and logical (e.g., Prolog) characteristics. As such languages come into more common use, it is reasonable to expect the evolution of more sophisticated development tools.

1.8   Development Process

The ES development process consists of several basic stages that are similar to the standard software engineering life cycle segments. These stages consist of problem identification, prototype construction, formalization, implementation, evaluation, and long-term evolution.

Without exception, the first task in any ES development is to establish that the proposed problem is suitable for, and requires, an ES solution. If the problem under consideration can be described in terms of direct definitions and algorithms, it is probably preferable to develop a traditional software solution. If it is ill-defined or requires intensive human judgment (e.g., judging an art contest), it is probably too complex for an expert system.

After the selection of an appropriate problem, a small prototype is constructed to assist in understanding the complete problem and estimating the task of building the complete solution. The next step in the development process is to formalize the problem statement and design the complete ES. Following the formalization, the implementation is conducted. It consists primarily of a continuing cycle of knowledge acquisition, knowledge base update, and test.

The evaluation phase, which follows implementation, is intended to evaluate the extent to which the system approaches the expert's behavior. Following evaluation and release, the ES enters a period of long-term evolution. During this period, the system continues to grow in competency (based on the experience of use) and is revised in response to changes in domain knowledge.

1.9   Current State of Expert System Development

Current ESs have been categorized as falling into three general classes [Davis, 1985]:

1. *Assistant.*   A small* knowledge-based system that performs an economically valuable but technically limited subset of an expert's task. Many "assistants" are PC-based.

2. *Colleague.*   A medium-size knowledge-based system that performs a significant subset of an expert's task. "Colleagues" are implemented on both PCs and larger platforms (e.g., specialized workstations and conventional mainframe computers).

3. *Expert.*   A large knowledge-based system that approaches an expert's level of performance within a given domain. Experts are normally implemented on powerful platforms by using sophisticated development tools.

In recent years the term "expert system" has been applied quite generally. All of the above classes of systems are called expert systems because they rely on an expert as a knowledge source and are implemented by using knowledge-based techniques. Most existing systems (and some of the most economically valuable ones) fall into the colleague or assistant class. Few existing systems could actually come close to replacing a human expert in a complex domain.

The concepts and functionalities described in this text are applicable to all of the above classes, although some may be omitted from assistant and colleague systems. It is also important to recognize that, although existing ESs are powerful and very useful, there is a very definite limit to the capabilities of the current state of the art. Typical systems have the following limitations:

- Knowledge is acquired from a small number of human experts.

- Application is to a limited specific domain or a small collection of domains.

- The application domain must have little need for temporal or spatial reasoning.

---

*Relative size factors are described in greater detail in later chapters.

- The task does not rely on the use of a large body of general or commonsense knowledge.

- The knowledge required to perform the task is reasonably complete, correct, and stable.

Although such limitations exist, there are still many domains that are appropriate for ES application. The remaining chapters of this book describe the AI concepts that are the foundation of ESs and then provide increasingly detailed descriptions of the internal operation and implementation of ESs.

Artificial Intelligence Problem-Solving Concepts

To understand the internal structure and workings of ESs, we must first develop an understanding of basic AI problem-solving concepts, because ESs are an application of AI techniques.* We begin by considering the question, "What is AI?"

AI represents a large body of concepts and techniques that has been developed by many researchers since the late 1950s. During this period, many definitions of AI have appeared, but none has been generally accepted. For the purposes of this text we will start with the following general definition:

> AI is the computer-based solution of complex problems through the application of processes that are analogous to the human reasoning process.

This definition is intended to serve as a launching point. Specifically, it attempts to skirt such interesting but traditionally controversial issues as "What is true intelligence?" and "Can a computer ever be made to actually think?"

---

* The focus of this discussion will be on AI concepts that relate to ESs.

2.1   The Two-Pail Problem

To observe different fundamental approaches to problem solving, consider the following classic problem:

> **Problem 2.1** We are given two empty water pails, one with a capacity of 6 gal and the other with a capacity of 8 gal. Given that we can fill either pail at will, how do we get the 8-gal pail exactly half full? (Assume there are no measuring marks on either pail.)

The first step in our solution process (using any approach) is to observe that several different actions would allow us to change the amount of water in each pail. The problem solution involves executing some sequence of those actions. Table 2.1 lists the actions, along with a description of the conditions under which each action can be applied.

The most straightforward approach would be to simply implement a *specific* solution to this particular problem. The developer would first determine, through whatever means necessary, a particular sequence of actions that would achieve the desired result. For example, one such sequence is 2, 6, 2, 7, 3, 6. The developer would then implement a program by simply encoding this sequence into a language recognized by the computer.

This approach results in a *hard-wired* implementation that executes more efficiently than any other type because it goes *directly* from beginning to end without any wasted effort along the way. In addition, it certainly meets the problem's stated requirements.

To approach this problem in a fundamentally different way, rather

TABLE 2.1   Operations for Prob. 2.1

Action number	Action	Condition for application
1	Fill the 8-gal pail.	8-gal pail is not full.
2	Fill the 6-gal pail.	6-gal pail is not full.
3	Dump the 8-gal pail.	8-gal pail is not empty.
4	Dump the 6-gal pail.	6-gal pail is not empty.
5	Empty the 8-gal pail into the 6-gal pail.	6-gal pail is not full, and the 8-gal pail not empty. The combined content is ≤ 6 gal.
6	Empty the 6-gal pail into the 8-gal pail.	8-gal pail is not full, and the 6-gal pail is not empty. The combined content is ≤ 8 gal.
7	Fill the 8-gal pail from the 6-gal pail.	8-gal pail is not full, and the 6-gal pail is not empty. The combined content is ≥ 8 gal.
8	Fill the 6-gal pail from the 8-gal pail.	6-gal pail is not full, and the 8-gal pail is not empty. The combined content is ≥ 6 gal.

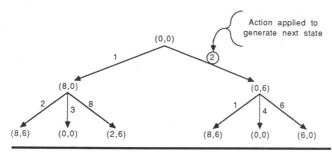

Figure 2.1   Partial state space for Problem 2.1.

than have the developer determine and encode a complete solution to the specific problem, we could provide a more *general* representation of the *problem environment* and allow the computer to *search* for a solution within the bounds of that environment.

The first step in this approach is to view the problem environment as a specific space that is composed of a collection of discrete states that represent possible configurations of the elements involved in the problem. For Prob. 2.1, consider states that represent the contents of the pails and define the pair (E,S) to represent the state that corresponds to a volume of E in the 8-gal pail and a volume of S in the 6-gal pail. Thus a state of $(1,2)$ indicates that the 8-gal pail contains 1 gal and the 6-gal pail contains 2 gal. Because the pails are originally empty, the starting state is $(0,0)$.

Given some known state, we can identify another valid state by applying the appropriate action from Table 2.1. For example, if we start with state $(0,0)$ and apply rule 1, the resulting state is $(8,0)$.

By using this concept, we can develop a *state space* (also called a *problem space*) that includes all the possible states for the given problem. Figure 2.1 shows a portion of the state space for Prob. 2.1, which is represented graphically as a tree. Given this problem representation, the solution process amounts to searching for a path that leads from the starting state to the required state (i.e., any state in which E has a value of 4).

2.2   Analysis of Artificial Intelligence Techniques

The first problem approach (the *direct method* from Prob. 2.1) represents an admittedly extreme example of the technique that has traditionally been used to develop software. A direct technique can be very loosely described as:

> Implementation of a program that executes, in a "prepackaged" form, the results of a developer's reasoning regarding a specific problem.

The *variability* of a direct program typically relates only to the program's ability to accept varying input data; the solution process is hardwired into the program. Some of the advantages of this technique are the following.

- A direct implementation is efficient in terms of both execution speed and required storage space. This advantage results from the fact that the program has been streamlined to address a localized problem. It makes no attempt to be all things to all people.

- It can be relatively easy to develop a direct implementation because it addresses a specific problem, especially when the problem is relatively simple.

- Direct techniques are well suited for solving problems whose difficulty is based primarily on the volume of data or the number of repetitions involved rather than on the complexity of the required reasoning. This type of problem is difficult for humans but easy for computers.

The following are the disadvantages of the technique.

- The reasoning process tends to be opaque. It is therefore difficult for an outside observer to understand how the program reasons.

- Direct implementations tend to be fragile. They are relatively inflexible, and any change to the problem statement normally requires at least some reanalysis and modification of the program by the developer.

- The problem and the required actions must be fully and exactly stated, and complete data must be available.

Many people have described the policies and procedures for highly bureaucratic organizations as plans designed by geniuses to be executed by idiots. Taken in the extreme, a direct computer implementation is analogous to this type of human plan.

In contrast to the direct approach, the AI approach is based on the following principle:

PRINCIPLE 2.1: AI techniques explicitly attempt to move the reasoning process into the program.

To actually develop an AI solution to Prob. 2.1, we would provide the system with the problem representation and the knowledge from Table 2.1 and encode the search process. Figure 2.2 shows the basic concept of an AI technique and the elements that are included.

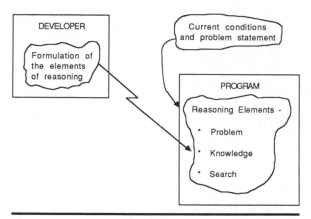

Figure 2.2 Artificial intelligence problem-solving method.

Some of the advantages of an AI approach (in a very idealized sense) are the following:

- Because the reasoning process is internal to it, an AI implementation can be made aware of its own reasoning. It can use this awareness to control the reasoning process and to make execution visible to the program developer and the user.

- An AI implementation is relatively flexible, and so it is less fragile. Because the system is applying flexible reasoning dynamically, it is often able to perform some portion of the task when faced with partially incomplete or inaccurate data, and it can often adapt to modified problem statements. Problems with varing requirements and partially incomplete or inaccurate data are relatively easy for a human, but they are relatively difficult for a computer using direct implementation methods.

- Because the knowledge is separated from the reasoning process, it can be updated without modifying the reasoning mechanism. This is impossible in canned solutions because the domain knowledge is intertwined with the reasoning process.

- AI techniques, because of the power of their internal reasoning processes, can be used to solve very complex problems, specifically, the problems that, because of their complexity, are the most difficult to solve through more direct methods.

In essence, AI implementations attempt to apply the well-established maxim that, in the long run, it is much better to teach a hungry man to fish than it is to simply give him a fish.

The disadvantages of an AI approach are the following:

- An AI implementation will generally run less efficiently than a corresponding direct implementation, primarily because of the overhead involved in searching for a solution. This difficulty is exacerbated by tasks that are highly repetitive.

- To develop an AI solution, the program developer must reason about his or her own reasoning. In many cases a developer can find a valid technique for solving a problem but can't actually describe how the solution was developed.

- If a problem is clearly deterministic, a complete, efficient solution algorithm can be defined, and it is unlikely that the problem will be changed significantly, then an AI implementation is probably a case of overkill; it is somewhat akin to the often-cited use of a sledgehammer to kill a fly.

- Although, as noted earlier, an AI implementation is able to explain its reasoning during execution, it is often difficult to develop an a priori description of the program's actions because they are determined dynamically.

2.3 Criteria for Success

A well-known procedure for evaluating the level of success of an AI program is the Turing test [Turing, 1963]. In the Turing test a human interrogator communicates, via text input and output, with an AI system and with another human who is participating in the test. The interrogator is not aware of which responses come from the computer and which come from the human. If, after sufficient questioning, the interrogator cannot differentiate between the human and the computer, then the AI system passes the test and is deemed successful. No existing AI system would pass a true Turing test, nor is it likely that there will be such a system in the foreseeable future.

Although the Turing test is interesting, especially from a philosophical viewpoint, it is, fortunately, possible for an ES (or any AI system) to be of great practical value even though it fails such a test. When considering the practical criteria for success of an ES, we begin with the following:

PRINCIPLE 2.2: An ES addresses a specific problem domain. It does not attempt to approach human capabilities in all areas.

The next step in establishing the criteria for success is to consider our expectations regarding ourselves as humans. When we go to the produce section of a grocery store to buy a tomato, we normally, after brief deliberation, select the first tomato that meets our standards (i.e., it looks and feels as a tomato is supposed to look and feel).

We could, of course, approach the problem in a more precise way. We could attempt to select the optimum tomato by first establishing specific definitions of desirable characteristics (e.g., acidity, color, firmness, sugar content, weight, and shoulder slope) and then precisely measure each candidate against the criteria.

We omit such precise evaluation because we associate little added utility with the selection of the optimum tomato vs. the selection of the first tomato that meets the general standards of acceptability.

PRINCIPLE 2.3: We expect consistently acceptable performance from a human, but we don't demand optimum solutions in all cases.

This concept is directly transferable to ESs:

PRINCIPLE 2.4: An ES seeks a *satisficing* [Simon, 1981] solution—one that is good enough to get the job done even though it may not be an optimum solution.

We have, historically, and frequently unknowingly, become adjusted to equating a "computer solution" with an extremely precise and accurate solution. This is due primarily to the fact that computers have traditionally been used to address numerical problems that require a high degree of precision.

PRINCIPLE 2.5: The level of accuracy and precision required for a solution to satisfice is dictated by the problem domain.

The term "satisfice" should not be confused with "sloppy" or "poor quality." Although the satisficing criteria for a tomato are quite general, we will probably insist on very stringent criteria when selecting a diamond or a heart surgeon.

2.4 Problem Solving in Artificial Intelligence

The following sections describe the components of AI problem solving in greater detail.

Before a problem can be solved, it must be formally represented. As an example of a formal problem representation consider a more formal description of the process for developing the *state-space representation* that was introduced for Prob. 2.1:

1. Define the problem environment as a collection of states in which each state corresponds to a unique configuration of the domain elements. This collection is called the *state space*.
2. Define the *start states* within the space. These correspond to the initial problem conditions, and they are used to initiate the search process.
3. Define the *goal states* that correspond to acceptable problem solutions. The search process terminates when it reaches a goal state.
4. Define a set of operators and rules that identify the conditions that must be met to apply the corresponding operator. Movement from one state to another is accomplished through the application of one operator.

It is frequently beneficial to use a state-space in a graphical form, as introduced in Fig. 2.1. We begin the development of such a graph by using the start state as a root node. We then develop, one by one, the states that result from applying each applicable operator to the start state. These resultant states are called *successor nodes*.

The graph is generated by entering the successor nodes and drawing directed arcs from the start state to the successor nodes. Each arc is labeled with the name of the operator that created it. This process continues, starting each time with the states that resulted from the previous construction. The generation of a path is complete when a goal state has been generated, and the overall process is complete when all goal states have been generated. Although the graphical representation shown in Fig. 2.1 is a tree, in general it is a directed acyclic graph (DAG)—a (possibly infinite) network structure where the allowable arcs between nodes are restricted only by the fact that the directions on the arcs must prevent cycles on the graph.

Although conceptually, and implicitly, we represent all possible states in the state space, the search process deals with only the *search space*—a limited portion of the complete space that is explicitly constructed during the search process.

The construction of the search space is controlled by an overall *control strategy* that systematically selects a path from multiple alternatives. At any given point, the job of the control strategy is to decide which operator to execute next. Many powerful strategies have been developed to support AI applications. In the following sections basic search concepts are illustrated by describing two fundamental strategies.

Breadth-first search

By using the basic control strategy of *breadth-first search,* we generate increasingly broad segments of the state space and check each generated level for a goal state. We begin the search process by *expanding* the start state (i.e., generating all possible successor nodes from the start state). If none of these nodes is a goal state, we then generate the next search level. This level is produced by taking, one by one, each of the nodes in the just-searched level and applying all applicable operators to produce all possible successor nodes for each of these nodes. This process continues until a goal state is discovered. By using this process, all nodes at a given level are searched before any node at a lower level is searched. That is illustrated in tree form by Fig. 2.3, which is based on Prob. 2.1.

This strategy could, in theory, be useful for solving many problems. On the surface it might even appear to be a flawless strategy because, given that the state space is finite, it will always find a solution as long as one exists. Moreover, it will always find the shortest path.

Unfortunately, if we look at it more closely with an eye toward real-world applications, we can observe that the number of nodes that must

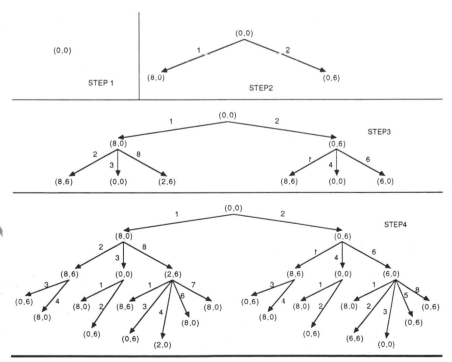

Figure 2.3 Breadth-first search.

be generated for every level grows exponentially with increasing depth. The time required for this search also grows exponentially, and therefore breadth-first search guarantees a solution only if we have unlimited time (and memory).

Depth-first search

For some problems the *depth-first* strategy avoids the problems associated with breadth-first search. In the depth-first strategy we select a path and follow it through increasingly deep levels until we discover a solution or the end of the path. (In reality we may have to give up on a path after reaching some predetermined depth because of the possibility of infinite paths.) Figure 2.4 displays a depth-first search for Prob. 2.1, where the choice of a node to be used in continuing the search path is based on random selection.

Depth-first search has several potential advantages over breadth-first search. It is less demanding of memory resources because it considers a more limited search space to reach any given level. For problems that have deep solutions, it will find a solution faster than breadth-first search.

Unfortunately, depth-first search also has several disadvantages. If the search of a path is stopped before reaching the end of the path (which may be required because of the possibility of infinite paths), then we may not find a solution even though one exists. If a solution path is located, there is no guarantee that it is the shortest available.

In reality, both strategies suffer from the same basic problem: Although in theory they can be used to solve many types of problems, in practice they are limited by time and space restrictions. Following a discussion of search directions, we will consider techniques for increasing the practical feasibility of searching.

Search direction

Another important characteristic of a search process is the *direction* in which the reasoning proceeds. All the search examples we have considered are examples of *forward reasoning*. Forward (or *data-driven*) reasoning starts at the initial conditions and works forward toward the goal. *Backward* (or *goal-directed*) *reasoning* starts at a goal state and proceeds back toward the start state.

As an informal example, consider a case of backward reasoning that is based on an old (and admittedly terrible) joke:

A resident of urban San Francisco goes for a leisurely drive outside Phoenix. Unfortunately, after passing through the small town of New River, he finds himself lost on a lonely desert road. Fortunately, he

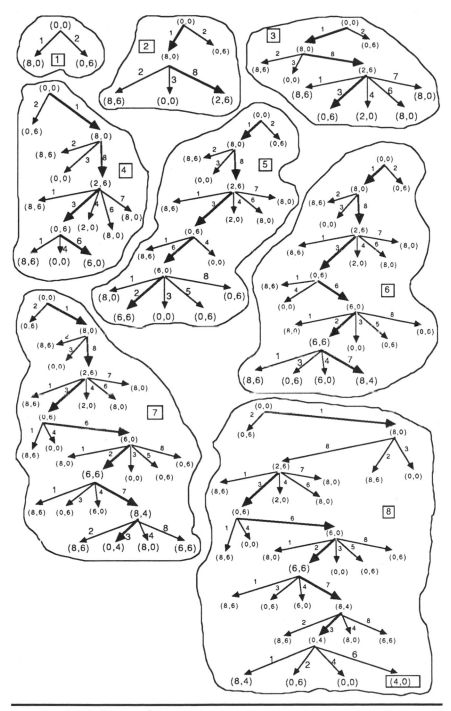

Figure 2.4   Depth-first search.

happens across an old cowboy and asks him how to get back to San Francisco. After scratching his head, and greatly pondering the question, the cowboy replies, "Well, I'd like to help you, but I'm afraid you just can't get there from here."

If we were in the above situation, we would probably, although perhaps subconsciously, employ backward reasoning to find a solution. We would first observe that, from a search viewpoint, finding Phoenix is equivalent to finding San Francisco, because we can easily establish a connection between the two large cities. Given that observation, our problem would reduce to one of finding Phoenix.

We would, however, still be lost because we don't know the way to Phoenix. To address the new problem of locating Phoenix, we would again query the cowboy. Not being inclined toward urban affairs, he, unfortunately, believes Phoenix to be as unreachable as San Francisco.

Our response to this new dilemma is to address it in terms of an even lower-level subgoal. We recall passing through the town of New River. Because there are road signs in New River that provide directions to Phoenix, reaching New River is equivalent, from a search viewpoint, to reaching Phoenix. We are no longer lost as soon as we find that the cowboy, fortunately, does know how to get to New River.

As a more formal example of backward reasoning consider Prob. 2.1, this time modified by the following statement: *The goal is to get exactly*

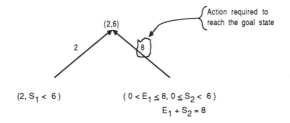

Notes on generation of required conditions:

RULE	CONDITION	REASON
2	$E = 2$	Goal is $E = 2$ and Rule 2 does not modify "E".
2	$S_1 < 6$	6-gallon pail must not be full for Rule 2 to apply.
8	$0 < E_1 \le 8$	8-gallon pail must not be empty and may be full.
8	$0 \le S_2 < 6$	6-gallon pail must not be full but may be empty.
8	$E_1 + S_2 = 8$	Rule 8 simply transfers water ; eight gallons must be present before rule execution.

Figure 2.5 Backward-reasoning tree.

2 gal in the 8-gal pail and 6 gal in the 6-gal pail. We can approach a goal-directed solution to this problem by using the rules from Table 2.1. Although they are the same rules that we used previously for forward reasoning, there is a significant difference in the way we select and apply them.

We begin by stating the final goal, in this case (2,6). Next we consider each of the rules and attempt to locate every rule whose action, if somehow we could apply it, would result in accomplishing our goal. In this example either rule 2 or rule 8 would be satisfactory, as shown graphically in Fig. 2.5. The lower-level states in Fig. 2.5 represent the conditions required to *enable* the execution of rule 2 or 8.

We now have two new subgoals to solve. The solution process now focuses on solving the subgoals and ignores the final goal. To solve the new subgoals, we look for rules whose action segments would, if executed, result in the conditions that match our subgoals. We continue this process until we generate a subgoal that is satisfied by the initial conditions. Figure 2.6 shows a solution for this example.

In some cases it may be desirable to employ *bidirectional search:* using forward search from the initial state while simultaneously using backward search from the goal states. Although bidirectional search

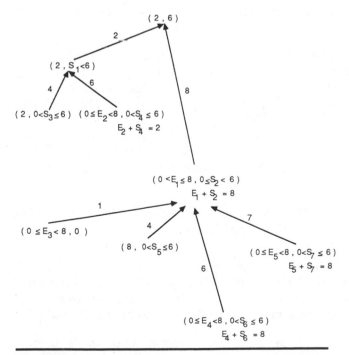

Figure 2.6 Backward reasoning.

can be very useful, it can also be much like starting a tunnel from both sides of a mountain without having precise surveying equipment—the search processes may pass each other without intersecting.

Applying knowledge to guide the search

If the search process had the benefit of an overall view of the complete state space, it could operate much like a person sitting on a mountain and observing the trails that cross a valley below. In most cases, given that strategic vantage point, we could quite quickly identify the paths that are likely to be the easiest to follow.

A search process, however, deals only with the developing search space. Given only the strategies that have been described so far, the search process must act much like a person looking for a trail by walking on the valley floor. At any given time the person can see only a very limited part of the valley and may therefore miss an excellent trail even though passing quite close to it.

These strategies are called *blind search* because they examine the search space exhaustively without visibility into the probability of success for one path vs. another.

PRINCIPLE 2.6: Because blind search has no way of fighting combinatorial explosion, it is useless for solving complex problems.

The primary use of heuristic knowledge is to increase the efficiency of a reasoning process by providing direction. Such direction has the effect of reducing the space that must actually be searched before a solution is found. This reduction allows us to address more complex problems within a given time.

Heuristics can be used for many purposes, including the elimination of entire branches from a search tree, selection of a general path to follow, and selection of the next node to expand. Regarding heuristics, we can also observe that:

- They are applied in the absence of more precise control mechanisms (e.g., if a highway marker specifically directs us to our goal, we should certainly follow it).

- *Heuristic search* focuses on the identification of solutions that satisfice. A heuristic, like any rule of thumb, will produce acceptable results in most cases. Unfortunately, because heuristics are not hard and fast, they will in some cases lead us down the wrong path.

For example, when attempting to locate a route while driving through unknown territory, we frequently apply the following heuristic: Select the route that seems to point most directly toward the goal. If we were to use this heuristic to select a route from Grand Canyon Village (on the south rim of Grand Canyon) to Bright Angel Point (13 miles away on the north rim) we would depart northbound on U.S. 180. The lack of a bridge across the canyon, however, means that the correct choice is actually south (on U.S. 180) to begin the 242-mile trip around Grand Canyon.

Although heuristic reasoning is not a panacea for problem solving (as the above example illustrates), it is a very powerful technique.

PRINCIPLE 2.7: Heuristic reasoning, when coupled with the concept of satisficing solutions, often allows us to find adequate solutions to problems that would classically be considered unsolvable because of their exponential complexity.

Chapter 12 describes techniques for using *best-first search* [Hart, 1972], which uses a *heuristic evaluation function*—a mathematical function that calculates heuristically determined values for the "goodness" of each possible node at every search choice point. For more information on artificial intelligence, see Rich, 1983, or Charniak, 1985.

The examples presented in this chapter involve only very simple problem knowledge (e.g., knowledge that if we fill an 8-gal pail, its resulting content will be 8 gal). In realistic problems a great deal of knowledge is required and the task of efficiently representing it is a major part of building an ES. The following chapter begins the investigation of schemes for representing knowledge.

Knowledge Representation and Formal Logic

As noted previously, knowledge forms the cornerstone of an ES's power. To actually realize this power, however, we must be able to abstractly represent knowledge and use the knowledge to support the system's reasoning process. This chapter and the following chapter present the basic issues of *knowledge representation* and describe several systems that are used to represent knowledge.

A knowledge representation encompasses:

- The *structure* used to describe elements of knowledge
- The *interpretive process* required to use the described knowledge

3.1 Knowledge Components

Most real-world domains include large quantities of both *factual* and *procedural* knowledge. *Facts* are the pieces of knowledge that tell us something about an *element* of the domain. Facts generally express a static "state of being" associated with an object; they tell us nothing about dynamic activities associated with the object.

Procedural rules are the pieces of knowledge that describe some dynamic action relative to domain elements (e.g., "If the roads are icy, then use tire chains."). As this example illustrates, most procedural rules are of the following form:

IF   (set of conditions)

THEN (actions to be taken)

The "set of conditions" portion of the rule, called the *antecedent* or *preconditions,* describes the conditions that must be met for the rule to be applied; the "actions to be taken" portion, called the *consequent* or *result,* describes the actions that occur as a result of the rule's application.

Although many different schemes are used for knowledge representation, there are several issues that are common to all. For example, using any representation, the knowledge engineering process consists of capturing the required knowledge, formulating it (at least mentally) as an English statement, and then coding it by using the selected representation.

PRINCIPLE 3.1: If a KE can't accurately represent a knowledge fragment by using English, then any subsequent structural representation will also be inaccurate.

This transition is also important because it may be necessary to use the English-language representation of a knowledge element for explanation purposes.

The remainder of this chapter relates to the specific structures that are used to actually code the knowledge represented by an English statement (by using a process that is somewhat similar to that of diagramming sentences from elementary English grammar).

3.2   Representation Evaluation Criteria

The representation schemes in common use today are primarily the result of extensive research and empirical analysis rather than the result of the philosophical consideration of some all-encompassing representation theory. There is no universally accepted "best" representation technique, and one scheme will be more applicable than another when evaluted relative to a specific domain.

However, even lacking such an exhaustive theory, we can still evaluate any given representation scheme relative to several general criteria. The evaluation can then be used to compare and contrast different schemes by their relative usefulness to a specific application. Some important general criteria are the following:

Transparency.   The extent to which we can easily identify stored knowledge.

Explicitness.   The extent to which knowledge is directly represented.

Naturalness.   The extent to which knowledge is represented in its native form.

Efficiency.   The relative ease with which we can access specific knowledge during execution.

Adequacy.   The extent to which a given structure can be used to represent all knowledge required for the system.

Modularity.   The extent to which knowledge fragments can be stored independently from one another.

3.3   Level of Representation

Knowledge involved in the reasoning process can be at many different levels of detail. The lowest-level elements, called *first principles,* form the fundamental building blocks on which domain expertise is based. The law of gravity is an example of a first principle.

From these principles, more specific principles, theorems, and action rules are developed. These, in turn, form the basis for additional knowledge derivation. This process is essentially one of *synthesis* (i.e., combining existing lower-level knowledge elements into more comprehensive elements).

Low-level knowledge is rarely of value when applied directly. Any student who has taken an open-book final exam without sufficient preparation is aware that it is an excruciatingly long way from reading lower-level knowledge to answering questions that require an application of higher-level knowledge generated from it. The ability to eventually derive a solution, given unlimited time, is not considered expert behavior.

Unfortunately, the flexibility of knowledge decreases with increasing level. This occurs because many specific components are combined in a very specific way to develop higher-level knowledge, and the knowledge is therefore useful only when the presupposed combination of components is present. Given only high-level knowledge, there is no way to respond to a new unanticipated situation; such a response requires original reasoning from lower-level knowledge.

PRINCIPLE 3.2: High-level knowledge is powerful but inflexible, whereas low-level knowledge is more flexible but less powerful.

In practice, an expert is able to deal effectively with real-world problems by first attempting to use compiled knowledge and relying on reasoning from lower-level knowledge when no applicable compiled knowledge is available.

To approach real problems, we must develop a compromise position regarding representation level that will allow the system to satisfice in terms of both flexibility and response time.

3.4 Knowledge Representation Schemes

Knowledge representations can be roughly classified as two different types: *declarative* and *procedural*. Declarative schemes emphasize the representation of knowledge as an accumulation of static facts along with limited information that describes how the knowledge is to be used. Procedural schemes emphasize the representation of knowledge in the form of dynamic rules that describe procedures for using the knowledge, with little stored directly as facts. Most practical representation schemes stress one technique over the other. In reality, however, elements of both are required for every ES.

Declarative representation

Declarative schemes stress the concept of a simple statement that states (or *asserts*) an element of truth (e.g., "Rover is a dog."). This has several desirable characteristics:

Transparency. The represented knowledge is stored in an explicit and unambiguous manner. It is relatively easy to revise the knowledge because of this transparency.

Storage efficiency. Each knowledge fragment is stored only once, even if it is used in several different ways.

Flexibility. The knowledge can be stored at a low level with an accompanying increase in flexibility.

Direct inference. The direct static nature of the representation allows for explicit, direct, mathematical-like inference.

The following sections informally describe the use of *formal symbolic logic* for knowledge representation.

3.5 Formal Logic

Formal logic, an outgrowth of early philosophical considerations, was one of the earliest forms of knowledge representation used in AI. The most widely used formal logic system, called *first-order predicate logic,* consists of four major components: an *alphabet,* a *formal language,* a set of basic statements called *axioms* (expressed in the formal language), and a set of *inference rules.* Each axiom describes one fragment of knowledge, and inference rules are applied to the axioms to derive new statements of truth.

Predicate logic: Alphabet

The alphabet for a formal language consists of the symbols from which statements in the formal language are constructed. The alphabets with which we will be concerned consist of *predicates, variables, functions, constants, connectives, quantifiers,* and *delimeters* such as parentheses and commas. The following sections define these symbols, and later sections describe how they are combined to build formulas.

Constant. A *constant symbol,* the simplest component in predicate logic, is used to represent a specific element from the domain. This element can be any named item of interest, including physical objects and abstractions such as ideas, viewpoints, or data sets. A string of uppercase letters is used for a constant symbol. Examples include:

ROVER	A dog
BLUE	A color
CONSERVATIVE	A political viewpoint

Variable. A variable symbol is used to represent a member of a set of domain elements without specifying a specific element. A string of lowercase letters is used for a variable symbol. Examples include:

dog	An element that is a dog, but with an unspecified identity
color	An unspecified color
viewpoint	Any of several viewpoints

Function. In addition to constant symbols and variable symbols, a *function* can be used to identify a domain element. A function describes an element by identifying it as the unique result of the application of a specified *mapping* between other elements in the domain. A lowercase string is used as the function symbol, and the arguments can be any legal term—where a term is a form for identifying a domain element. A term is defined inductively as a variable, a constant, or a function (where, as noted above, the arguments of the function can themselves be terms).
    Examples of functions include:

father(CHAD)	A function invocation that specifies the unique element, in this case a man, that is the father of CHAD

mother(father(CHAD))   The unique element that is the mother of the father of CHAD—CHAD's grandmother

killer(x)   The unique individual who killed the unspecified element represented by x

Predicate. Predicates are used to represent *relations* within the domain; they indicate that one element is related to another in some specified way. A predicate has a value of true if the specified elements are related in the specified way and false if they are not.

Predicates (strings of uppercase letters), along with terms that identify the related elements, are used to form *atomic formulas* (or *atoms*), which are among the basic building blocks of predicate logic. (A more formal definition for complex formulas is presented in a later section.) Examples of predicates include:

MAN(TOM)   Tom is a man.

BIGGER(TOM,BOB)   Tom is bigger than Bob.

BIGGER(TOM,father(TOM))   Tom is bigger than his father.

Predicate logic: Interpretation

Given the above components, we can form many interesting atomic formulas. For a formula to be useful, however, we must be able to accurately determine what it represents. To compose a formula, the developer first selects a set of specific component symbols and then establishes a *correspondence* between each selected symbol and the associated domain element or relation. This set of correspondences establishes the semantics that allow us to *interpret* a formula.

In the case of simple atomic formulas the interpretation may be obvious. For example, consider the simple formula, DOG(ROVER). Even if no interpretation is specified, we may assume that this formula represents the fact that "Rover is a dog." Our unsupported belief in this interpretation is probably based on the fact that DOG was chosen as a predicate symbol, coupled with the fact that ROVER is typically the name of a dog.

Note, however, that P(A) is an equally valid, although less obvious, formulation and that "My land-rover does not run well" is potentially an equally valid, although more obscure, interpretation.

Because of the possibility of confusion, when composing well-formed formulas (WFFs) in predicate logic, it is desirable to select symbols with mnemonic significance.

Predicate logic: Connectives

The components described to this point have little value for representing comlex compound statements. For example, it would be quite difficult to represent the statement, "My house is a blue, two-story Victorian with yellow shutters on a corner lot." Although we could define a predicate B2VYC to indicate all of the above attributes and then compose a formula, B2VYC(MY-HOUSE), the formula, although technically correct, would be cumbersome and completely useless for independent syntactical manipulation.

To express *compound propositions,* we use *connectives* that combine formulas to build more complex WFFs. The component formulas can be WFFs or atomic formulas. Commonly used connectives include:

$\wedge$	and
$\vee$	inclusive or
$\rightarrow$	implies
$\equiv$	is equivalent to
$\sim$	not

They are described as follows:

$\wedge$ $\wedge$ is used to build formulas that indicate that several components must be true for the entire WFF to be true. Each of the component formulas in such an expression is called a *conjunct,* and the expression overall is called a *conjunction.* For example,

BLUE(MY-HOUSE) $\wedge$ TWO-STORY(MY-HOUSE) $\wedge$ VICTORIAN(MY-HOUSE) $\wedge$ YELLOW-SHUTTERS(MY-HOUSE) $\wedge$ CORNER(MY-HOUSE)

$\vee$ $\vee$ is used to build formulas whose truth depends only on the truth of any component. Each component formula is called a *disjunct,* and the overall expression is called a *disjunction.* For example, "Harry bought a car or a truck," is represented by the disjunction

BOUGHT(HARRY,CAR) $\vee$ BOUGHT(HARRY,TRUCK)

$\sim$ The not symbol ($\sim$), which is sometimes considered a pseudo-connective because it does not actually connect formulas, is used to change the truth value of a WFF from true to false or from false to true. When a $\sim$ is applied to a formula, the formula becomes a *negation.* For example, $\sim$BOY(LEE) represents the phrase, "Lee is not a boy."

$\rightarrow$ $\rightarrow$ is used for developing if-then constructs called *implications.* The fact that the antecedent is true implies that the consequent is also true. For example,

[PRESENT(SPARK) $\wedge$ PRESENT(FUEL) $\wedge$ PRESENT(AIR)] $\rightarrow$ COMBUSTION(FUEL)

$\equiv$ $\equiv$ is used to indicate the *logical equivalence* of two formulas. A formula such as X $\equiv$ Y indicates that the truth states of the left- and right-hand sides are equivalent, regardless of how they are interpreted (as long as the variables are interpreted consistently).

Predicate logic: Quantification

We are using *propositional logic,* a subset of predicate logic, if we employ only the constructs described up to this point and exclude the use of variables in expressions. Unfortunately, although the use of connectives greatly increases our expressive power, we still can't express the simple fact, "All people need air." To aid in forming such expressions, we use *quantifiers.* The *universal quantifier* $\forall$x is used to assert that a formula is true for all values of the associated variable. For example, "All people need air" can be represented as

$$\forall x[\text{PERSON}(x) \rightarrow \text{NEED\_AIR}(x)]$$

The *existential quantifier* $\exists x$ is used to assert that there exists at least one assignment for x that will make the associated formula true. For example, "The owner of the car also owns the boat," can be represented as

$$\exists x[\text{OWNER}(x,\text{CAR}) \wedge \text{OWNER}(x,\text{BOAT})]$$

In this case, the formulas is true if there is one owner who owns both the car and the boat. It is also true if several (or all) individuals from the domain own both (e.g., they are owned by a partnership).

The variable associated with a quantifier is the *quantified variable,* and the *scope* of the quantifier is the formula that follows it. Variables that are referenced in quantifiers are called *bound,* and those that are not are *free.* Most formulas of interest in ESs are those called *sentences,* which are formulas that have only bound variables.

Predicate logic: Language

The formal language associated with first-order predicate logic is the set of all formulas that can be legally constructed from the alphabet symbols (i.e., the set of all statements that could be made given the subject symbols).

A legally constructed formula in the language is called a *well-formed formula* (WFF) and is defined (inductively) as follows:

1. An atomic formula is a WFF.
2. The following are WFFs: $(\sim F)$, $(F \wedge G)$, $(F \vee G)$, $(F \rightarrow G)$ where:

    F and G are WFFs

3. The following are WFFs: $(\forall x F)$ and $(\exists x F)$ where:

    F is a WFF and x is a variable

Given this definition, we can construct arbitrarily complex WFFs, for example,

$$(\exists x)((\forall y)[P(x,y) \wedge Q(y, x) \wedge R(x,x) \rightarrow R(x,y)])$$

However, other simple expressions that are formed from the symbols of the alphabet are not WFFs. For example, ~f(A) is not a WFF according to the above rules. More important, the following are not WFFs:

$$(\forall P)P(A) \quad \text{and} \quad (\exists f)f(A)$$

The form of logic described in this section is called first-order because it does not allow quantification over predicates or functions.

Predicate logic: Evaluation

The concepts of *truth* and *formal proof* are important in a formal logic system. The process of inferring new knowledge is structured as a proof that is similar to the proofs developed in mathematics. This process, which depends only on *syntactical manipulations* and closely matches the theoretical ideal for an ES, is a method for rigorously demonstrating the truth of a proposed statement based on truth that is already known. This process, of course, depends on our ability to determine whether any given WFF is true or false.

The truth value of an atomic formula is determined by applying the interpretation of the predicate: If, given the intended interpretation of the predicate in the subject domain, the relation described by the predicate is true of its arguments, then the truth value of the atom is true; otherwise, the truth value of the atom is false. For example, if the predicate TALL(x) is interpreted to mean "x is at least 6 ft tall," then to find the truth value of the formula TALL(JACK), we measure Jack. If he is at least 6 ft tall, then the formula is true; otherwise, it is false.

In propositional logic, the truth value of a complex formula can be established by using the *truth table method,* which is based on the *truth table* shown in Table 3.1. Note that the truth definition for the "implies" connective is not intuitively clear. An implication's truth value is true, by definition, whenever the antecedent is false or the consequent is true. The truth value applies to the implication overall and tells us nothing about the truth of any component. Therefore, HORSE (ROVER) → CAT(ROVER) is true.

To determine the truth or falsity of a complicated compound formula in predicate logic, we successively apply the relations from the truth

TABLE 3.1   Formula Truth Table

X	Y	X ∧ Y	X ∨ Y	X → Y	~X	X ≡ Y
T	T	T	T	T	F	T
T	F	F	T	F	F	F
F	F	F	F	T	T	T
F	T	F	T	T	T	F

table to reduce the component formulas, starting from the "inside" out. For example, given the knowledge that some predicate P is false and that the predicates Q and R are true,* to establish the truth value of the expression

$$[(P \lor (Q \land R)) \land \sim P] \to (Q \land P)$$

we first use the truth table to determine that $Q \land R$ is true. The compound expression then reduces to

$$[(P \lor tt) \land \sim P] \to (Q \land P)$$

We then establish that $P \lor tt$ is true and reduce the expression to

$$(tt \land \sim P) \to (Q \land P)$$

This expression is then reduced to final form using the following sequence:

$$(tt \land tt) \to (Q \land P)$$

$$tt \to (Q \land P)$$

$$tt \to ff$$

$$ff$$

Thus it is established that the overall expression is false.

The process required to establish the truth value of formulas that involve variables (i.e., predicate logic) is more complicated and is explained in Chap. 11.

3.6 Knowledge Engineering When Using Formal Logic

When using formal logic, the basic knowledge engineering process consists of the following steps:

1. Develop an understanding of the knowledge.

2. Formulate the knowledge as English statements.

3. Break the statements into their component parts.

4. Choose symbols to represent the elements and relations in each component.

---

*For this and following discussions of propositional logic it is assumed that all example predicates have the same constant as an argument [e.g., P(A), Q(A), R(A)].

5. Build WFFs, by using the above symbols, that represent the statements.

As we select the formal logic symbols and the interpretation for each symbol, it is important to remember that later we must be able to properly interpret the formal logic—to recapture the original meaning solely on the basis of the formal symbolic representations and interpretations. The following examples illustrate this process.

Example 3.1 Formulate the following expression in predicate logic: "Rover is a black dog."

The structure of this sentence is clarified by restructuring it as two sentences: (1) "Rover is a dog" and (2) "Rover is black." One predicate, DOG, is used for the first sentence, and another, BLACK, for the second. The WFF is then DOG(ROVER) $\wedge$ BLACK(ROVER).

Example 3.2 Formulate the following expression in predicate logic: "John is a computer science student but not a pilot or a football player."

To state this sentence unambiguously, we must deal with the possible ambiguity introduced by the "or." We can make the meaning of this sentence more explicit, and therefore less ambiguous, by using "nor" (meaning "and not") rather than "or": "John is a computer science student but not a pilot nor a football player." The sentence can then be restated in the following subparts, each of which refines our knowledge and understanding of John:

1. John is a computer science student.
2. John is not a pilot.
3. John is not a football player.

We compose the WFF as

COMPUTER_SCIENCE(JOHN) $\wedge$ ~PILOT(JOHN)

$\wedge$ ~FOOTBALL_PLAYER(JOHN)

Example 3.3 Formulate the following expression in predicate logic: "You will gain weight unless you exercise."

This sentence can be restated as "If you do not exercise, then you will gain weight." Using a universal quantifier, because the statement is implicitly asserted for all individuals, we can formulate this as

$$\forall x[\sim\text{EXERCISE}(x) \rightarrow \text{GAIN}(x)]$$

Example 3.3 Formulate the following expression in predicate logic: "LeeAnn would be happy to find a $1 bill or a $5 bill."

In considering this statement, we can observe that the "or" is intended as a "logically inclusive or." This observation is based on our belief that the statement may be accurately structured as follows:

1. LeeAnn would be happy if she found a $1 bill.
2. LeeAnn would be happy if she found a $5 bill.
3. LeeAnn would be happy if she found both a $1 bill and a $5 bill.

The resulting WFF is

[FIND-ONE(LEEANN) $\lor$ FIND-FIVE(LEEANN)] $\longrightarrow$

HAPPY(LEEANN)

Example 3.4 Formulate the following expression in predicate logic: "Studying expert systems is exciting and applying logic is very fun if you are not going to spend all of your time slaving over a terminal."

This statement can be composed as

$\forall x(\sim\text{SLAVE}(x) \to [\text{ES\_EXCITING}(x) \land \text{LOGIC\_FUN}(x)])$

In this formulation we have dropped some of the knowledge that was represented by the English-language statement; namely, that logic is "very fun," vs. simply "fun," and that the subject is "going to be spending time," vs. "is spending time," slaving over a terminal. This loss of knowledge may or may not be acceptable, depending on how we employ the knowledge during use.

Example 3.5 Formulate the following expression in predicate logic: "Every voter either favors the amendment or despises it."

In this case it is important to recognize that the "or" is being used in the sense of a "logically exclusive or"; any given voter, we believe, will not both favor and despise an amendment. The formulation of this statement is therefore significantly different from the simple WFF of Example 3.4:

$\forall x[\text{VOTER}(x) \to ([\text{FAVOR}(x,\text{AMENDMENT})$

$\lor \text{DESPISE}(x,\text{AMENDMENT})]$

$\land \sim[\text{FAVOR}(x,\text{AMENDMENT}) \land \text{DESPISE}(x,\text{AMENDMENT})])]$

3.7 Inference Processes

As introduced in Sec. 3.5, inference in formal logic is the process of generating new WFFs from existing WFFs through the application of rules of inference. The most common rule of inference, *modus ponens,* is expressed symbolically as:

$$[P1 \wedge (P1 \rightarrow P2)] \rightarrow P2$$

or in English as: "If P1 is true, and P1 being true implies that P2 is true, then P2 is true." For example, if we realize that the presence of smoke implies the presence of fire, then, by applying modus ponens, we can infer the presence of fire by observing smoke.

Another common rule of inference [Klenk, 1983], *universal specialization,* is used to generate the WFF F(INDIVIDUAL) from the WFF $(\forall x)[F(x)]$. This rule can be stated symbolically as

$$\text{INDIVIDUAL} \wedge (\forall x)[F(x)] \rightarrow F(\text{INDIVIDUAL})$$

We can use this rule to conclude that a tree requires water, based on the facts that all plants require water.

We can also use another form of inference called *substitution* to produce new WFFs. Substitution is based on the recognition of equivalence laws that are true for all formulas. Several of these laws for *propositional logic,* developed by using the truth table definitions of Table 3.1, are shown in Table 3.2, and Example 3.8 illustrates their use to develop a *proof* of a desired fact.

TABLE 3.2 Equivalence Laws for Propositional Logic

(3.1)	$P1 \rightarrow P2 \equiv \sim P1 \vee P2$	
(3.2)	$P1 \vee P2 \equiv P2 \vee P1$	(Commutative)
(3.3)	$P2 \wedge P1 \equiv P1 \wedge P2$	(Commutative)
(3.4)	$P1 \vee (P2 \wedge P3) \equiv (P1 \vee P2) \wedge (P1 \vee P3)$	(Distributive)
(3.5)	$P1 \wedge (P2 \vee P3) \equiv (P1 \wedge P2) \vee (P1 \wedge P3)$	(Distributive)
(3.6)	$(P1 \vee P2) \vee P3 \equiv P1 \vee (P2 \vee P3)$	(Associative)
(3.7)	$(P1 \wedge P2) \wedge P3 \equiv P1 \wedge (P2 \wedge P3)$	(Associative)
(3.8)	$P1 \rightarrow P2 \equiv \sim P1 \rightarrow \sim P2$	
(3.9)	$\sim(\sim P1) \equiv P1$	
(3.10)	$\sim(P1 \vee P2) \equiv \sim P1 \wedge \sim P2$	(DeMorgan's)
(3.11)	$\sim(P1 \wedge P2) \equiv \sim P1 \vee \sim P2$	(DeMorgan's)
(3.12)	$P1 \vee \text{FALSE} \equiv P1$	
(3.13)	$P1 \vee \text{TRUE} \equiv \text{TRUE}$	
(3.14)	$P1 \wedge \text{TRUE} \equiv P1$	
(3.15)	$P1 \wedge \text{FALSE} \equiv \text{FALSE}$	
(3.16)	$P1 \vee \sim P1 \equiv \text{TRUE}$	
(3.17)	$P1 \wedge \sim P1 \equiv \text{FALSE}$	

Example 3.6 We are given the following facts:

1. When an airplane runs out of fuel, the engine stops.
2. If an airplane's engine stops, a forced landing is required.
3. At a given point in time, Captain J. G. Smith's airplane runs out of fuel.

Use the above facts, and the equivalence rules from Table 3.2, to show that the airplane's engine stops and a forced landing is required when it runs out of fuel.

We can begin the solution for this problem by defining three predicates:

RD   Captain Smith's airplane has run out of fuel.

ES   The engine on Captain Smith's airplane has stopped.

FL   Captain Smith must execute a forced landing.

The first given facts can be represented as RD → ES and ES → FL. At the time the airplane's fuel is exhausted, we can add the fact RD and express our collective knowledge as a conjunction:

$$(RD \rightarrow ES) \wedge (ES \rightarrow FL) \wedge RD$$

we can now apply substitution:

Transformation	Justification
$(RD \rightarrow ES) \wedge (ES \rightarrow FL) \wedge RD$	Given
$(\sim RD \vee ES) \wedge (\sim ES \vee FL) \wedge RD$	3.1
$RD \wedge (\sim RD \vee ES) \wedge (\sim ES \vee FL)$	3.3
$[(RD \wedge \sim RD) \vee (RD \wedge ES)] \wedge (\sim ES \vee FL)$	3.5
$[FALSE \vee (RD \wedge ES)] \wedge (\sim ES \vee FL)$	3.17
$(RD \wedge ES) \wedge (\sim ES \vee FL)$	3.12
$[(RD \wedge ES) \wedge \sim ES] \vee [(RD \wedge ES) \wedge FL]$	3.5
$(RD \wedge ES \wedge \sim ES) \vee (RD \wedge ES \wedge FL)$	3.7
$(RD \wedge FALSE) \vee (RD \wedge ES \wedge FL)$	3.17
$FALSE \vee (RD \wedge ES \wedge FL)$	3.15
$RD \wedge ES \wedge FL$	3.12

The last formula in the table, RD $\wedge$ ES $\wedge$ FL, represents the desired condition. We could, alternatively, solve this problem by applying modus ponens twice:

$$[RD \wedge (RD \rightarrow ES)] \rightarrow ES \quad \text{and} \quad [ES \wedge (ES \rightarrow FL)] \rightarrow FL$$

We can also observe that in this case it would behoove Captain Smith to directly store the higher-level knowledge that running out of fuel ultimately implies a forced landing.

One of the greatest advantages of representation using formal logic is that syntactic inference is possible and is guaranteed to be valid (given that the starting formulas are valid). This characteristic makes it possible to develop automatic inference systems that are extremely powerful.

Unfortunately, although all inferences are guaranteed to be correct, there is certainly no guarantee that they will all be valuable. In fact, they are often completely useless. The number of such useless inferences can be infinite, and even directed processes can be very time-consuming. Note, for example, the number of steps required to solve the simple problem of Example 3.6.

Fortunately, several powerful techniques for performing inference by using formal logic have been developed. Resolution, an example of such a technique, is described in Chap. 11. For further information on formal logic, see Mendelson, 1979.

The following chapter describes several less formal (and more flexible and widely used) schemes for representing knowledge.

Nonformal
Knowledge Representation

This chapter describes knowledge representation schemes that are less formal than the symbolic logic scheme described in Chap. 3. Within this chapter several schemes are presented in an order that corresponds roughly to their dependence on declarative information.

4.1   Semantic Networks

A *semantic network* focuses on the graphical representation of relations between elements in a domain. The basic components of a semantic net are *nodes* and *links*. Nodes are used to represent domain elements. They are shown graphically as rectangles and are labeled with the names of the represented elements. Links (or *arcs*) represent relations between elements. A link is shown as a vector from one node to another; it is labeled with the name of the relation represented. The simple net shown below represents the statement, "Horses eat grass."

$$\text{HORSE} \longrightarrow \text{eat} \longrightarrow \text{GRASS}$$

A link can be viewed as something we assert to be true about one element relative to another. Because an assertion can be only true or false, a link is fundamentally a *binary relation*.

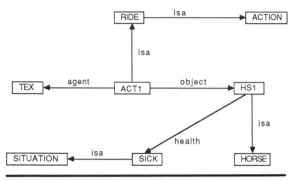

Figure 4.1 Comprehensive semantic network.

Two of the most common binary relations used in semantic nets are *isa* and *partof*. The isa link is used to represent the fact that an element is a member of a class of elements that have a collection of distinguishing *properties* in common. A node that represents a specific example of a class is an *instance* of that class. For example, the following net represents the fact that a horse is a type of mammal:

$$\text{HORSE} \relbar \text{isa} \longrightarrow \text{MAMMAL}$$

The following net represents the fact that a tail is a part of a horse:

$$\text{TAIL} \relbar \text{partof} \longrightarrow \text{HORSE}$$

These network fragments can be combined to form one net:

$$\text{TAIL}$$
$$\vert \quad \text{partof}$$
$$\text{HORSE} \relbar \text{isa} \longrightarrow \text{MAMMAL}$$

The concepts of a class and an isa link can also be used to represent situations, actions, and events. In Fig. 4.1 the node labeled ACT1 represents the specific ride taken by the *agent* TEX. In this case, ACT1 is a specialization of an action. The *object* of the action represented by node HS1 is an unnamed instance of a HORSE. The horse in question is further described by the presence of the SICK node.

Property inheritance

Any defining characteristic, such as color, size, and texture, can be represented as a property associated with a node.

Example 4.1   Expand the HORSE network to include an instance of a black horse named TRIGGER and show that he is an animal.

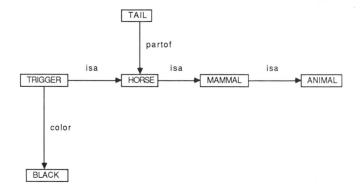

Considering Example 4.1, we can observe that, in addition to being black, TRIGGER also has a tail. Although this fact is not explicitly included in the network, we can conclude that it is true by noting that a TAIL is a part of a horse and, because TRIGGER is a HORSE, a TAIL must be part of TRIGGER. This description is an example of *property inheritance,* one of the most important concepts in semantic nets.

Property inheritance tells us that any property we assert to be true for a class of elements should also be true for any instance of the class; properties "trickle down" to connected lower levels through *property inheritance links.* This concept makes semantic nets particularly useful for representing domains that can be structured as *taxonomies.*

Reasoning with semantic nets

Reasoning based on semantic nets is generally straightforward because associations can be made simply by tracing the linkages in the system. For example, we can apply *linkage inference* to the following simple net and conclude that 12 is greater than 3:

$$12 \longrightarrow \text{is greater} \longrightarrow 7 \longrightarrow \text{is greater} \longrightarrow 3$$

Unfortunately, no rigorous semantic rules guide such reasoning. In a system such as predicate logic, reasoning proceeds on the basis of uninformed syntactic manipulation of the representation symbols. Inferences that result from this process may be irrelevant, but they will always be valid. That is not always true of semantic nets.

If we simplistically navigate the links in a semantic net, we can develop inferences that are not valid because the relations represented are not totally rigorous, primarily because of unrecognized exception conditions. For example, although all horses are mammals and almost all horses have tails, there are horses, known as bobtails, that don't have tails [Brachman, 1985].

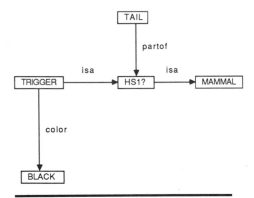

Figure 4.2 Matching in semantic networks.

PRINCIPLE 4.1: The meaning of a semantic net is established, at least in part, by the procedures that interpret the net.

Another common reasoning technique for semantic nets is inference through *matching*. A matching procedure relies on the construction of a network fragment that has a mixture of nodes with defined values and nodes whose values are desired but unknown. The desired values are represented by variables. An example of such a fragment is shown in Fig. 4.2. It is designed to answer the question, "What kind of black mammal has a tail and is named TRIGGER?"

When this fragment is applied, the matching procedure looks for a network that will perfectly match the fragment it has constructed. When such a match is found, the procedure *binds* each variable to the value of the corresponding node in the matched network. Thus, in the network of Fig. 4.2, the variable HS1? would be bound to the value HORSE to satisfy the query.

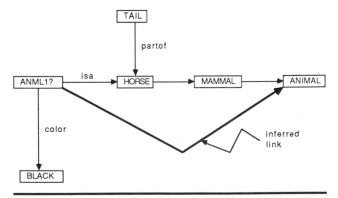

Figure 4.3 Inference of links.

In many cases it is necessary for the matching procedure to infer new links from existing links when constructing a matching fragment. For example, to answer the question, "Which animal is a black horse with a tail?" it would be necessary to infer the ANML1?-to-ANIMAL link as shown in Fig. 4.3. For more information on semantic networks see Findler, 1979.

4.2 Frames

Humans have the important ability to interpret new situations on the basis of knowledge gained from experience in similar situations. This ability allows our knowledge to grow with each experience rather than start from the initial conditions in every case.

For example, based on our past experience with them, we expect cars to have wheels and an engine, to require fuel, and to move. These elements are *defining characteristics* that, when taken as a whole, constitute our understanding of "car." They are our *expectations* regarding a car—the things that, unless there is evidence to the contrary, we expect to be true of all cars.

We maintain large mental collections of knowledge structures that include these expectations as *default values* for the corresponding characteristics.

PRINCIPLE 4.2: People frequently react to a new situation by applying expectations based on past experience.

A *frame*, first introduced in Minsky, 1975, is a structure for organizing knowledge—with an emphasis on default knowledge. Frames share several concepts in common with semantic nets. Each frame represents a class of elements in the same way that a class node is used to represent such elements in a sementic net. It is common to develop networks in which the nodes are frames (as described in Chap. 12).

PRINCIPLE 4.3: Frames are used for organizing our basic understanding of the things that are typically true of some general class of elements.

A frame consists of a series of *slots* each of which represents a standard property or attribute of the element represented by the frame. A slot gives us a place to systematically store one component of our past experience regarding the represented class of elements.

Each slot is identified by the name of the corresponding attribute and includes the value, or range of values, that can be associated with the slot. A default value for the slot may also be indicated. Figure 4.4 shows a frame that provides a partial description of the class of objects

```
Frame: CAR
  Specialization of: LAND VEHICLE
    Model:
      Range: (sedan, convertible, 2-door,
              station wagon)
      Default: sedan
    Body: steel
    Windows: glass
    Mobility: self-propelled
    Mobility Mechanism: has wheels
    Tires: rubber
    Fuel:
      Range: (gasoline, diesel, propane)
      Default: gasoline
    Number of Seats:
      Range: (1-9)
      Default: none
```

Figure 4.4 A car frame.

called CAR. For complex domains, slots can be divided into increasingly detailed subslots. Slots may also be filled by lower-level frames. A frame system is composed of the interrelated frames that are required to represent a domain.

Property inheritance

A frame system relies heavily on the concept of inheritance in the same sense that a semantic net does. Any given class of objects can be included in several different frames that represent objects at different levels of spcification. For example, the class of cars can be included in frames named PHYSICAL OBJECT, VEHICLE LAND VEHICLE, and CAR.

A frame that represents a class of objects at a given level of specification can include slots, and values in slots, that are inherited from frames that represent a higher level of abstraction. The CAR frame, for example, inherits the attributes of "mobility" and "mobility mechanism" from the fact that it is a specialization of a LAND VEHICLE frame. The use of default and inherited slot values allows for efficient reasoning because such use obviates the need for expensive reasoning processes to rediscover old facts in new situations.

Procedural information

Procedural information also can be associated with slots. The most common examples of such *attached procedures* are *if-needed* and *if-added*. If-needed procedures describe the process required to establish a value for the associated slot (i.e., "fill in" the slot) when a value is

```
Frame: CAR
   Specialization of: LAND VEHICLE
      Body: steel
      Windows: glass
      Fuel Remaining:
         Range: (empty, 1/4 tank, 1/2 tank, full)
         Default: none
         IF-NEEDED: check fuel gauge
      Type of Wreck:
         Range: (fender-bender, serious, total)
         Default: none
         IF-ADDED: call insurance agent
```

Figure 4.5   Event-driven processes in frames.

required. If-added procedures are event-driven processes that are triggered by the fact that the associated slot has been assigned a value. Figure 4.5 shows a frame that includes if-needed and if-added procedures.

Reasoning with frames

Representing knowledge with a frame system allows us to reason, at least to some extent, even though the information available is incomplete, and it allows us to quickly infer facts that are not explicitly observed. For example, we can immediately assume that an object has a steering wheel as soon as we identify it as a car.

To begin this type of reasoning process, we first select a frame to represent the current situation. Because in most cases we will not have a frame that is exactly applicable in the current context, we must often begin with a "best fit" based on the available partial evidence. We must then *instantiate* the selected frame on the basis of the specific current conditions.

In general, this process of instantiation associates a particular individual with a class. The process builds an *instantiation,* an individual description formed by applying the specific individual characteristics to the generic class description.

One of the difficulties with frame representation is the problem of establishing the default values for a frame accurately. There is never exact agreement among any group of observers as to the typical characteristics of any object. Each individual's view of "typical" is colored by personal experience and biases. When presented with the word "car," one person conjures up an image of an old wood-grained station wagon and another develops an image of a new sports convertible. Even though it may appear obvious to most people that we should assume a tree has leaves, someone from the Pacific northwest may expect a tree to have needles rather than leaves. In addition to the above situation, we must also deal with questions such as, "Is a small plastic model of a car a 'car'?"

In spite of these difficulties, the frame representation scheme remains a powerful mechanism for knowledge representation and is gaining increasing use. For further information on frames see Winston, 1984; Goldstein, 1979; and Lenat, 1982.

4.3 Scripts

Similar to our expectations regarding objects, we have certain expectations about sequences of events that are likely to occur in any given situation. These expectations are based on our observation of recurring patterns in the events of similar situations that we have observed in the past.

A *script,* which is a specialization of the general concept of a frame,

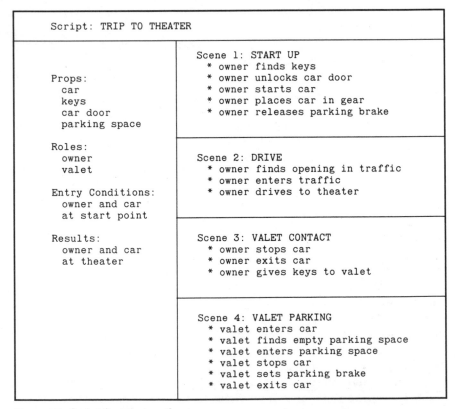

```
Script: TRIP TO THEATER


                                  Scene 1: START UP
                                   * owner finds keys
        Props:                     * owner unlocks car door
         car                       * owner starts car
         keys                      * owner places car in gear
         car door                  * owner releases parking brake
         parking space


        Roles:
         owner                    Scene 2: DRIVE
         valet                     * owner finds opening in traffic
                                   * owner enters traffic
        Entry Conditions:         * owner drives to theater
         owner and car
         at start point


        Results:                  Scene 3: VALET CONTACT
         owner and car             * owner stops car
         at theater                * owner exits car
                                   * owner gives keys to valet


                                  Scene 4: VALET PARKING
                                   * valet enters car
                                   * valet finds empty parking space
                                   * valet enters parking space
                                   * valet stops car
                                   * valet sets parking brake
                                   * valet exits car
```

Figure 4.6 Script for trip to a theater.

is a structure that is used to store *prototypes* of expected sequences of events. Many different components can be used to construct a script. Some of the most common include:

Entry conditions.   The conditions that must exist for the script to be applicable.

Script results.   Conditions that will be true after the events in the script have occurred.

Props.   Slots that represent objects that are involved in the script.

Roles.   Slots that represent agents (e.g., people) that perform actions in the script.

Scenes.   Specific sequences of events that make up the script.

Figure 4.6 shows a script that represents the process of driving to a theater.

There are no absolute rules for defining the generic content of a script or for identifying the specific entries. We may, for example, decide to include entries regarding *time factors, places of occurrence,* or *points of view.*

Reasoning with scripts

To reason on the basis of a script, we must first select an appropriate script. The selection process, which is similar to the selection of a condidate frame, can be based on establishing a best-fit match between the observed conditions and the entry conditions of a specific script.

Once we have a script that models the existing conditions, we can use the scenes to infer the existence of unobserved events. For example, considering the script of Fig. 4.6, if we observe that the valet has parked the car, we can, on the basis of the sequence of events in the VALET PARKING scene, infer that the valet must have first found a parking space.

This type of reasoning is not, however, equally reliable for predicting future events on the basis of a scene. The fact that the valet has found a parking space does not necessarily imply that he or she will continue to follow the scene and park the car. (The valet may, for example, decide to steal the car instead.)

It can also be useful to view the event sequences in a script as a series of *cause-effect* relations that establish a complex *causal chain.* For example, consider the following actions: (1) John insults Luther's wife; (2) Luther strikes John; (3) John falls to the ground. From this fragment we speculate that event (1) caused event (2), which in turn caused event (3). By using this type of reasoning, we may be able to establish the root cause of an observed event.

We should, however, be aware that, strictly speaking, what we have labeled "causes" may actually simply be antecedents that are required to enable later actions. "Cause" implies possible intent or forcing action. Arbitrarily selecting an antecedent and labeling it the "cause" of an event is risky business. There is, for example, fairly general agreement as to the major events that occurred prior to World War II; there is not, however, an equal level of agreement regarding the actual cause of the war.

For more information on scripts see Schank, 1977.

4.4   Production Systems

A *production system,* the most commonly used scheme in ESs, uses rules for knowledge representation. A production system consists of:

- An area of memory that is used to track the *current state* of the universe under consideration

- A set of *production rules (condition-action pairs)*

- An *interpreter* that examines the current state and executes applicable production rules

One common production system programming language, OPS5 [Brownston, 1985], refers to the first two items as working memory and production memory, respectively. (The syntax used for illustration in this section is similar to that of OPS5. Additional examples of production systems include YAPS [Allen, 1983] and OPS83 [Forgy, 1984].)

Global memory elements

The *global memory* area that is used to track the current system state is composed of a series of individual *memory elements.* Conceptually, each memory element describes the state of one item of interest. A memory element consists of a symbol that identifies the described element as is followed by a series of *attribute-value* pairs, each of which describes the current value (i.e., state) of the associated attribute of the element.

For example, Fig. 4.7 shows a memory element that describes a car that belongs to a person named John.

```
John car | ^color brown ^type sedan ^brake off
^motion moving ^fuel gas ^location home
```

Figure 4.7 Example of a memory element.

Production rules

The condition portion of a production rule, sometimes called the LHS for left-hand side, consists of a series of *condition elements* that describe the conditions that must be true for the rule to be applicable. These conditions are described by identifying required global memory patterns: *memory element identifiers* along with associated *attributes* and *required values*.

The *action* portion of the rule, sometimes known as the RHS for right-hand side, describes the actions to be taken when the rule *fires* (i.e., executes). The possible actions generally include activities such as entering new state descriptions in global memory, modifying existing state descriptions, and performing a user-defined action that is unique to the specific production.

The syntax of a production rule in a typical production-system programming language is:

```
(p ⟨production name⟩
   ( ⟨condition element⟩ )
         .
         .
   ( ⟨condition element⟩ )
              →
            ( ⟨action⟩ )
              .
              .
              .
```

where ⟨production name⟩ :: = name that identifies the production
⟨condition element⟩ :: = ⟨memory element identifier⟩
$^\wedge$⟨attribute identifer⟩ ⟨value⟩
.
.
.
$^\wedge$⟨attribute identifier⟩ ⟨value⟩

where ⟨attribute identifer⟩ :: = the attribute whose value is to be compared
⟨value⟩ :: = ⟨constant⟩ or ⟨variable⟩ that identifies the value the associated attribute must have for the condition to be met

where ⟨constant⟩ :: = a specific value
⟨variable⟩ :: = a value determined by *binding* during execution. A variable is bound (to the current value of the corresponding attribute in the memory element) when first encountered in a production. The

bound value is then used as the variable's value for any later occurrence of that variable in that production.

→ :: = "implies"

⟨action⟩ :: = action to be taken by the production.

Typical actions include:

make	Add a new element to global memory.
remove	Delete an element from global memory.
modify	Modify the value of the specified attribute of the specified memory element.
compute	Calculate a value from specified variables.
read	Accept input from the user.
write	Provide output to the user.
call	Execute a specific user-defined procedure (but not another production).

Although not specifically shown above, condition elements can also include various AND/OR combinations of attribute values and negation of condition elements.

Example 4.2 Develop a rule, based on Fig. 4.7, that represents the following statement: "Applying the brake stops John's car."

```
(p brake-action
(John car ^brake on) →
(modify ^motion stopped))
```

This production, named brake-action, indicates that if the value of the "brake" attribute for the "John car" memory element ever becomes equal to the value "on," then the value of the "motion" attribute should be modified to a value of "stopped."

Factual and procedural representation

Both factual and procedural knowledge can be represented in the form of production rules.

Example 4.3 Develop a production rule that represents the following fact: "Milk is white."

```
(p color of milk
(xf(p (SUBSTANCE ^type mile) →
              (modify SUBSTANCE ^color white))
```

This production, named "color of milk," indicates that if the attribute "type" for the SUBSTANCE element in global memory has a value of "milk," then the "color" attribute of the SUBSTANCE element should be modified to "white." From this example, we can observe that some "mental manipulation" is required to realize that this rule actually represents this simple fact.

PRINCIPLE 4.4: Factual knowledge that is represented as production rules is stored implicitly.

Example 4.4 illustrates the representation of procedural knowledge.

Example 4.4 Develop a production rule that represents the following statement: "Always check the traffic before entering a freeway."

```
(p check traffic
(ROAD POSITION ^state ck_traffic)
(TRAFFIC CONDITION ^state clear) →
    (MODIFY ROAD POSITION ^state enter freeway))
```

One of the advantages of a production system is that it stores knowledge in a uniform and modular form. Each production is essentially a separate, independent entity and productions never call each other. This eases the burden of adding, deleting, or modifying productions.

Interpreter

The interpreter in a production system, in its most essential form, simply recognizes and executes a production whose LHS has been satisfied. To recognize applicable rules, the interpreter compares LHS attribute-value patterns to the current state of global memory. The reasoning process continues because the execution of a production normally changes the content of global memory and thereby activates additional productions. Example 4.5 illustrates the process.

Example 4.5 Develop the production rules required to perform the reasoning, and to recommend an action, for the problem described in Sec. 1.3.

The set of production rules could be formulated as the following (where text following a semicolon is a comment and the possibility of uncertain states is ignored):

```
(p VERIFY LIGHT
    (warning_light ^state on) →
; ''verify_light'' is a user-defined procedure that returns a
; value of ''valid'' or ''invalid.''
        (modify warning_light ^status (call verify_light)))
(p BAD_LIGHT
    (warning_light ^state on ^status invalid) →
        (write ''The warning light is invalid. Log the failure
                of the light and continue normal flight.''))
```

```
(p CHECK_ENGINE
    (warning_light ^state on ^status valid) →
;  ''check_engine_status is a user-defined procedure that
returns
;  ''one_bad'' or ''>1 bad.''
    (makes engines ^status (call check_engine_status)))
(p ONE_ENGINE_BAD
    (warning_light ^state on ^status valid)
    (engines ^status one_bad) →
        (write ''One engine has failed. Stop the bad engine and
        continue flight in a degraded mode.''))
(p MANY_ENGINES_BAD
    (warning_light ^state on ^status valid)
    (engines ^status >1 bad) →
        (write ''A multiple-engine failure has occurred.
        Execute an emergency landing immediately.''))
```

At the beginning of execution, global memory contains the following (as established by an external source):

```
| warning_light | ^state on |
```

After execution of VERIFY LIGHT, global memory will be either:

```
| warning_light | ^state on ^status valid |
```

or

```
| warning_light | ^state on ^status invalid |
```

If the light is invalid, the process reports the error and terminates. If the light is valid, the content of global memory, after execution of CHECK_ENGINE, will be either:

```
| warning_light | ^state on ^status valid |
| engines | ^status one_bad          |
```

or

```
| warning_light | ^state on ^status valid |
| engines | ^status >1_bad            |
```

Processing terminates after reporting appropriately. Note that, although the productions were presented in execution order in this example, the interpreter is not actually sensitive to the order in which the rules appear.

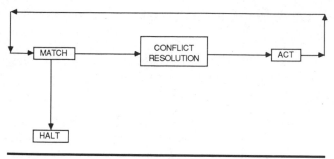

Figure 4.8 Production system interpreter.

Conflict resolution

If we consider the interpreter in greater detail, we find that it generally operates in a recognize-act cycle. A diagram of this cycle is shown in Fig. 4.8. The cycle is described as:

Match. During the match process, the interpreter first instantiates each rule. It then compares the values in the condition elements from the instantiation of each rule with the corresponding memory elements to identify the rules whose applicability conditions have been satisfied. (In reality, the interpreter is often implemented so that only a specified subset actually has to be scanned for a match during any given cycle [Forgy, 1982]. If no match is found, the interpreter halts.)

Conflict resolution. In a large production system, the match cycle will frequently identify many matches. The interpreter adds all matching instantiations to a group called the *conflict set* and considers them to be candidates for execution.

    Conflict resolution is the process of selecting the *dominant instantiation,* that is, the specific instantiation that is to be executed. This selection is based on a specific *conflict resolution strategy.* Many different strategies have been used in various systems. A typical strategy, which is similar to that used by default in OPS5, is described as follows:

1. Discard every instantiation that has already fired.
2. Select the production whose LHS references memory elements that were most recently added to global memory. This rule is included to assist in forcing the execution of sets of rules that are intended to be chained together to represent long sequences of events.
3. Select the most specific instantiation (i.e., the instantiation with the most detailed LHS).
4. Select an instantiation pseudo-arbitrarily.

Act. Carry out the actions described in the RHS of the dominant instantiation.

> **Example 4.6** Given the following classic problem, develop the production rules required to solve the problem and explain their operation.

In the midst of a journey, a farmer, along with his goat, a wolf, and a cabbage, come to a river that they must cross. There is a boat on the near side of the river, but it is only large enough to accommodate the farmer and one other item (i.e., the goat, the wolf, or the—presumably large—cabbage). The farmer must contrive a sequence of river crossings that will result in a safe crossing, recognizing that the wolf, if left unattended, will eat the goat and that the goat, if left unattended, will eat the cabbage. (We will assume that it does not occur to the wolf to eat the farmer and then the goat.)

We can approach this problem by recognizing that only a limited number of different states are legal. If we represent the elements with the symbols M, W, G, and C, we can then represent states as (⟨symbols for elements of the near side⟩ – ⟨symbols for elements of the far side⟩).

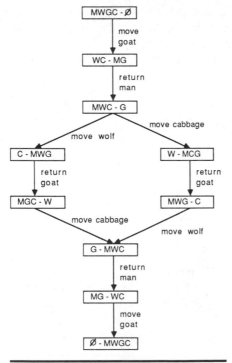

Figure 4.9 The man-wolf-goat-cabbage problem.

Using this representation, the initial state is (MWGC – φ) and the required state is (φ – MWGC). The legal states are:

(MWGC – φ), (φ – MWGC), (MWG – C), (MG – WC), (WC – MG),

(C – MWG), (MWC – G), (W – MGC), (MWG – C), (G – MWC)

Given the above states, and recognizing the operations required to move from one state to another, we can develop the graph shown in Fig. 4.9 (which ignores cycles) to represent this problem and then form production rules:

```
(p start
     (man ^location near_bank)
     (wolf ^location near_bank)
     (goat ^location near_bank)
     (cabbage ^location near_bank) →
         (write ''Move the goat.'')
         (modify man ^location far_bank)
         (modify goat ^location far_bank))
(p return_man 1
     (wolf ^location near_bank)
     (cabbage ^location near_bank)
     (man ^location far_bank)
     (goat ^location far_bank) →
         (write ''Return to the near side.'')
         (modify man ^location near_bank))
(p move_wolf 1
     (man ^location near_bank)
     (wolf ^location near_bank)
     (cabbage ^location near_bank)
     (goat ^location far_bank) →
         (write ''Move the wolf.'')
         (modify man ^location far_bank)
         (modify wolf ^location far_bank))
(p move_cabbage 1
     (man ^location near_bank)
     (wolf ^location near_bank)
     (cabbage ^location near_bank)
     (goat ^location far_bank) →
         (write ''Move the cabbage.'')
         (modify man ^location far_bank)
         (modify cabbage ^location far_bank))
(p return_goat 1
     (cabbage ^location near_bank)
     (man ^location far_bank)
     (wolf ^location far_bank)
     (goat ^location far_bank) →
         (write ''Return the goat.'')
         (modify man ^location near_bank)
         (modify goat ^location near_bank))
(p return_goat 2
     (wolf ^location near_bank)
     (man ^location far_bank)
     (cabbage ^location far_bank)
     (goat ^location far_bank) →
         (write ''Return the goat.'')
         (modify man ^location near_bank)
         (modify goat ^location near_bank))
```

```
(p move_cabbage 2
    (man ^location near_bank)
    (goat ^location near_bank)
    (cabbage ^location far_bank)
    (wolf ^location far_bank) →
        (write ''Move the cabbage.'')
        (modify man ^location far_bank)
        (modify cabbage ^location far_bank))
(p move_wolf 2
    (man ^location near_bank)
    (wolf ^location near_bank)
    (goat ^location near_bank)
    (cabbage ^location far_bank) →
        (write ''Move the wolf.'')
        (modify man ^location far_bank)
        (modify wolf ^location far_bank))
(p return man 2
    (goat ^location near_bank)
    (man ^location far_bank)
    (wolf ^location far_bank)
    (cabbage ^location far_bank)
        (write ''Return to the near side.'')
        (modify man ^location near_bank))
(p final
    (man ^location near_bank)
    (goat ^location near_bank)
    (wolf ^location far_bank)
    (cabbage ^location far_bank) →
        (write ''Move the goat.'')
        (modify man ^location far bank)
        (modify goat ^location far bank))
```

Production execution begins when we put the starting conditions into global memory. Execution will continue, following a single path, up to the point of (MWC – G). Selection of a production for execution at (MWC – G), according to the conflict resolution scheme described in Sec. 4.4, will be pseudo-arbitrary. After the execution of "final," no LHS will be satisfied and execution will halt.

From Example 4.6 we can observe the following principle:

PRINCIPLE 4.4: All management of control in a production system occurs through LHS satisfaction.

In a production system it is difficult to represent algorithmic information because of the lack of transparency in the control mechanism. Because of the concept of the independence of production rules, it can become very difficult to force the execution of a specific sequence of events.

To force a given sequence, we may have to add interpreter control information to production rules that will force the interpreter to select and execute the rules in the desired order. This process, which, even given a detailed understanding of the conflict-resolution scheme, can

```
; Begin configuration for IOUs (IO units) by making a starting
; element for each IOU.

(p io2
  (config ^state ious)→ ; config is an overall control
                          ; element
     (make iouno ^count 4)) ; make a new element, iouno,
                             ; that will be used as an
                             ; iteration control variable.

;*************** iteration will loop to this point ******

(p io4
  (config ^state ious)
  (iouno ^count ⟨c⟩) ; ⟨c⟩ is bound to the current value of
                       ; the count attribute for the iouno
                       ; element.
 -(iouno ^count 8) ; loop variable check. If the count has
                     ; reached 8 (i.e., the loop has executed
                     ; 4 times) then this production will no
                     ; longer match and production io6, which
                     ; will match, will execute.

 →

; enter a new IOU element for IOU ⟨c⟩ (Note that ⟨c⟩ is
; still equal to the value established by the binding in the
; oooond condition element.)

     (make IOU ^id ⟨c⟩ ^status present))

;
; The following action will increment the ''loop count'' by
; adding 1 to the current value of ⟨c⟩ and storing the
; result as the new value for the ^count attribute of the
; iouno element.

     (modify iouno ^count (compute ⟨c⟩ + 1))

;********************** end of looping ****************

(p io8
  (config ^state ious)
  (iouno ^count 8)→               ;all IOUs have be n done
     (modify config ^state start memory)) ; start new
                                            ; activity
```

Figure 4.10 Control in a production system.

become very complex, makes it more difficult to develop and update
any productions that may be involved in this opaque control sequence.
It is, in addition, sometimes difficult to distinguish between productions that represent procedural domain knowledge and productions
that are simply encoding control. There is, in general, no control nest-
ing hierarchy in a production system.

Figure 4.10, a slight modification of a fragment of the computer configuration system described in Rolston, 1986*b*, illustrates the use of productions for control purposes.

For additional information regarding production systems see Nilsson, 1980; Buchanan, 1983; and Buchanan, 1984*a*. For additional information regarding knowledge representation in general see Brachman, 1985*c*.

The following chapter describes schemes for organizing ESs and begins to present them as overall problem-solving systems.

5

Problem-Solving
Strategies

This chapter provides an initial internal glimpse of ESs as problem-solving systems. Specifically, it presents a conceptual overview of several system architectures—overall problem-solving and organizational concepts—that are used as the framework for combining the basic components into a complete system.

The descriptions proceed from straightforward approaches that are sufficient for relatively simple tasks with limited reasoning requirements to more sophisticated approaches that are used for very complex situations.

5.1 Exhaustive Search

Simple exhaustive search is a direct application of search to every possible problem state. It is an organized procedure for trying all possibilities.

PRINCIPLE 5.1: Exhaustive search can be applied only when the problem is *immediately tractable*.

An immediately tractable problem is one with a reasonably small problem space, no need for backtracking to retract mistakes, and

knowledge and data that are complete and reliable. XCON (J. Mc-
Dermott, 1982), a well-known system for configuring VAX computers,
relies on a very limited degree of exhaustive search.

5.2 Large Search Spaces

Exhaustive search could, in theory, be used to solve any noninfinite
search problem. In reality, however, a useful system must not only
solve the specified problem, it must solve it within specific time and
resource limits. For most real-world problems the space is much too
large to allow exhaustive search. In Stefik, 1982, it is suggested that
the practical upper bound for exhaustive search is very restrictive—
about 10! possible solutions.

Two basic methods are commonly used for problems with a large
problem space:

- Develop an efficient process for dealing with the large space (Sec.
  5.3).

- Transform the space into a more manageable form. For example, it
  may be possible to divide a complex problem into a collection of
  relatively simple components, each of which can then be addressed
  separately—possibly by using exhaustive search on each section (Sec.
  5.4).

5.3 Generate and Test

One method for increasing the efficiency of a search process, called
heuristically guided search, relies on the use of a heuristic evaluation
function to guide the search process as it moves through the search
space (e.g., to decide which node to expand). Although this process
effectively illustrates the use of heuristics in processing, the actual
technique is most widely used in AI applications outside of ES.

Conceptually, it is also possible to structure search as *generate and
test*. In its most basic form, generate and test is a type of depth-first
search that is used to perform classical *reasoning by elimination*. It
relies on a *generator* that develops complete candidate solutions and
an *evaluator* that tests each proposed solution by comparing it with
the required state. This process of generation followed by evaluation
continues until a solution is discovered.

Ideally, a generator should be *complete*—to generate all possible
solutions—and *nonredundant*: each solution (or equivalent solution)
should be generated only once. The difficulty with this form of generate
and test is, again, the time required for execution; it is actually simply
a technique for structuring exhaustive search.

In some cases, however, it is possible to provide the generator with knowledge that will allow it to recognize that an entire class of proposed solutions will not meet some specified *elimination constraint*. When such a recognition is possible, the size of the search space can be greatly reduced by *pruning:* dropping an entire class of elements from further consideration. This process is called *hierarchical generate and test* (HGT).

Example 5.1   One of the biggest problems for a police detective is knowing where to start in an attempt to locate an unknown criminal. To solve this problem, a detective often begins by looking for clues, for example, fingerprints, to focus the search process.

Consider the design of a system that would assist in fingerprint matching. The task in this case is to locate a given pattern within a large number of possibilities. The search tree that corresponds to this identification might look like this:

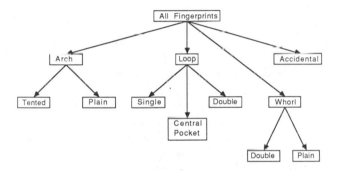

Each of the nodes in the figure represents a type of fingerprint. It is often possible to identify a whorl after analyzing only a small part of the print. It is then possible to prune entire branches (i.e., arch, loop, and accidental) from the search tree.

PRINCIPLE 5.2: HGT is effective only when it is possible to *factor the solution space* and *evaluate partial solutions.*

To factor a solution space, it must be possible to divide the space into classes that can be considered independently. The value of HGT derives from the quick reduction gained from early pruning of partial solutions. Therefore, it must be possible to predict that the final version of a solution would be unacceptable by comparing a partial version against some specified constraint.

HGT is frequently used for *data interpretation* problems that attempt to identify reasonable interpretations (i.e., make identifications) from a large volume of data. It is especially effective when the set of acceptable solutions is a small subset of all the possibilities. The most frequent condition blocking the use of HGT is the lack of an effective evaluator for partial solutions.

Dendral [Lindsay, 1980], an ES that infers molecular structures from mass spectrogram data, is well known for using a specialized form of HGT. Other examples include GA1 [Stefik, 1978] and AM [Davis, 1982b].

5.4 Space Transformation

Many strategies deal with the problem of a large problem space by changing the space into a more manageable form through the use of *abstraction* and *problem decomposition*. Abstraction is the process of concentrating on a generalized representation of the most important elements of a problem. This allows a problem solver to ignore the minor details and focus on big decisions.

PRINCIPLE 5.3: Searching an abstracted search space can greatly reduce combinatorial explosion.

Problem decomposition is the process of breaking a large, complex problem into a collection of smaller subparts. By using *hierarchical* problem-solving concepts, it is possible to define several levels of abstraction, each with an increasing level of detail. Such decomposition attempts to break the overall problem into smaller subtasks, solve each subtask independently, and then combine the separate pieces to form a solution to the original problem.

The most commonly cited example of problem abstraction and decomposition is that of planning a long cross-country drive. Rather than attempt to search for the optimum route by using a very large collection of state and city maps, we typically begin with a single-page abstraction of the highways in the United States (i.e., a map showing primarily the interstate highways). After planning the overall route, we then consider more detailed maps for the exact routing within congested areas.

This process quickly produces a satisficing solution to the problem. The key point is that little is to be gained by studying a detailed map to look for the absolute optimum when a quick search of the abstraction produces an adequate solution.

Processing subproblems

The most direct form of space transformation is simply to divide a complex problem into a collection of *independent* subproblems.

PRINCIPLE 5.4: Subproblems are independent iff the decisions made within one subproblem have no effect on any other.

In most cases the subproblems that result from decomposition will have interactions among them. The following sections describe techniques for dealing with such interactions.

Fixed order of subproblems.   It is sometimes possible to define a *fixed order of execution* for subproblem processing that will control the interaction between subproblems.

For example, Syscon [Rolston, 1986*a*) is an ES that has been used since 1984 to configure mainframe computers. Syscon's task is to develop a specification and configuration of the low-level components that are required to produce a system that is initially described as a collection of major components (e.g., "two processors, an I/O controller, two main memory units, etc.").

There are approximately 479 different types of components in the target system (a DPS 90) that range in complexity from a simple cable to a power-supply assembly. The configuration process typically requires about one week of effort when performed by a human expert and involves between 500 and 800 decisions. The output of the configuration process is a document (typically 40 to 80 pages in length) that lists the required components and describes the interconnections among them.

Although it is true that a DPS 90 is composed of thousands of occurrences of individual components, it is possible to view the system abstractly as a composition of no more than 24 different "major functional units" (some of which correspond to physical cabinets). Given this abstraction, the overall space can be partitioned into a set of subspaces that correspond to the major units.

The configuration problem is solved by first configuring a collection of major units (which identifies the units and the connections between them) and then scheduling a series of subtasks (one for each subspace) to configure the internal components of each unit.

Unfortunately, although the set of possible subproblems is fixed, the subproblems are not independent. There are many potential interactions among them. To address the problem of subproblem interaction, the subproblems are scheduled in a specific predetermined order. Actions taken in the processing of the early subproblems constrain the possibilities in the later subproblems, and thus the process becomes increasingly deterministic as processing continues. Note that this approach is possible in Syscon only because it is possible to define a predetermined set of subtasks and an ordering for their execution.

Dynamic subproblem development

Unfortunately, it is frequently impossible to identify an invariant order for subproblems that will suffice in every situation. In such a case it is necessary to increase the reasoning power of the system by including a mechanism for dynamically forming the subproblem set during execution. (An architecture based on a constant order is simply a subset of the general structuring case in which the developer applies the intelligence required to structure the set and then directly encodes the results.) The following two sections present techniques for structuring this reasoning process.

5.5 Planning

To understand the significance of planning and its application to dynamic subproblem analysis, first consider the significance of mistakes within a given domain.

PRINCIPLE 5.5: Incorrect decisions are *ignorable*, *recoverable*, or *irrecoverable*.

In some domains incorrect decisions are ignorable in the sense that they affect only efficiency and not the actual correctness of a solution. For example, when choosing a path through an unfamiliar city, we may realize that we have selected a route that results in the long way around. Although it may be desirable to return to some previous choice point and select another route, it is generally not necessary to do so. We can ignore the mistake, declare to our passengers that we are on the scenic route, and continue on the long way around. Nothing is lost but time and, possibly, credibility with passengers.

In other domains mistakes are not ignorable (i.e., must be corrected) but they may be recoverable; an incorrect decision, when detected, can be retracted and replaced by another without irreparable damage resulting. For example, if when attempting to pack travel baggage into the trunk of a car we discover that the items have been entered in the wrong order, we can simply remove them and try again. Nothing is lost but time and, possibly, tempers.

There are, however, domains in which mistakes are irrecoverable. For example, a crisis management system for a military aircraft [Anderson, 1984] cannot advise the pilot to eject and then recognize an error and attempt to retract the decision at a later time.

Planning is the process of deciding on sequences of actions prior to executing the actions. Planning systems operate by *simulating* actions within a *model* of the domain. As each action is simulated, its effect on the domain is observed. Actions that would be irrecoverable in the real world are easily withdrawn in a simulated environment.

PRINCIPLE 5.6: Planning can increase efficiency in domains in which mistakes are ignorable or recoverable, and it is imperative when mistakes are irrecoverable.

Basic Planning

Planning systems frequently attempt to work on one subproblem (resulting from problem decomposition) until it is completely solved and then tackle another. However, difficulties arise if the subproblems *interact*. For example, a planner for a large construction job might solve the "set the main girder" subproblem by planning to use a ground-based crane for a period of 3 days, whereas a later subproblem solution plans to remove the crane to pour a concrete floor during the same 3 days.

Planners rely on dynamic resolution of subproblem interactions to deal with this type of problem. The first step in the process is to recognize that, although it is theoretically possible to have extensive interaction between goals, in many actual cases—the *nearly decomposable problems* [Simon, 1981)—there are only infrequent conflicts between subproblems. In such cases it is often reasonably efficient to assume initially that the problem is completely decomposable and then to use special processing to detect and resolve interactions only as they actually occur.

The early basic planning system Strips [Fikes, 1971] uses the above general approach. Like many early planning systems, it was based on the *means-ends analysis* paradigm that was originally used in the historically significant system General Problem Solver (GPS) [Newell, 1963]. This paradigm operates by identifying the *difference* between the current state and the goal state and then heuristically selecting operations that will reduce the identified difference.

Strips combines means-ends analysis with the use of a *goal stack*. The goal stack contains both goals and the operators that are intended to achieve the goals. In addition to the goal stack, a Strips-like planner uses a predicate logic representation of the current system state and a set of operators that is used to modify the state.

A major issue of concern for any planning system is the *frame problem* [McCarthy, 1969]: deciding how much of the domain representation to include for each operator. In the simple example of Sec. 2.2 the complete system state (two elements) is described for each node. In a complex situation, such as the representation of a factory floor, many elements may have to be represented to describe the entire state.

Many times the application of an operator changes only a few of the many items present in the system state description, yet if the operator lists all before and after conditions, all of the unchanged elements will be needlessly repeated for each operation. Strips addresses this problem with what has come to be known as the *Strips assumption* [Wilkins, 1984]: All elements in the state are assumed to be unchanged except for those explicitly listed as changing.

Associated with each operator is a *precondition* list that describes the elements that must be present in the state description for the operator to apply, an *add* list that describes the elements to be added

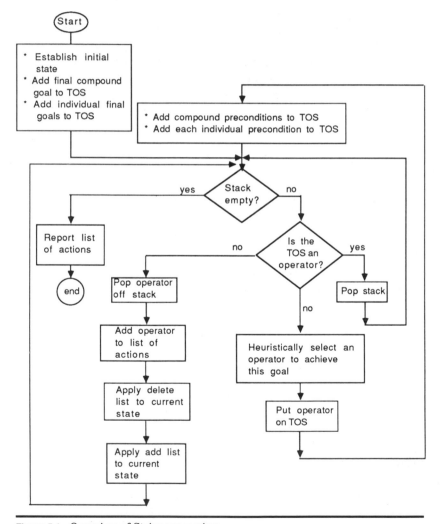

Figure 5.1 Overview of Strips processing.

to the state description when the operator is applied, and a *delete* list that describes the elements to be deleted. The overall operation of a Strips-like planner is shown in Fig. 5.1 and is described in Example 5.2.

Example 5.2 Consider the hypothetical application of a Strips-like system for planning the actions of an automated cargo arm that moves large supply cylinders to and from a space shuttle that is docked with a permanent space station. The station includes a platform that has two resting areas on which cylinders can be placed. The shuttle cargo bay is similarly equipped with two cylinder-resting areas. The cargo movement arm is attached to the space station and moves objects back and forth between the station and the shuttle, and it can place one cylinder on top of another. (This example is a revision of the *blocks world* domain that is frequently used to describe the operation of a planning system. In the blocks world a robot manipulates blocks on a table top by using a few specified operations.)

The state of the system at any given time is described using the following:

```
ON(X,Y) - Cylinder X is on top of Cylinder Y.
ONSTATION(X) - Cylinder X is resting on the space station plat-
form.
INBAY(X) - Cylinder X is in the shuttle's cargo bay.
CLEAR(X) - There is nothing on top of cylinder X.
ARMEMPTY - The cargo arm is not holding anything.
HOLDING(X) - The arm is holding cylinder X.
```

The following operators, with associated precondition, add, and delete lists, are available:

```
STACK(X,Y) - Place cylinder X on cylinder Y.
    P: CLEAR(Y) ∧ HOLDING(X)
    D: CLEAR(Y) ∧ HOLDING(X)
    A: ARMEMPTY ∧ ON(X,Y)
UNSTACK(X,Y) - Remove cylinder X from cylinder Y.
    P: On(X,Y) ∧ ARMEMPTY ∧ CLEAR(X)
    D: ON(X,Y) ∧ ARMEMPTY
    A: HOLDING(X) ∧ CLEAR(Y)
GETFROMBAY(X) - Pick up cylinder X from the cargo bay
    P: CLEAR(X) ∧ INBAY(X) ∧ ARMEMPTY
    D: INBAY(X) ∧ ARMEMPTY
    A: HOLDING(X)

GETFROMSTATION(X) - Pick up cylinder X from the station platform.
    P: CLEAR(X) ∧ ONSTATION(X) ∧ ARMEMPTY
    D: ONSTATION(X) ∧ ARMEMPTY
    A: HOLDING(X)
PUTINBAY(X) - Put cylinder in the cargo bay.
    P: HOLDING(X)
    D: HOLDING(X)
    A: INBAY(X) ∧ ARMEMPTY
PUTONSTATION(X) - Put cylinder X on the station platform.
    P: HOLDING(X)
    D: HOLDING(X)
    A: ONSTATION(X) ∧ ARMEMPTY
```

Given the following starting state:

```
CLEAR(B)  ^  ON(B,A)  ^  ONSTATION(A)  ^  CLEAR(E)  ^  ON(E,D)  ^  ON(D,C)  ^
INBAY(C)  ^  ARMEMPTY
```

find a set of operators that will produce the following final state:

```
CLEAR(D)  ^  ON(D,E)  ^  ON(C,B)  ^  ONSTATION(E)  ^  CLEAR(A)  ^  INBAY(A)  ^
ONSTATION(B)
```

Because we are using backward reasoning, the first step is to enter the final compound goal as the first entry on the goal stack. It is then followed by each of the individual goals.

```
CURRENT STATE                    GOAL STACK
CLEAR(B)                         CLEAR(A)
ON(B,A)                          INBAY(A)
ONSTATION(A)                     ONSTATION(E)
CLEAR(E)                         ON(C,B)
ON(E,D)                          ON(D,E)
ON(D,C)                          ONSTATION(B)
INBAY(C)                         CLEAR(D)
ARMEMPTY          CLEAR(D)  ^  ONSTATION(B)  ^  ON(D,E)  ^  ON(C,B)  ^
                    ONSTATION(E)  ^  INBAY(A)  ^  CLEAR(A)
```

Each of the seven individual goals is now treated as an independent subproblem. Operations required to achieve the goal on the *top of the stack* (TOS) are derived on the basis of the independence assumption (i.e., without regard for the potential for impact on other goals). The presence of the compound goal as the last entry on the stack is a very basic technique for *dynamically dealing with interactions between subproblems*.

If the subproblems are actually independent, then, because each of the subgoals has been achieved, the compound goal will be met when it is reached. In the case of independent subproblems, solving the subproblems is equivalent to achieving the overall goal. If, however, the subproblems are not actually independent, the compound goal will not be satisfied when it is reached because the operator applied to achieve one subgoal may undo the results of another subgoal solution. (A specific example of this occurs later in this discussion.)

The following steps are now applied:
Action Taken: Consider the TOS CLEAR(A). It is not in the current state and, therefore, an operator must be selected to achieve CLEAR(A).

In general, several operators may apply and the selection will strongly influence the time required to find and execute a solution. Many heuristics can be applied to this selection. For example, one heuristic is that the applicable operator with the greatest number of preconditions should be selected. For the sake of brevity, in the remainder of this example operators will be selected without explanation.

In this case, UNSTACK(B,A) is selected. The operator, UNSTACK(B,A), replaces the goal, CLEAR(A), on the TOS because the goal is guaranteed to be satisfied after the operator is executed. The situation after the operator selection is as follows (where * is used to represent "unchanged from previous" and ⟨final⟩ represents the final compound goal).

```
STATE                 STACK
                      UNSTACK(B,A)
    *                 INBAY(A)
                          *
                          *
                      ONSTATION(B)
                      CLEAR(D)
                      (final)
```

Next Action: The preconditions required to execute UNSTACK(B,A), determined from the precondition list for UNSTACK, are pushed onto the stack; first in a compound form and then individually. The resulting situation is:

```
STATE                          STACK
                               ON(B,A)
                               ARMCLEAR
                               CLEAR(B)
    *       ON(B,A) ∧ ARMCLEAR ∧ CLEAR(B)
                               UNSTACK(B,A)
                                   *
```

Next Action: ON(B,A) is in the current state and is therefore popped from the TOS and discarded. ARMCLEAR is also in the current state and is popped, as are CLEAR(B) and the compound goal. The TOS is now UNSTACK(B,A), so it is "executed" against the simulated environment and the operator is popped from the stack. The elements from UNSTACK's delete list are deleted from the state, and then the elements from the add list are added:

```
DELETE: ON(B,A) ∧ ARMEMPTY    ADD: HOLDING(B) ∧ CLEAR(A)
```

The result is:

```
ACTIONS       STATE         STACK
UNSTACK(B,A)  CLEAR(B)      INBAY(A)
              ONSTATION(A)  ONSTATION(E)
              CLEAR(E)      ON(C,B)
              ON(E,D)       ON(D,E)
              ON(D,C)       ONSTATION(B)
              INBAY(C)      CLEAR(D)
              HOLDING(B)    (final)
              CLEAR(A)
```

Next Action: Replace INBAY(A) with the operator PUTINBAY(A).
Next Action: Add preconditions for PUTINBAY(A).

Next Action: Replace HOLDING(A) with GETFROMSTATION(A) followed by its preconditions.

Next Action: Replace ARMEMPTY with PUTONSTATION(b) followed by its preconditions.

Next Action: Pop HOLDING(B) and execute PUTONSTATION(B):

```
DELETE: HOLDING(B)          ADD: ONSTATION(B) ∧ ARMEMPTY
ACTIONS             STATE           STACK
UNSTACK(B,A)        CLEAR(B)        ONSTATION(A)
PUTONSTATION(B)     ONSTATION(A)    CLEAR(A)
                    CLEAR(E) CLEAR(A) ∧ ONSTATION(A) ∧ ARMEMPTY
                    ON(E,D)         GETFROMSTATION(A)
                    ON(D,C)         HOLDING(A)
                    INBAY(C)        PUTINBAY(A)
                    CLEAR(A)        ONSTATION(E)
                    ONSTATION(B)    ON(C,B)
                    AREMPTY         ON(D,E)
                                    ONSTATION(B)
                                    CLEAR(D)
                                    ⟨final⟩
```

Next Actions: Pop ONSTATION(A), CLEAR(A), and the compound goal.

Execute GETFROMSTATION(A):

D: ONSTATION(A)   ∧   ARMEMPTY   A: HOLDING(A)

Pop HOLDING(A) and execute PUTINBAY(A):

D: HOLDING(A) A: INBAY(A) ∧ ARMEMPTY

```
ACTIONS             STATE           STACK
UNSTACK(B,A)        CLEAR(B)        ONSTATION(E)
PUTONSTATION(B)     CLEAR(E)        ON(C,B)
GETFROMSTATION(A)   ON(E,D)         ON(D,E)
PUTINBAY(A)         ON(D,C)         ONSTATION(B)
                    INBAY(C)        CLEAR(D)
                    CLEAR(A)        ⟨final⟩
                    ONSTATION(B)
                    INBAY(A)
                    ARMEMPTY
```

Next Actions: Replace ONSTATION(E) with PUTONSTATION(E) and add the precondition, HOLDING(E).

Replace HOLDING(E) with UNSTACK(E,D) and its preconditions.

Pop CLEAR(E), ARMEMPTY, ON(E,D), and the compound goal.

Execute UNSTACK(E,D):

D: ON(E,D) ∧ ARMEMPTY A: HOLDING(e) ∧ CLEAR(D)

Execute PUTONSTATION(E):

D: HOLDING(E) A: ONSTATION(E) ∧ ARMEMPTY

Replace ON(C,B) with STACK(C,B) and its preconditions.

Replace HOLDING(C) with GETFROMBAY(C) and it preconditions.
Pop ARMEMPTY and INBAY(C).
Replace CLEAR(C) with UNSTACK(D,C) and its preconditions.
Pop CLEAR(D), ARMEMPTY, ON(D,C), and the compound goal.
Execute UNSTACK(D,C):
   D: ON(D,C) $^\wedge$ ARMEMPTY A: HOLDING(D) $^\wedge$ CLEAR(C)

ACTIONS	STATE	STACK
UNSTACK(B,A)	CLEAR(B)	CLEAR(C) $^\wedge$ INBAY(C) $^\wedge$ ARMEMPTY
PUTONSTATION(B)	CLEAR(E)	GETFROMBAY(C)
GETFROMSTATION(A)	INBAY(C)	CLEAR(B)
PUTINBAY(A)	CLEAR(A)	CLEAR(B) $^\wedge$HOLDING(C)
UNSTACK(E,D)	ONSTATION(B)	STACK(C,B)
PUTONSTATION(E)	INBAY(A)	ON(D,E)
UNSTACK(D,C)	CLEAR(D)	ONSTATION(B)
	ONSTATION(E)	CLEAR(D)
	HOLDING(D)	(final)
	CLEAR(C)	

Note that the resulting situation is an example of the interaction among subgoals. The execution of PUTONSTATION(E) accomplished the ARMEMPTY subgoal, but the latter execution of UNSTACK(D,C)—to accomplish CLEAR(C)—undoes the ARMEMPTY subgoal. To resolve this problem, the ARMEMPTY goal must again be put on the stack and resolved. This results in:

ACTIONS	STATE	STACK
		ARMEMPTY
		CLEAR(C) $^\wedge$ INBAY(C) $^\wedge$ ARMEMPTY
*	*	GETFROMBAY(C)
		*

Final Actions: Replace ARMEMPTY with STACK(D,E) and its preconditions.
Execute STACK(D,E):
   D: CLEAR(E) $^\wedge$ HOLDING(D) A: ARMEMPTY $^\wedge$ ON(D,E)
Execute GETFROMBAY(C):
   D: ARMEMPTY $^\wedge$ INBAY(C) A: HOLDING(C)
Pop CLEAR(B) and the compound goal.
Execute STACK(C,B):
   D: HOLDING(C) $^\wedge$ CLEAR(B) A: ON(C,B)
Pop ON(D,E), ONSTATION(B), and CLEAR(D).

The final goal has now been reached and is satisfied.
   Not all basic planning systems use means-ends analysis and a goal stack. Some operate by dividing the task into subproblems and then

assuming (possibly incorrectly) that the subproblems are independent. The final solution that results from such assumed reasoning is then analyzed. The problem-solving system is called recursively to reduce the difference between the previous results and the desired goal. Hacker [Sussman, 1975] is a planning system based on this paradigm. Hacker searches for appropriate sequences and then notes the areas where such attempts have failed. It then treats each such failure as a *bug* and applies a specific *bug-correction routine* (from a library of such routines) to attempt to remove the bug.

Other basic planning systems include Interplan [Tate, 1975], a system that is based on the dynamic reordering of subgoals, a IrisII [Fox, 1982], a system that performs job shop scheduling.

Hierarchical planning

The basic planning systems described above are hierarchical only in the sense that they rely on *hierarchical goal structures;* each goal is subdivided into subgoals, which are then further divided. The result is a hierarchical set of subgoals. Figure 5.2 shows a portion of a structure that represents the goals from Example 5.2.

Basic planning systems also have in common the fact that they do not initially distinguish between actions that are important and those that are less important. This means that important decisions can be masked by superfluous detail. As a result, considerable detailed plan-

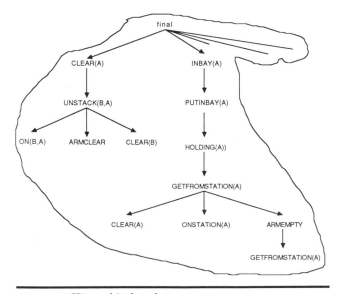

Figure 5.2 Hierarchical goal structure.

ning effort can be wasted as the planner works its way down paths that ultimately turn out to be dead ends. *Hierarchical planning systems* attack this problem by using abstraction, problem decomposition, and a top-down problem-solving problem approach.

PRINCIPLE 5.7: Hierarchical planners develop several complete plans, each at a more detailed level of abstraction.

The highest level represents a complete solution to an abstraction of the most important aspects of the problem. Insignificant details are simply ignored. This high-level plan is then successively refined, each time by considering additional details, until an acceptable plan at an acceptable level of detail is developed.

Abstrips [Sacerdoti, 1974] is a well-known extension of Strips to hierarchical planning. To assist in deciding which elements of the domain are most important, in Abstrips a *criticality value* is associated with each component of the preconditions and delete list for each operator. Things that are hard to accomplish are assigned a high value, and those that are easy receive a low value. In the problem shown in Example 5.2, ONSTATION would receive a high value and ARM-EMPTY, which is very easy to accomplish, would be assigned a low value.

Execution in Abstrips begins with the initial "current" criticality level" set to the maximum level of criticality. The planning operation that follows is identical to Strips except that preconditions whose criticality value is below the current level are invisible to the planner and, when an operator is executed, any delete list elements with criticality values lower than the current level are not deleted.

After a complete plan has been formed, the criticality level is decremented and the planning process is restarted by using the plan developed during the previous planning process as a guide. This plan is passed down to the lower level by starting the process with a goal stack that consists of the final goal and each of the operators along with its *visible* preconditions (based on the new lower-level criticality value), which were identified by the preceding level. The purpose of these goals on the goal stack (rather than having a stack that consists of only the final goal) is, in effect, to assist the planning system when it has to make a choice as to which of several operators to select or which of several orders to include on the stack. This assistance constrains the planning process and assists in reducing combinatorial explosion.

There are, however, several problems with this procedure. Because the items that would normally be deleted by the execution of an operator may be hidden, it is possible to end up with an inconsistent state description. (This condition can be ignored and will be resolved by later execution.) Sometimes the planning process within a given level will fail to find a solution. When that occurs, it is necessary to return to the next higher level and develop a new plan.

A much more significant difficulty is the need to make an a priori assignment of the criticality value for each operator. Moreover, this assignment must be equally applicable for all domain problems that the system might be called upon to solve.

5.6   Least-Commitment Principle and Constraint Propagation

All of the planning systems discussed up to this point produce *linear plans*: The actions required to accomplish each goal are started and completed before the planning system begins work on the next goal. In many complex cases it is useful to produce a *nonlinear plan* by which actions relative to a goal can be suspended and then restarted following the completion of another goal.

PRINCIPLE 5.8: Nonlinear plans often allow for tighter interleaving of tasks and reduce schedule "holes."

One approach for generating such plans is to apply the *least-commitment principle:* Decisions should be postponed to the last possible moment, when the maximum amount of information is available. This has the effect of coordinating decision-making activity with the availability of information and avoids the possibly negative impact of arbitrary decisions.

Noah [Sacerdoti, 1977] is an example of a hierarchical planner that uses least commitment to produce nonlinear plans. Problem solving in Noah is accomplished by developing a *procedural net,* a sophisticated structure for representing both action and state information. The problem-solving process begins with a single node that represents the goal to be achieved. This parent node includes a pointer to a collection of functions that expand goals into subgoals. Each of the subgoals is linked to every other subgoal and back to the parent goal.

Each subgoal also includes a pointer to a set of functions that are used to further expand the subgoals. They also include a declarative representation of the effects, if any, of executing the expansion functions. Noah employs the least-commitment principle by expanding subgoals without any regard for ordering until the possibility of an interaction is detected. The possibility of such interaction is detected by one of several *critics*—small programs that review plans for potential conflicts.

This principle is extended even further in Mologen [Stefik, 1981] through the use of *constraint posting*. Rather than explicitly selecting

objects, the planner *partially describes* them by simply identifying relations between domain elements. These relations serve to constrain
the possible choices (e.g., the selection of which of several possible
cylinders to unstack in Example 5.2).

This process focuses on the selection of *objects* (rather than actions)
that are involved in operations. For example, when designing a custom
home that includes an indoor spa, a planning system might generate
the following constraints:

$$LARGER(D,S)$$

$$SMALLER(S,R)$$

where D = width of the door
     S = width of the spa
     R = width of the room

For additional information on the theoretical aspects of constraint
satisfaction planning systems, see Fox, 1982, Mackworth, 1985, and
D'Ambrosio, 1985.

The above concepts have also been used in more recent applications.
For example, many planners show acceptable performance only in the
specific domain for which they were developed (or for closely related
domains). Sipe [Wilkins, 1984] uses hierarchical, constraint-based, interactive planning to achieve greater domain independence.

Express [Hankins, 1985] is a constraint-based system that develops
time, resource, and task plans for assembling space shuttle payloads
at the Kennedy Space Center.

5.7 Classification Model

The *Classification Model* (CM) is a framework for structuring rules
that has been widely applied, especially for diagnostic and interpretation tasks. The CM is used to organize reasoning (from observations
to conclusions) that is based on *classification:* the selection of a conclusion from a prespecified list of possible conclusions. It is typically
implemented as a modified production system with a knowledge base,
control mechanism, and working memory. Each of these segments is
described below.

Knowledge base

A CM knowledge base consists of:

- A list of possible observations. (This includes both *initial observed
conditions* and *findings* that result from some form of test or experiment that is executed to gather information.)

- A list of possible conclusions. (This includes both *intermediate conclusions* and *final conclusions*. In most cases the reasoning process will move through several levels of intermediate conclusions before reaching a final conclusion.)
- A set of rules that relate the observations to the conclusions.

Control

The primary role of the control segment is to order the collection of evidence.

Working memory

Working memory is a global memory area that stores initial observations, findings that have been made, and conclusions that have been reached.

Note that the working memory segment of the CM is simpler than the corresponding segment of a typical production system (Sec. 4.5). The global memory area in a production system is used to store object-attribute-value triples to implement a form of predicate logic. The CM uses the global area to store simple propositions (i.e., statements that are either true or false) and so implements a form of the more simple propositional logic.

The reasoning process in a CM uses a conceptually simple form of inference based on the representation of implication by rules and the application of modus ponens based on collected evidence (Sec. 3.8).

This process begins at the initial observations and applies rules to develop new findings or intermediate hypotheses based on the initial observations. It then proceeds through several levels of intermediate analysis until a final conclusion is reached.

Two general types of rules are used in a CM:

- *Evidence-to-conclusion.* These rules are used to list the conclusions that are indicated by the evidence and to drive the reasoning process described above. An example of this type of rule is:
  IF   the heating element in an oven is glowing red,
  THEN conclude that the element is very hot.
- *Conclusion-to-evidence.* This type of rule describes the evidence that should be present if a given condition exists. These rules are used to describe evidence to look for to confirm a suspected hypothesis. An example of this type of rule is:
  IF   the lights went off because the utility company lost power,
  THEN the neighbors' lights should also be off.

Within these general classes several specific types of rules are used:

- *Finding-to-finding.*   This type of rule describes the fact that one finding can be inferred from another. (For example, a rule that says that once you have made the finding that a car's battery is dead, then you can also conclude that the finding "headlights fail to light" also is true.) This is an example of the application of a general principle:

PRINCIPLE 5.8: Avoid asking questions to retrieve information that could be inferred from information that is already available.

- *Finding-to-hypothesis.*   This type of rule is used to generate intermediate hypotheses from observations or findings. (For example, if the circuit breaker has popped, then conclude that there is an electrical problem.)
- *Hypothesis-to-hypothesis.*   This type of rule is used to move from intermediate hypothesis to other hypotheses or final conclusions. For example:
  IF   all power went off suddenly and all the power in the neighborhood is off,
  THEN conclude that the electric utility has lost power.

For more information on classification systems see Weiss, 1984, and Clancey, 1984*b*.

5.8   Blackboard Model

The *Blackboard Model* (BBM), which was developed as an abstraction of the techniques used in the Hearsay [Erman, 1980] and Hasp [Nii, 1982] systems, is a system architecture that is used to structure reasoning in complex domains.

An overview of the BBM is shown in Fig. 5.3. To structure a problem-solving task by using the BBM, the solution space is first divided into a hierarchy of partial solutions, each at a different level of abstraction. For example, in the Hearsay system (which interprets spoken words) the partial solution levels included sounds, segments, syllables, words, word sequences, phrases, etc. An ES for diagnosis of difficult system-level problems in a mainframe computer complex might include partial solution levels of individual unit hardware errors, individual unit software errors, subsystem errors, and intersystem errors.

The *blackboard* in a Blackboard System (BBS) is a global memory structure that is used to contain the emerging partial solutions as shown in Fig. 5.3. The knowledge in a BBS is divided among several

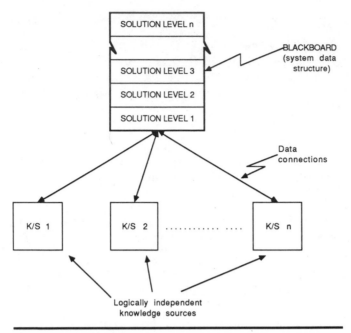

Figure 5.3 Blackboard model.

separate *knowledge sources* (KS) that can observe and modify the content of the BB but cannot communicate directly among themselves.

Processing in a BBS is based on the concept of *independent cooperating experts*. When faced with complex problems, experts frequently work together; each contributes partial solutions that result from his or her own expertise. (For example, in the diagnostic situation mentioned above, a hardware expert, software expert, and systems expert are frequently involved in solving system-level computer problems because any given problem can manifest itself in many different forms.)

PRINCIPLE 5.9: The BBM is useful for structuring complex problem-solving tasks that require multiple experts.

Each KS represents an individual expert who observes the current content of the BB and tries to develop a new (typically higher-level) partial solution based on the application of his or her knowledge to the current state. Thus in the Hearsay system, once a set of syllables appears on the BB, the word-level expert can begin to form words from the syllables.

Another key concept in a BBS is the notion of *opportunistic scheduling*. Conceptually, production systems are based on the general concept of opportunistic scheduling; rules fire when they are appropriate without a priori ordering.*

This concept is developed in a very specialized and powerful form in BBS. There is no control flow because each expert is a self-activating ("demon") process that watches the BB and seizes the opportunity to add solutions when possible. Nii, 1986*a*, gives the example of several people working together on a jigsaw puzzle to illustrate the concept of BBS.

In this way the complete high-level solution evolves naturally without the need for explicit a priori control.†

For more information on BB, see Nii, 1986*a* and 1986*b*.

In the following chapter techniques for dealing with partially incomplete or inaccurate information are described.

---

* In actuality, almost all production systems use at least some specific rule ordering. Many systems which are called production systems are rule-based but have completely abandoned the concept of opportunistic scheduling.

† BBS implementations include some control, such as arbitration of contention for the right to write on the BB.

6

Dealing with Uncertainty

One of the most important capabilities of a human expert, and one of the most difficult to faithfully replicate in an ES, is the ability to deal effectively with imprecise, incomplete, and sometimes uncertain information.

There are many different types of uncertainty that are common in expert domains:

Uncertain knowledge. Frequently the expert will have only heuristic knowledge regarding some aspect of the domain. For example, the expert may know only that a certain set of evidence probably implies a certain conclusion.

Uncertain data. Even when we are certain of the domain knowledge, there may still be uncertainty in the data that describes the external environment. For example, when attempting to infer a specific cause from an observed effect, we may have to rely on questionable test results.

Incomplete information. It is frequently necessary to make decisions based on incomplete information. This can occur for several reasons. For example, we must make such decisions in the course of processing incrementally acquired information.

Randomness.   Some domains are inherently random; even though the available knowledge and information is complete and the knowledge is certain, the domain still has stochastic properties.

ESs using current technology are not capable of dealing with uncertainty as effectively as their human counterparts, and this subject remains an important research topic. The following sections describe several methods for handling uncertainty. Although, as noted above, these methods will not completely duplicate human capabilities, each has proved to be useful in the development of actual systems.

6.1 Reasoning Based on Partial Information

Reasoning systems based on predicate logic (as described in Chap. 3) are conceptually elegant and intellectually appealing because they are precise and rigorous. By using formal logic, truth can be given or derived with equal assurance. Once established, truth is always true. Moreover, derived truth will never produce a contradiction, given that no contradictions exist within the axioms.

Because of these characteristics, predicate logic is a *monotonic* reasoning system. "Monotonic," which means to "move in one direction only," is used in describing a predicate logic system to convey the idea of a reasoning process that moves in one direction only—that of continuously adding additional truth.

PRINCIPLE 6.1: In a monotonic reasoning system the number of facts known to be true at any specified time is always increasing, never decreasing.

Unfortunately, although they provide a basis for consistent, reliable inference, these characteristics also limit the extent to which pure logic systems can be applied in the real world. As introduced in Sec. 6.1, reasoning processes that are to be applied to practical, unstructured problems must recognize at least the following:

- Available information is frequently incomplete, at least at any given decision point.
- Conditions change over time.
- There is frequently a need to make an efficient, but possibly incorrect, guess when reasoning reaches a dead end.

6.2 Nonmonotonic Reasoning

In dealing with these difficulties, human problem solvers often augment absolute truth with beliefs that are subject to change given further information. These *tentative beliefs* are generally based on *default assumptions* that are made in light of the lack of evidence to the contrary. For example, even though the decision to board a commercial airliner is very important, when we actually make the decision, we will probably assume that the pilot is competent and that the aircraft is airworthy, unless there is something that indicates otherwise. A *nonmonotonic reasoning system* (NMRS) is based on this concept.

PRINCIPLE 6.2: A nonmonotonic reasoning system tracks a set of tentative beliefs and revises those beliefs when new knowledge is observed or derived.

An NMRS typically includes a set of *premises* that are held to be immutably true (analogously to the axioms in a predicate logic system). In addition to premises, the system keeps a collection of tentative beliefs: pieces of knowledge that are explicitly recognized to be potentially incorrect because they are either assumptions or beliefs inferred from assumptions. For each tentative belief the system maintains a *dependency record* that tracks the belief vs. its *justification:* the facts, beliefs, and inferences that were used to generate the tentative belief.

Example 6.1 Consider the following rather contrived situation: A woman who has never been out of the United States wakes from unconsciousness on a deserted bank of a very large river in unfamiliar territory. She can remember (somehow) only that she is near a large city and that the city is at the mouth of the river. Although it is dark, she can sense that the area surrounding her is warm, humid, and tropical.

Given that she can recall the facts listed below (from past study of world geography) and that she assumes she is in the United States (given the lack of evidence to the contrary), describe the set of beliefs and associated justifications that she would probably develop.

```
fact 1     The sky is blue.
                                  .
                                  .
                                  .

fact 37    The Amazon river—
           A    flows from west to east
           B    empties into the South Atlantic Ocean
           C    ends at Almirim, Brazil
fact 38    Most of the area near the mouth of the Amazon is warm, hu-
           mid, and tropical.
fact 39    The mouth of the Nile is in Egypt.
fact 40    The Columbia River—
           A    flows from east to west
           B    empties into the Pacific Ocean
           C    ends at Astoria, Oregon
fact 41    The Nile river—
           A    flows from south to north
           B    empties into the Mediterranean Sea
           C    ends at Cairo, Egypt
fact 42    Most of the area near the mouth of the Nile is hot and dry
           with sparse vegetation.
```

```
fact 43    The predominate language in the United States is English.
fact 44    The Mississippi river—
           A    flows from north to south
           B    empties into the Gulf of Mexico
           C    ends at New Orleans, Louisiana
fact 45    The predominant language in Brazil is Portuguese.
fact 46    The Columbia river is in the United States.
fact 47    The Mississippi river is in the United States.
fact 48    The predominant language in Egypt is Arabic.
fact 49    Most of the area surrounding the mouth of the Columbia river
           is cool, moist, and includes large conifers.
fact 50    The Amazon river is in Brazil.
fact 51    Most of the area surrounding the mouth of the Mississippi
           river is warm, humid, and tropical.

                                              .
                                              .
                                              .

fact N     It is dark after sunset.
```

Given the above information, the woman could, using the following beliefs, quite reasonably conclude that she was traveling south, toward New Orleans and the Gulf of Mexico:

Belief number	Belief	Justification
6	Traveling south	Fact 44A and belief 3
5	Traveling toward Gulf of Mexico	Fact 44B and belief 3
4	Traveling toward New Orleans	Fact 44C and belief 3
3	The river is the Mississippi	Fact 47, fact 51, belief 2, and belief 1
2	The surrounding area is warm, humid, and tropical	External observation
1	The area is in the United States	Assumption based on lack of contrary information

Because an NMRS includes tentative knowledge, it is possible to add a new piece of knowledge that will cause a previously believed tentative truth to become false.

PRINCIPLE 6.3: When a belief in an NMRS is revised, then any beliefs that rest on it, directly or indirectly, must also be revised.

The *belief revision* portion of an NMRS propagates the effect of any change in belief through the use of *dependency-directed backtracking*.

Example 6.2: Given the situation from Example 6.1, what belief revisions would occur as a result of the woman's finding several public notices written in Portuguese?

Having observed such a sign, the woman would be forced to replace the assumption that she is in the United States with the belief that she is in Brazil. The cascading effect of this change is illustrated by the following set of revised beliefs:

Belief number	Belief	Justification
6	Traveling east	Fact 37A and belief 3
5	Traveling toward South Atlantic	Fact 37B and belief 3
4	Traveling toward Almirim, Brazil	Fact 37C and belief 3
3	The river is the Amazon	Fact 38, fact 50, belief 2, and belief 1
2	The surrounding area is warm, humid, and tropical	External observation
1	The area is in Brazil	Fact 45

Her conclusion, which changed radically as the result of adding a small piece of knowledge, is now that she is heading east on the Amazon toward Almirim and the South Atlantic Ocean.

PRINCIPLE 6.4: The addition of a small piece of new knowledge can result in a great deal of belief revision.

The increased power and flexibility of default reasoning makes an NMRS especially useful for problem-solving domains, such as planning and design, that require a large number of tentative assumptions based on partial information. This increased usefulness is not, however, without cost. Specifically, an NMRS can require a large amount of memory to store the dependency information and a large amount of processing time to propagate changes in beliefs.

For additional information on nonmonotonic reasoning, See D. McDermott, 1980, Winograd, 1980, and Davis, 1980.

6.3 Truth Maintenance System

The Truth Maintenance System (TMS) is an implementation of an NMRS [Doyle, 1979a and 1979b]. TMS operates as a knowledge base management system and is called every time the reasoning system generates a new truth value. TMS, using belief revision, takes any action required to modify dependent beliefs to maintain consistency in the knowledge base. TMS's role is purely passive; it never initiates the generation of inferences.

In TMS a *node* represents one unit of knowledge: a fact, rule, assertion, etc. At any point in execution, every node is in one of two conditions:

IN   Currently believed to be true.

OUT   Currently believed to be false. A node can be OUT because there is no possible condition that would make it true or because the conditions required to make it true are not currently IN.

Support list justifications

Associated with each node are *justifications* for the node's truth value. (We will assume one justification per node for simplicity's sake.) For each node that is IN, TMS records a *well-founded support:* proof of the validity of the node, starting from the system's facts and justifications.

The simplest form of justification is a *support list* (SL), which has the following form:

$$[\text{ SL (in\_nodes)(out\_nodes) }]$$

where (in_nodes) :: = list of all nodes that must be IN for this node to
              be true

    (out_nodes) :: = list of all nodes that must be OUT for this node
              to be true

Example 6.3 Develop a set of nodes, and associated SL justifications, for the following:

1. It is sunny.
2. It is daytime.
3. It is raining.
4. It is warm.

Node number	Knowledge	Justification
1	It is sunny.	[SL (2) (3)]
2	It is daytime.	[SL ( ) ( )]
3	It is raining.	[SL ( ) (1)]
4	It is warm.	[SL(1)(3)]

The content of the IN and OUT lists at any time describe a snapshot of the system's belief. As system execution proceeds, the content of each of these lists is changed by TMS to ensure consistency.

Example 6.4 Given the nodes and justifications from Example 6.3 and the following IN and OUT lists:

IN   1, 2, 4

OUT 3

What is the effect of the reasoning system passing to TMS the following: "It is raining."?

The content of the IN and OUT lists will become:
IN   3, 2
OUT 1, 4
Several different types of nodes can be justified by a support list.

Premise. A premise is a fact that is always valid. The in_list and out_list portions of the SL for a premise will always be empty. Given that we ignore time of day, node 2 in Example 6.3 is a premise.

Normal deduction. A normal deduction is an inference that is formed in the normal sense of a monotonic system. The out_list portion of the SL for a normal deduction will always be empty; the belief in the deduction follows from the belief in the nodes listed in the in_list portion of the SL. Example 6.3 could be extended to include a belief, "It is wet," with an SL of [SL (3) ( )] that would be an example of a normal deduction.

Assumption. An assumption is a belief that is supported by the lack of contrary information. The out_list portion of the SL for an assumption will never be empty. The nodes that are on in_list can be viewed as the *reasons* for making the assumptions, and the nodes on the out_list are the nodes whose presence would provide contrary information that would invalidate the assumption.

Assumptions provide the basis for default reasoning in TMS. Node 1 in Example 6.3 is an example of an assumption. Its justification can be interpreted as, "Assume that it is sunny given that it is daytime and that nothing suggests that it is raining."

Conditional proof justifications

A *conditional proof* (CP) is a second type of justification that is used to support hypothetical reasoning. The format of a CP is:

$$[CP\langle consequent\rangle\ (in\_hypothesis)]$$

(A CP also includes an out_hypothesis entry, but it is almost always empty and is ignored in this discussion.) A CP justification is valid if and only if the consequent node is IN whenever all of the nodes on in_hypothesis are IN. The usefulness of such justification is illustrated in the following section.

Dependency-directed backtracking in TMS

When TMS discovers an inconsistency in the current set of beliefs, as a result of a newly added justification, it invokes dependency-directed backtracking to restore consistency. This backtracking activity is based on the following principle:

PRINCIPLE 6.5: Contradictions in a set of beliefs occur as a result of incorrect assumptions.

To restore consistency, TMS must retract belief in one or more assumptions. This process consists of the following:

1. A node is marked as a *contradiction* when it is discovered that belief in it causes inconsistencies. Well-founded support in a contradiction is unacceptable, and, therefore, backtracking must continue until the contradiction becomes OUT.

2. The backtracker traces backward through the well-founded support for the contradiction, attempting to find a possible cause. Because all normal deductions are correct, the cause of the inconsistency must be a bad assumption, and, therefore, the backtracker looks only for such assumptions. The result of this activity is the accumulation of the set of suspects

$$S_a = \{A_1, A_2, A_3, \ldots, A_n\}$$

the assumptions in the well-founded support for the contradiction.

3. The backtracker creates a new node, *nogood,* that indicates that S_a is inconsistent [e.g., representing the fact

$$\sim(A_1 \wedge A_2 \wedge A_3 \wedge \ldots \wedge A_n)]$$

S_a is then called the *nogood-set.*

The justification for the nogood node is generally represented by using the CP form:

node# nogood [CP (contradiction) (S_a)]

We know that "nogood" should be IN because, if all of the nodes in the nogood-set S_a are simultaneously IN, then the contradiction node will also be IN. This stores the relationship between the assumptions and the contradictions. (The use of the term "condition proof" for this form of justification corresponds to this usage. The truth of the nogood node is implied as a result of a specific type of proof technique—called conditional proof—of the contradiction from the nogood-set [Klenk, 1983].)

4. The backtracker uses the information from the nogood-set to identify an assumption that must be retracted to resolve the inconsistency and so remove the contradiction.

Example 6.5 Assuming that each fact from Example 6.1 is now represented as a premise node (where node numbers for nodes shown in this list correspond to the fact numbers from Example 6.2), the following set of beliefs are IN—in addition to nodes 37 to 51 (which are premises):

Node number	Belief	Justification
6	Traveling south	[SL (3 , 44A) ( )]
5	Traveling toward Gulf of Mexico	[SL (3 , 44B) ( )]
4	Traveling toward New Orleans	[SL (3 , 44C) ( )]
3	The river is the Mississippi	[SL (26,2,47,51) ( )]
2	The surrounding area is warm, humid, and tropical	[SL ( ) ( )]
26	The area is in the United States	[SL (21) ( )]
21	The predominant language is English	[SL ( ) (20, 22)]

The following nodes are OUT:

24 The area is in Brazil.
25 The area is in Egypt.
20 The predominant language is Portuguese.
21 The predominant language is Arabic.

After the observation of the Portuguese signs occurs, a contradiction is eventually observed and a contradiction node is added:

50 contradiction-1 [SL (26, 24) ( )]

Backtracking is invoked as a result of the recognition of the contradiction. The backtracker looks backward through the well-founded support for node 50 in search of an assumption that could have caused the inconsistency. The backtracker creates a node, nogood-1, by using a CP justification to represent the inconsistent assumption:

56 nogood-1 [CP 55 (21,20)]

This node can be interpreted as, "The contradiction called contradiction-1 results from assuming node 21." To remove the assumption, the backtracker must move a node (from the out_list of the assumption) from OUT to IN. Once this move occurs, the faulty assumption will be forced out. Any nodes that depended on the faulty assumption will also be forced OUT. In this case all of the IN list will be removed (except for nodes 20 and 2 and the premises), and a new IN list will be generated.

Several modifications of Doyle's TMS have been developed (e.g.,

Charniak, 1979, Martins, 1984, and Petrie, 1985.) For a history of such development see Doyle, 1980.

6.4 Reasoning Based on Probability

The techniques of *probability theory* have been widely used in many different disciplines in attempts to quantify uncertainty. The appeal of probability is based in part on the fact that it has a solidly established mathematical basis; techniques for using probabilities are widely published.

$P(E)$ is the probability that an event E will occur; it represents a quantification of the likelihood of this occurrence. In most cases the value of $P(E)$ is established by statistical analysis (e.g., measuring the frequency of occurrence of E in a random series of tests).

Probabilities have a value from 0 to 1, where 1 represents absolute knowledge of E and 0 represents absolute knowledge that E will not occur. When an event being considered has several possible outcomes (e.g., rolling a pair of dice) a probability is associated with each outcome. The sum of the probabilities for all possible outcomes for an event must equal 1.

An *objective probability* is a probability that is measured by using frequency ratio techniques described above. Unfortunately, in most ES domains it is impossible to preform such measurements. It is much more common to attempt to collect estimates of the probability values, called *subjective probabilities,* by interviewing experts.

There are several problems that make it difficult to use probability for dealing with uncertainty in ES. For example, even though a person is an expert in a domain, it can still be very difficult for that person to accurately estimate probabilities.

Because the actions of an expert system are typically the result of piecing together many different fragments of knowledge, each with different probability characteristics, we must be able to combine probabilities. Probability values can be combined by using many established techniques. For example, a commonly used formula

$$P(E_1 \text{ and } E_2) = P(E_1) * P(E_2)$$

can be used to find the probability that both E_1 and E_2 will occur, given the individual probabilities of E_1 and E_2. For example, if the probability of drawing an ace of spades from a deck of cards is $\frac{1}{52}$, and the probability of drawing any diamond from a separate deck is $\frac{13}{52}$, then the probability of drawing both the ace of spades and a diamond is $\frac{1}{52} * \frac{13}{52}$.

Bayes's rule is used for more complicated situations. It employs the following terms:

B_i ::= a specific belief

$P(B_i)$ ::= the a priori probability that B_i is true; this is the probability that B_i is true, given no specific evidence

$P(B_i|E)$ ::= the *conditional probability* that B_i is true, given evidence E; this indicates our revised belief in B_i upon finding that E is true.

$P(E|B_i)$ ::= the probability of of observing E, given that B_i is true

k ::= total number of possible beliefs

Bayes's rule states:

$$P(B_i|E) = \frac{P(E|B_i) * P(B_i)}{\sum_{i=1}^{k} P(E|B_i) * P(B_i)}$$

A typical use of Bayes's rule is in diagnostic domains. In such cases, B_i represents a cause of the effect E. $P(B_i|E)$ is, in effect, inferred belief that B_i is the cause of effect E. We can use this relation to quantify the extent to which we should believe B_i given the available evidence E. For this reason, Bayes's rule is often referred to as the *probability of causes theorem* [Spiegel, 1975].

Probability theory has been successfully applied in several ESs, for example, Page-1 [Strandberg, 1985] and most notably the Prospector system [Duda, 1980].

6.5   Certainty Factors

A *certainty factor* (CF) is a relatively informal mechanism for quantifying the degree to which, based on the presence of a given set of evidence, we believe (or disbelieve) a given conclusion. Certainty factors have been most widely applied to domains that use incrementally acquired evidence.

The concept of CF was developed for Mycin [Buchanan, 1984a], and it has been used successfully in many other systems [Buchanan, 1983]. For Mycin it was decided, after much discussion, to use a new technique for certainty quantification rather than the more traditional probabilistic methods, primarily because of the difficulty of accurately estimating the a priori and conditional probabilities required for the application of Bayes's rule. (See Adams, 1984, for a discussion of the use of CF vs. formal probability.)

Description of certainty factors

A CF is a numerical value that expresses the extent to which, based on a given set of evidence, we should accept a given conclusion. A CF with a value of 1 indicates total belief, whereas a CF with a value of -1 indicates total disbelief.

Component certainty factors

For each rule in the system, a CF is assigned by the domain expert. It is based on the expert's knowledge and experience.

PRINCIPLE 6.6: A CF is a subjective quantification of an expert's judgment and intuition.

> **Example 6.6** The following simple rule for diagnosing the failure of a table lamp illustrates the use of a CF (in this case, 0.8).
> IF   a table lamp is plugged into a receptacle,
>   the receptacle has current, and
>   the lamp's switch is on,
> THEN there is suggestive evidence (0.8) that the light bulb is faulty.

The CF that is included in a rule is a *component certainty factor* (CF_{comp}), and it describes the credibility of the conclusion, given only the evidence represented by the preconditions of the rule.

Typically, in a large rule-based system, many different rules will relate to the same conclusion. The following principle relates an important constraint regarding these multiple rules:

PRINCIPLE 6.7: In a system that uses CFs, the rules must be so structured that any given rule either adds to belief in a given conclusion or adds to disbelief.

A *measure of belief* $MB[c,e]$ is a number that indicates the degree to which our belief in conclusion c is increased, based on the presence of evidence e. By definition: $0 \le MB[c,e] \le 1$.

Similarly, a *measure of disbelief,* $MD[c,e]$, is a number that indicates the degree to which our disbelief in c is increased, based on the presence of e.

Because of the restriction described in Principle 6.7, for any given rule if $MB[c,e] > 0$, then $MD[c,e] = 0$, and if $MD[c,e] > 0$, then $MB[c,e] = 0$. The component certainty factor can now be more formally described as:

$$CF_{comp}[c,e] = MB_{comp}[c,e] - MD_{comp}[c,e] \qquad (6.1)$$

Ranjit Kaur

where: $c ::=$ the conclusion under consideration
$\quad\quad e ::=$ the evidence relating to c

Note that either the MB term or the MD term must equal zero.

Because there are many rules that relate to any given conclusion, each of which can add to our *overall* belief or disbelief in a conclusion, a *cumulative certainty factor* is used to express the certainty of the conclusion, at a given point in execution, in light of *all* of the evidence that has been considered up to that point.

Calculation of certainty factors

The cumulative certainty factor, which provides a means of assessing the certainty of a conclusion from a global viewpoint, is formed by combining global degrees of belief and disbelief represented by the *cumulative measure of belief* and the *cumulative measure of disbelief* for the conclusion.

Specifically, a cumulative certainty factor is defined, for a specified point during system execution, as follows:

$$CF[c,e_c] = MB[c,e_f] - MD[c,e_a] \quad\quad (6.2)$$

where $c ::=$ the conclusion under consideration
$\quad\quad e_c ::=$ *all* of the evidence that relates to c that has been considered up to the specified point of execution
$\quad CF[c,e_c] ::=$ the cumulative certainty factor for c given e_c (the net belief in the conclusion, given the current evidence)
$\quad\quad e_f ::=$ all of the evidence *for* c that has been considered
$\quad\quad e_a ::=$ all of the evidence *against* c that has been considered
$\quad MB[c,e_f] ::=$ cumulative measure of belief for c given e_f
$\quad MD[c,e_a] =$ cumulative measure of disbelief for c given e_a

The above definition implies the need for calculating MB and MD for each possible conclusion in the system. This calculation is performed by first initializing both terms to zero and then incrementally including the effect of each applicable rule. Every time an additional rule is considered, a new MB and MD is calculated on the basis of the effect of the new rule combined with the existing MB and MD.

Combining functions for performing this activity are based on the constraint that the collections of evidence being considered are independent. For example, in an automotive diagnostic system, "a low battery" and "dim lights" do not individually contribute new evidence because they routinely occur together. All pieces of *related* evidence must occur in the same rule.

The measure of belief that results from considering two sources of evidence can be calculated by using the following formula:

$$MB[c,s_1 \& s_2] = \qquad (6.3)$$

IF $MD[c,s_1 \& s_2] = 1$, THEN 0
ELSE $MB[c,s_1] + MB[c,s_2](1 - MB[c,s_1])$

where $MB[c,s_1 \& s_2] ::=$ the measure of belief based on a pair of sources

In the elementary case, s_1 and s_2 are simply two individual rules r_1 and r_2. In general, s_1 may represent a set of rules whose cumulative effects have previously been considered and s_2 represents a new rule whose effect is to be added to the previously existing cumulative belief. ($MD[c,s_1 \& s_2]$ is the measure of disbelief for the same pair of sources and is equal to 1 if and only if the conclusion is known to be false with absolute assurance).

Similarly, MD is defined by using

$$MD[c,s_1 \& s_2] = \qquad (6.4)$$

IF $MB[c,s_1 \& s_2] = 1$, THEN 0
ELSE $MD[c,s_1] + MD[c,s_2](1 - MD[c,s_1])$

The reasonableness of this function is clear when we recognize that the addition of new evidence that supports belief in a conclusion increases, but does not absolutely establish, the credibility of the conclusion. As a large number of elements of supporting evidence are combined, the overall MB grows asymptotically toward unity.

The factor

$$MB[c,s_2](1 - MB[c,s_1])$$

in Eq. (6.3) describes the contribution to MB provided by a new piece of evidence. This factor can be viewed as a measure of the extent to which the new evidence mitigates the doubt that remained after the previous evidence had been considered. The degree of mitigation is, quite reasonably, proportional to the strength of the new evidence. A similar argument holds for MD.

Example 6.7 Given that there are only four rules that suggest conclusion c, find the cumulative certainty factor for c, given the following component certainty factors:

Rule	CF
1	0.8
2	0.3
3	-0.2
4	0.7

For rule 1, using Eqs. (6.1) and (6.2):

$$MB = MB_{comp} = 0.8 \qquad MD = MD_{comp} = 0$$

Equation (6.2) is then used to include the effect of rule 2:

$$MB = 0.8 + 0.3(1 - 0.8) = 0.86 \qquad MD = 0$$

After considering rule 3,

$$MB = 0.86 \qquad MD = -0.2$$

Finally, the effect of rule 4 is included:

$$MB = 0.86 + 0.7(1 - 0.86) = 0.96 \qquad MD = -0.2$$

and the final certainty factor is developed:

$$CF = 0.96 - 0.2 = 0.76.$$

The following formulas are used to calculate MB and MD on the basis of the combination of separate conclusions rather than separate evidence:

Conjunction of conclusions:

$$MB[c_1 \text{ or } c_2, e] = \max(MB[c_1, e], MB[c_2, e]) \qquad (6.5)$$

$$MD[c_1 \text{ or } c_2, e] = \min(MD[c_1, e], MD[c_2, e]) \qquad (6.6)$$

where c_1 = conclusion 1
c_2 = conclusion 2
e = all available evidence

Disjunctions of conclusions:

$$MB[c_1 \text{ or } c_2, e] = \max(MB[c_1 e], MB[c_2, e]) \qquad (6.7)$$

$$MD[c_1 \text{ or } c_2, e] = \max(MD[c_1, e], MD[c_2, e]) \qquad (6.8)$$

Example 6.8   Given that with TR, the results of an automotive diagnostic test, the following conclusions can be drawn, each with the associated CF:

C1   The problem requires immediate attention (0.8).
C2   There is a problem in the electrical system (0.6).
C3   There is a short in the electrical system (0.4).
C4   There is a fault in the flow control computer (0.2).

Find the measure of belief that there is a problem in the electrical system that requires immediate attention and that the problem is either a short or a computer fault.

Using Eqs. (6.5) and (6.7):

$$MB[C1\&C2\&(C3 \text{ or } C4),TR] = min(MB[C1,TR], MB[C2,TR],$$
$$MB[C3 \text{ or } C4,TR])$$
$$= min(MB[C1,TR], MB[C2,TR],$$
$$max(MB[C3,TR], MB[C4,TR]))$$
$$= min(0.8,0.6,max(0.4,0.2))$$
$$= min(0.8,0.6,0.4)$$
$$= 0.4$$

The domain expert assigns a CF to a rule based on the assumption that all conditions in the premise are known with certainty. If there is uncertainty regarding the conditions, then the CF normally associated with the rule is not fully applicable. In this case, the following formulas can be used to calculate the revised CF for the rule. The calculation is based on a CF that describes our degree of belief in the required condition (i.e., the evidence for the rule).

$$MB[c,s] = MB'[c,s] * max(0,CF[s,e]) \tag{6.9}$$

$$MD[c,s] = MD'[c,s] * max(0,CF[s,e]) \tag{6.10}$$

where $c ::=$ conclusion of the rule
    $s ::=$ evidence required for the rule
$MB'[c,s] ::=$ MB in the conclusion, given complete confidence in s
$CF[s,e] ::=$ actual degree of belief in s (established by some prior evidence e)

The situation described above typically occurs in one of two ways:

1. There is less than total confidence in the evidence when it is provided to the system (e.g., the evidence represents the conclusions of a test that had mixed results).

2. The evidence is a conclusion that resulted from previous execution of a different rule with which a CF was associated.

The second case frequently occurs during the process of chaining rules. To calculate the CF for the final conclusion in a chaining process, it is generally necessary to use both the combining functions for strength of evidence [Eqs. (6.9) and (6.10) and the combining functions for conjunction and disjunction of hypothesis [Eqs. (6.7) and (6.8.)].

Example 6.9 Given the following rules from an ES for diagnosis of electrical problems:

1. IF   a system fault has been reported and the WPLMI board is reporting low voltage,
   THEN there is suggestive evidence (0.7) that there is a problem in the power supply in the WPLMI board.
2. IF   there is a problem in the power supply to the WPLMI board, the CPU port has been closed, and the voltage at the input to the CPU is less than 4.5 V,
   THEN there is suggestive evidence (0.9) that the CPU power supply has failed.
3. IF   the CPU is not responding to port commands and a system fault has been reported,
   THEN there is suggestive evidence (0.4) that the CPU port has been closed.
4. IF   a system fault has been reported and the WPLMI board is the source of the system fault,
   THEN there is suggestive evidence (0.6) that there is a problem in the power supply to the WPLMI.

Given also the following observations, each of which is known with complete certainty:

E1 A system fault has been reported.
E2 The CPU is not responding to port commands.
E3 The voltage at the input to the CPU is 3.8 V.
E4 The WPLMI board is the fault source.

find the certainty with which we can conclude that the CPU power supply has failed.

From rule 1, we conclude C1—there is a problem in the power supply to the WPLMI board—with a CF of 0.7. Rule 4 is then applied to C1:

$$CF_{c1} = 0.7 + 0.6(1 - 0.7) = 7.2$$

Using rule 3, we conclude C2—the CPU port has been closed—with a CF of 0.4.

We can conclude C3—the voltage at the input to the CPU is less than 4.5 V—with absolute certainty, based on E3. By using these conclusions as evidence for rule 2, the rule, including the CFs for each condition, can now be written as:

IF   there is a problem in the power supply to the WPLMI board (7.2),
      the CPU port has been closed (0.4), and
      the voltage at the input to the CPU is less than 4.5 V (1.0),
THEN there is suggestive evidence (0.9) that the CPU power supply has failed.

The measure of belief in the desired conclusion can now be characterized as:

$MB[C_{final}, C1\&C2\&C3]$

$$= MB'[C_{final}, C1\&C2\&C3] * max(0, CF[C1\&C2\&C3, E_p])$$

where $E_p ::=$ previous evidence (in this case, E1, E2, E3, and E4)

$$MB[C_{final}, C1\&C2\&C3] = 0.9 * max(0, CF[C1\&C2\&C3, E_p])$$

Using Eq. (6.5):

$$CF[C1\&C2\&C3, E_p] = min(CF[C1, E_p], CF[C2,_p], CF[C3, E_p])$$

$$= min(7.2, 0.4, 1.0)$$

$$= 0.4$$

$$MB[c_{final}, C1\&C2\&C3] = 0.9 * max(0, 0.4)$$

$$= 0.36$$

$$CF[c_{final}, C1\&C2\&C3] = 0.36 - 0 = 0.36$$

The use of CFs as described in this section is essentially a technique for supplementing existing reasoning processes with information regarding uncertainty.

6.6 Fuzzy Reasoning

Fuzzy reasoning is specifically designed to deal with the inexactness (or fuzziness) that is present in the knowledge used by human experts [Zadeh, 1965].

In conventional mathematics, a set has clearly defined boundaries that specifically identify an exact, although potentially infinite, group of elements (e.g., the set of integers larger than 2 and smaller than 10). Given a correct understanding of a set's definition, it is possible to determine whether a given candidate is or is not a member of the set. Unfortunately, it is very difficult, if not impossible, to develop exact set definitions for many of the concepts and classification mechanisms that are used by humans:

PRINCIPLE 6.8: Humans routinely and subconsciously place things into classes whose meaning and significance are well understood but whose boundaries are not well defined.

In fuzzy reasoning the concept of a *fuzzy set* corresponds to such a class. A fuzzy set is a class of elements with loosely defined boundaries.

Examples of fuzzy sets include the set of "large cars," "fast horses," and "rich people." To identify the members of a fuzzy set, we associate a *grade of membership* with each element that could potentially be a member. The grade of membership is a number, between 0 and 1, that indicates the extent to which an element is a member of the set. A grade of 1 indicates that the candidate is definitely a member, whereas a grade of 0 indicates that the candidate is definitely not a member. The transition between these extremes is gradual rather than distinct.

PRINCIPLE 6.9: Grades of membership for fuzzy sets are subjectively assigned on the basis of context.

For example, we might assign a value of 0.2 as the grade of membership for a 28-year-old college freshman in the set of "young college freshmen." Note that there is no deterministic procedure for establishing the validity of this value; rather it can be viewed as an intuitive statement, expressed on a scale of 0 to 1, of the extent to which the label "young college freshman" applies to the subject person. Overall, a fuzzy set is defined by a *membership function* that associates a grade of membership with each candidate element. A membership function for the example mentioned above is shown in Fig. 6.1.

In some cases the grade of membership may itself be inexactly represented as a *fuzzy number* (e.g., a membership grade that is "near 0.2" or "about 0.5"). A fuzzy set that uses fuzzy values in its membership function is called an *ultrafuzzy set*. An example of a membership for an ultrafuzzy set is shown in Fig. 6.2.

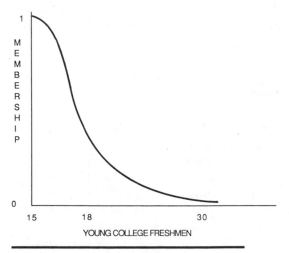

Figure 6.1 Membership function for a fuzzy set.

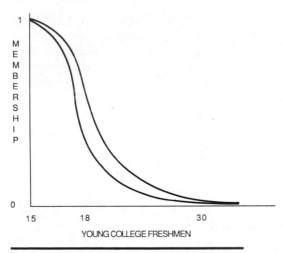

Figure 6.2   Membership function for an ultrafuzzy set.

Conceptually, membership grades are not intended to correspond to probabilities. Rather than representing the probability of an element being a member of a given set—based on an analysis of randomness in the data—a grade of membership is intended to quantify an intuitive understanding of the extent to which a given element is compatible with a given concept.

Manipulation of fuzzy sets

Fuzzy logic is a well-defined reasoning system that is based on the use of fuzzy sets rather than on the binary values associated with traditional bivalent logic.

PRINCIPLE 6.10: In a fuzzy logic system only the elements being manipulated are fuzzy; the rules of logic are well defined.

The task of translating human expressions in fuzzy logic systems is relatively simple because humans tend to communicate ideas and quantifications by using verbal rather than numeric descriptions. These verbal expressions are based on the use of *linguistic variables* such as big, old, and fast. To translate these values in a fuzzy logic system, we simply describe a membership function that represents them. Once the basic membership functions have been established, *fuzzy modifiers* can be used to modify a membership function (e.g., very old). Figure 6.3 illustrates the use of the modifiers "very" and "not."

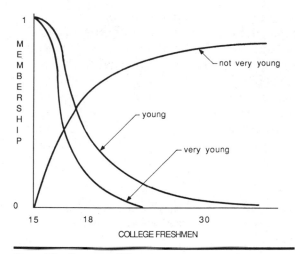

Figure 6.3 Fuzzy modifiers.

Fuzzy quantifiers are used to represent approximate quantification in fuzzy logic. Fuzzy quantifiers are frequently used for *dispositions*, statements that include implied fuzzy quantification. For example, the statement, "Horses have tails," actually implies the use of the fuzzy quantifier "most" (e.g., "Most horses have tails").

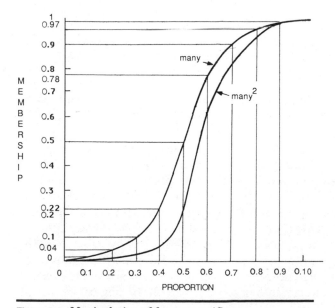

Figure 6.4 Manipulation of fuzzy quantifiers.

Frequently, it is necessary to combine fuzzy quantifiers when forming an inference. For example, if it is known that "Many of A. B. Jones's crimes are bank robberies" and that "Many bank robberies endanger innocent people," then we can conclude that many^2 of A. B. Jones's crimes endanger innocent people. The term "many^2", as shown in Fig. 6.4, is the square of the fuzzy quantifier "many" and, as would be expected, it represents a quantification that is fuzzier than the original "many." (Note that the representation of "very old" in Fig. 6.3 is equivalent to old^2.)

It is also possible to combine the effects of independent fuzzy sets, as illustrated in Example 6.9.

Example 6.10   Given the following condition/action rule (for an aviation domain): If the rate of climb is near zero and the altitude is somewhat too high, then make a slight negative throttle adjustment.
Given also the following membership functions:

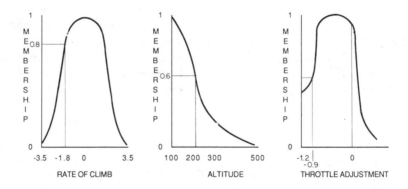

If the measured rate of climb is -1.8 %/hr and the altitude is 200 ft above normal, find the throttle adjustment that should be made.

We must first determine the extent to which the preconditions are satisfied. We do so by finding the grade of membership for each of the preconditions by using the given membership functions. From the given information, we can determine that the "rate of climb" precondition is satisfied to an extent of 0.8 and the "altitude above normal" precondition is satisfied to an extent of 0.6, as shown in the above figure.

Thus, a value of 0.6 is used for the overall extent to which the preconditions have been met. This is based on the fact that 0.6 is the minimum of the observed precondition grades. To determine the extent of the action to be taken, the model action (a slight negative throttle adjustment) is scaled by a value of 0.6, as shown in the figure. The final result is a value of -0.9.

For further information on the human aspect of fuzzy reasoning see Bandler, 1983, Gupta, 1982, and Kandel, 1986. For more information on hardware developed for fuzzy reasoning, see Johnson, 1985.

The following chapter describes how an ES explains its reasoning process.

7

Explanation Facilities

The explanation facility in an ES describes the system's reasoning to the user. The presence of a powerful explanation facility, which is often one of the most important parts of an ES, tends to distinguish ESs from more traditional software systems.

Historically, software systems have taken what might be called the oracle approach: The user presents a problem, and the system metaphorically "goes away to work the problem" and eventually returns with a response that is to be accepted without explanation. During this exchange, it is tacitly assumed (by the user) that the system's analyst, developer, and tester have constructed the system correctly. It is further assumed (by the developers) that the user is not interested in understanding the system's reasoning process or would be incapable of understanding it if it were presented.

Based on these assumptions, traditional software tends to provide an explanation only in the sense of debugging aids that produce status and trace information intended to assist the developers.

The first assumption is generally valid for traditional systems. Because such systems deal only with complete information by using only predefined, well-understood operations, they will, ignoring the possibility of implementation errors and hardware failures, always produce correct results. The second assumption is also generally valid because the typical user:

1. Is interested only in results and not how the results are developed

2. May have little knowledge of the subject domain and therefore will not understand descriptions that are based on domain-specific terminology

3. Is not attempting to learn about the domain from the system (e.g., the person executing a payroll program is not trying to do payrolls)

The first assumption is generally not valid for ESs because ESs are designed to produce satisfying results, possibly on the basis of incomplete or partially incorrect information. Even if an ES is perfectly implemented, it can still produce incorrect results (e.g., make a bad guess).

The second assumption is not generally applicable to ESs which are intended to be used, at least in part, as training vehicles.

PRINCIPLE 7.1: If there is a possibility of the system producing incorrect results, then the user cannot blindly accept system results.

Thus, explanation systems are of less importance for ESs that are fully autonomous. For these systems explanation may be limited or even nonexistent. On the other end of the spectrum, explanation systems are very important for ESs that are used as advisers or consultants.

PRINCIPLE 7.2: The importance of user involvement and accompanying explanation facilities increases as the following factors increase:
- The probability of incorrect results being produced
- The cost of being wrong
- The desire to transfer the system's expertise to the user

Specifically, explanation within an ES is intended to accomplish one or more of the following:

1. Assisting in debugging the system

2. Informing the user of current status

3. Increasing the user's confidence in (and acceptance of) the system

4. Clarification of terms and concepts used by the system

5. Increasing the user's personal level of expertise

7.1 Basic Explanation—Focus on Debugging

This section describes a hypothetical explanation system called Fixit that is similar to that included in many existing consultation systems (e.g., Mulsant, 1984). This type of explanation has grown from work in early ESs such as Mycin [Buchanan, 1984*b*], Prospector [Duda, 1984], and Teiresias [Davis, 1982*b*].

The most fundamental concept in explanation implementation is that explanation is based on the processing of *meta-knowledge*—knowledge that a system has about its own internal knowledge. When using meta-knowledge, ESs are operating in an *introspective mode*—looking at their own operation from the viewpoint of an outside observer.

For any form of explanation to be effective, there must be a *framework for explanation* that is mutually understood by both the system and the user. This framework includes such things as a general understanding of the inference paradigm used by the system and an understanding of the domain-specific vocabulary used in explanations.

Fixit is a hypothetical ES that diagnoses problems in automotive systems. In this case the framework is that of a rule-based, goal-driven system which constructs a goal tree that describes the goals that are to be achieved during a given diagnostic session. The following is a sample of Fixit rules:

RULE 1   IF   the headlights are bright and spark is present at the engine cylinders,
         THEN the electrical system is working normally.

RULE 2   IF   the car will not start,
                  the electrical system is working normally,
                  the starter is cranking normally, and
                  air is reaching the engine cylinders,
         THEN fuel is not reaching the cylinder.

RULE 3   IF   the fuel gauge is working normally and
                  the fuel gauge shows fuel in the tank,
         THEN there is an adequate supply of fuel.

RULE 4   IF   fuel is not reaching the engine cylinders,
                  there is an adequate supply of fuel, and
                  the fuel pump is working normally,
         THEN the fuel filter is clogged.

Figure 7.1 shows the goal tree that corresponds to these rules. Fixit offers two primary explanation options: HOW and WHY. The following is an example of a mechanic using the WHY option while trying to determine why a car won't start:

[Fixit asks:]

    Is there air reaching the engine cylinders?

[The mechanic asks for an explanation:]

    WHY

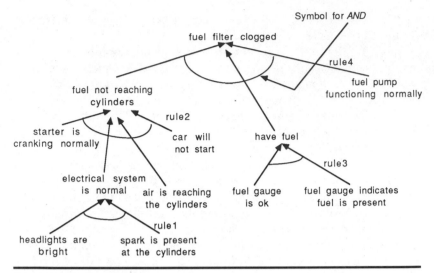

Figure 7.1 Fixit goal tree.

[Fixit responds by explaining why it is asking the question:]

```
It has already been established that:
      The electrical system is normal.
Therefore, if:
      The starter is cranking normally and
      Air is reaching the engine cylinders
Then, by RULE 2:
      Fuel is not reaching the engine cylinders.
```

The following is an example of the use of HOW:

[The mechanic enters:]

```
HOW ''Electrical system is normal.''
```

[Fixit responds (by using RULE 1):]

```
Rule 1 was used to establish that:
      Electrical system is normal.
Because:
      Headlights are bright.
      Spark is present at the cylinders.
```

Usefulness of a basic explanation system

Fixit's explanation system is most useful for providing program visibility in support of debugging and knowledge base verification. (The original purpose for creating explanation systems in ESs was for support of incremental knowledge base construction [Buchanan, 1984b].)

In a theoretical sense, the code in any program is used in some sense to *model* the subject domain. One of the primary difficulties in developing any software is understanding the mapping between such codes and the domain elements (i.e., understanding the *significance* of any given code).

This problem is most pronounced in assembly-language programming. Because assembly languages focus on representing *sequencing* and *replacement,* the meaning of a program element often must be established by the physical characteristics or physical position of the element within a program (e.g., recognizing something because it is located at some offset from a given base address). During any given computation, the programmer recognizes the specific domain elements from the fact that they are dynamically contained in certain registers. Given the code LDR $R1, = 25 (i.e., load register one with the number 25) the programmer must mentally associate $R1 with the element (e.g., number of items to process).

Most important, this symbol is associated with this element for only a short time. In a large assembly-language program the significance of register symbols is constantly changing; therefore, $R1 will represent thousands of different elements during a long computation. The programmer is required to "mentally execute" at least part of the program to recognize the current significance of a register, an extremely complex task for a large program.

One of the advantages of a high-level language such as Fortran is in the use of variables to represent domain elements. If a unique variable is used to represent each element, the programmer is able to recognize the significance of a variable by its name. More modern languages such as Pascal and Ada have improved on this concept by allowing very long and descriptive variable names and have thus eased the problem of establishing the meaning of program code.

Unfortunately, even with these improvements, hopefully aided by comments and a symbolic debugger, the programmer will still have to remember the meaning of each of potentially thousands of variable and procedure names. Moreover, this is simply a small example of a much larger problem: The programmer must somehow relate program execution to the real world. An explanation system greatly assists in this area by *dynamically describing* the program's execution to the programmer and so eases the burden of mental bookkeeping required to understand it. The value of an explanation system increases even more when we try to involve the expert in knowledge base construction and verification.

PRINCIPLE 7.3: Without an explanation system, only someone familiar with the program's implementation can understand or modify it.

Given an explanation system, anyone can, at least to some significant degree, understand the system's operation given that they understand the framework for explanation and the subject domain. The visibility provided by the explanation system also makes assumptions explicit and assists the expert in predicting the impact of possible changes and in correcting errors.

Limitations of a basic explanation system

Although a basic explanation system is useful, it is limited in several ways:

It will respond only to specific predefined types of queries. There is little capability for *natural-language* understanding. Another problem is that it has no sense of an overall continuing dialog. For example, the scope of the WHY facility is limited to the current rule. The explanation is essentially simply a paraphrase of the rule whose premise Fixit is trying to satisfy with the premises divided into those that are satisfied and those that remain to be satisfied. The HOW option operates by moving to, and paraphrasing, the rule that has the desired statement as its conclusion.

To develop a more complete understanding of the overall line of reasoning, the user must enter a series of HOW or WHY questions, as shown in the previous examples. (Systems that automatically combine sequences of such questions to generate summaries of complete reasoning chains have been constructed [Wiener, 1980].)

Similarly, to develop a more complete understanding of what the system has established (and how it was established), the user enters a series of HOW questions. This has the effect of sequentially unwinding and explaining the elements of a *history list* that is used to track system activity.

Example 7.1 Suppose that processing of the network shown in Fig. 7.1 had proceeded as follows: The primary goal, "fuel filter clogged," was selected. It is necessary to establish "fuel not reaching cylinders" (along with other conditions) to confirm the primary goal; therefore, the secondary goal is pushed on a "goal stack" over the primary goal. Eventually the system will reach a state with the following goal stack:

- Spark is present at the cylinders. ← top of stack
- Electrical system is normal.
- Fuel not reaching cylinders.
- Fuel filter clogged.

The system will ask the question "Is there a spark present at the cylinders?" as a part of processing the top goal. If the user responds with WHY, the system simply responds that it is attempting to determine if spark is present at the cylinders (the immediate goal).

If the user again responds with WHY, the system takes it to mean that the user is requesting a deeper explanation of the system's purpose at this point. The system will respond by describing the next level down on the goal stack: "Spark is present at the cylinders" is needed to prove "electrical system is normal." This process of unwinding the goal stack continues until the primary goal is reached. This process gives the user a sense of the overall system strategy.

Another problem with the Fixit explanation system is that it lacks a complete awareness of the overall *problem-solving context*. The reason is that the entire development activity is a process of abstracting reality (in this case, into compiled rules) with the resultant loss of many of the details that were originally present in the physical scene. As a result of dropping that knowledge, it generally is not possible for a system based on compiled knowledge to provide deep explanations.

PRINCIPLE 7.4: Explanation is fundamentally a process of translating knowledge from one form to another; therefore, an ES can only articulate knowledge that it possesses in one form or another.

The effect of this principle is most evident when the use of an explanation system to reassure or train a user is considered.

PRINCIPLE 7.5: The *depth of explanation* in an ES should be sufficient to satisfy intended users as to the basic soundness of the knowledge and the underlying reasoning process.

The required depth depends on the type of person for whom the system is intended. Gaining acceptance from an expert can actually be easier than gaining acceptance from a less knowledgeable user. The expert already understands the knowledge and simply needs to be shown that the system is aware of it. The expert has a tendency to accept the system's validity as soon as it is recognized that the expert and the system share knowledge regarding the important aspects of the domain. A less knowledgeable user is not able to quickly discern the validity of knowledge through recognition and therefore requires a more complete explanation to be assured of the system's correctness.

Convincing such a user of the system's validity requires the ability to reconstruct a rational line of argument that establishes the *reason-ableness* of the conclusion. This in turn requires the ability to connect the inference steps with the domain principles that are the *justifications* for each of the corresponding steps. (Justification can take many forms, including justification by definition, observation, inference, or appeal to established authority. Although most ESs focus on justification through inference, some such as Mycin and Casnet cite published references in support of conclusions.) Justification in terms of first (or low-level) principles is generally not possible because ESs lack knowledge of such principles.

To provide more persuasive explanations in the face of missing principle knowledge, in addition to typical *retrospective reasoning* (explaining what the system has already done), explanation can be based on *counterfactual* reasoning—answering WHY NOT. This type of explanation describes what prevented the system from using rules that would have established specified facts. Example 7.2 is based on Fixit.

> **Example 7.2** [During the course of execution, a mechanic enters] WHY NOT "fuel filter clogged."
> [The system responds] Rule 4 could have been used to show "fuel filter clogged" except that "have fuel" could not be shown.

It is also possible to use *hypothetical reasoning*—answering what-if questions—to enhance explanation capabilities. Explanation of this type provides responses to questions such as: "What rules would apply if it could be shown that 'spark is not present' at the cylinders?" This allows the user to move freely about the system to establish a deeper understanding of the knowledge base. It also allows for the identification of missing findings that, if added, would strengthen belief in the rule.

7.2 Causal Models

Another very powerful technique for extending explanation is to associate specific *causal models* (for explanation purposes only) with the active portion of the knowledge base. These causal models, which are frequently represented in the form of semantic nets, are used to store information describing the basic objects in the system and the relations between those objects. Several types of relations are recognized in such models; for example:

cause-effect The conclusion follows from the preconditions. For example:
IF   the fuel gauge is working and
        the fuel gauge shows fuel,
THEN there is fuel in the tank.

effect-cause The cause can be inferred from the presence of the effect. For example:
IF   an area is blackened,
        there is a strong smell of smoke, and
        ashes are present,
THEN there has been a fire in the area.

associative The preconditions and the conclusion are related but there is no sense of causal direction. For example:
Rising wage rates are associated with inflation. (Note that this

does not take a position on the perennial question as to whether rising wages cause inflation or result from it.)

definitional The conclusion further describes the precondition, frequently identifying an object as a member of a class (i.e., a form of isa relation).

When a query is presented, the system responds by dynamically traversing the causal model. Figure 7.2 shows an example of part of a causal model for an automotive diagnostic system. Because the model is for a diagnostic system, many of the links are cause-effect (C/E) or effect-cause (E/C). Conceptually, any C/E link could also be modeled as an E/C link. In practice, the choice is based on intended usage (e.g., "car will not start" is an observed effect for which causes will be inferred). It is also generally not possible to establish equal certainty in both directions (e.g., a broken belt definitely causes a "fan not turning," but it is not equally certain that "broken belt" can be inferred from "fan not turning").

Note that the network includes associative relations. For example, engine problems are associated with cooling system problems: A plugged water jacket (an engine problem) can cause overheating, and cooling system problems can cause the block to crack (an engine problem). The network also includes causes with multiple possible effects, depending

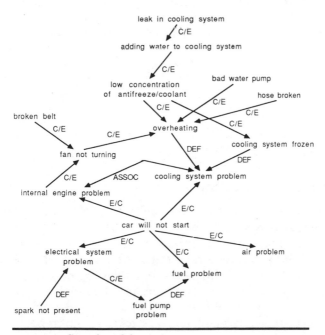

Figure 7.2 Causal model.

on external conditions (e.g., low antifreeze). Example 7.3 shows how the HOW and WHY options can be extended by using hypothetical reasoning based on the causal model from Fig. 7.2:

EXAMPLE 7.3:   [User asks:] HOW can a leak in cooling system cause "car will not start?"

The system traverses the links in the causal model and responds:

```
Leak in cooling system can cause
   adding water to cooling system, which can cause
      low concentration of antifreeze, which can cause
         overheating,  (a  cooling  system  problem),   which   can
            cause
            car will not start.
```

or

```
Leak in cooling system can cause
   adding water to cooling system, which can cause
      low concentration of antifreeze, which can cause
         cooling system freezing (a cooling system problem), which can
            cause
            car will not start.
```

Note that, given the network in Fig. 7.2, the system has no knowledge, and therefore no way of explaining, when overheating rather than freezing would occur. For example, at some point during execution, after it has been established that there is a cooling system problem, the user asks: WHY "car will not start?" The system responds:

```
Car will not start is caused by
   cooling system problem, which is associated with
    engine problem, which includes
      overheating problems, and
      cooling system frozen.
```

For additional information on this form of causal network see Wallis, 1984.

7.3   Press—Explanation Focus on Status

Press [Rolston, 1986*b*] is an ES that resolves software problems that occur in GCOS, an operating system for a mainframe computer. GCOS is a very large and complex software system that is used in many different customer environments. As a result, and as is invariably the case with such systems, long-term maintenance is an extremely large and expensive undertaking. Many Stars (software problem reports) are received every month, and because of the fact that any given problem can be detected by several different users, many Stars represent repeats of problems that have previously been reported and resolved.

Press is used to analyze information associated with Stars (e.g., memory dumps and operator console logs) in an attempt to recognize known problems and to provide the expert with a running start for new problems. To achieve these goals, Press is used as a Star screening system. All incoming Stars (within specific subsets of GCOS) are analyzed by Press.

When Press detects a known problem, it provides the identifying number of the fix that should be applied and thereby allows a response to be made to the Star without requiring any involvement from GCOS experts. When Press fails to recognize a problem, it provides a summary of the general information that it has developed during analysis. This information, which includes such things as abort codes and locations and names of affected modules, allows a GCOS expert to analyze the problem without starting from ground zero.

This capability, which has proved to be of at least as great a value as the known problem recognition capability, is provided by an explanation system that focuses on providing detailed status information. The explanation system, although it does provide a WHY option, is not primarily intended to describe the system's reasoning strategy or to rationalize or justify that strategy. It is intended to provide the user with visibility to the current status at any point during execution.

PRINCIPLE 7.6: Explanations focusing on status are particularly useful for data interpretation tasks and situations in which it is not clear which information is most important.

As an example of the above principle, Press, when working with new error situations, is assisting the expert in finding every valid interpretation of the error data. Because the error has not been identified, it is not immediately clear which set of information is most valuable for developing such interpretations; therefore, information of a type that has proved valuable for error resolution in the past is made generally available. It is focused to the extent that the current situation will allow.

Overview of press design

Following initialization and retrieval of general information, Press uses a *known error list* (which lists all known errors vs. the major error class that each error can appear as) plus system state information derived from the dump to establish a *working error list* of errors that should be considered further.

The working error list is exhaustively searched for a known error that matches the new problem situation. This process works by selecting the head of the working error list as a *primary hypothesis* and then attempting to prove the hypothesis. This proof process locates a *primary rule* that lists the primary hypothesis vs. the facts that must be established to prove the hypothesis. These facts are then processed as conjunctive subgoals.

Global facts, which are universally recognized and have significance to several errors, persist once they are established. *Local facts,* which apply only to the error being considered, are discarded after processing of the corresponding hypothesis.

Explanation in press

The explanation mechanism is accessed by entering "explain" in response to any given question asked by Press. In response, the user receives a menu, as shown in Example 7.5—a sample of Press execution.

Option 1 (from the menu shown in Example 7.5) prints the known error list. Option 2 prints the current class and the current working list. Example 7.5 shows the use of option 3.

EXAMPLE 7.5   The following is an example of the use of the Press explanation system.

```
Enter the content of location 1110, bits 0-17 ::→ 0
Enter the content of location 1101, bits 0-17 ::→ 0
   ** FYI ... The following questions do general classification.**
Enter the content of location 13, bits 27-35 ::→ 2
Enter the content of safestore location 5, bits 12-17 ::→ 0
Enter the content of location 15334, bits 12-17 ::→ 22
   ** FYI ... The following class is now being processed: UNKNOWN
ABORT**
   ** FYI ... Beginning processing of SER 67198 **
Search the system trace table for the fault entry. Enter
the ISR base for the fault entry ::→ 650373
Go to location 650773 and enter the module name that occurs
at that location ::→ MEXTM
Is there a STRT CC entry in the system trace table for TSS
that occurs before the fault entry? yes
Enter the ''Entry Point'' from the trace table entry ::→
explain

The following explanation options are available:
   1) List all the errors recognized by the system.
   2) List the errors that are currently being considered.
   3) What is the current goal and why is it being considered?
   4) Which facts are currently known?
   5) Which conclusions have been reached?
   6) Start trace explanation.
   7) Stop trace explanation.
   8) Return to normal execution.
Please enter the menu number for the desired option → 3
   We are attempting to show that the problem is a repeat
   of SER 67198. The following conclusions must be reached
   to show that this is a repeat of 67198:

   There is an IPR present in the current safestore frame.
   The fault occurred outside of TSS.
   The content of the UST save area is 27.
```

Options 3, 4, and 5 focus on current system status. Option 4 lists the currently known global and local facts. The following is an example of part of the output from Option 4:

```
The following global facts are currently known:
    The ISR is located at 65330.
    The load map is located at 15334.
    The value of abort type is 0.
    The MME field is undefined.
    The release identifier is 2300.
The following local facts are known:
    The value of TSSN size if 4084.
```

Option 5 lists the conclusions that the system has inferred from the given facts. Its output has a format similar to that of option 4.

Option 6 starts the detailed explanation (trace) mode, in which each question is preceded by a simple explanation of why the question is being asked.

PRINCIPLE 7.7: Status explanation is greatly simplified if facts and conclusions are stored separately and explicitly.

One of the disadvantages of structuring a system to capture status information is that the system may not correspond to the way a human problem solver normally resolves problems.

PRINCIPLE 7.8: Explanation is more difficult if the reasoning system used by the system is different from that used by the expert.

The technique used by human experts was not followed by Press because it does not explicitly track facts that are established during analysis and it discards all facts that are not significant to the current hypothesis.

7.4   Clear—Explanation Focus on Clarification

As noted in Sec. 7.1, many existing explanation systems are based on retrospective analysis; they focus, in one way or another, on the reasoning the system has done. This form of explanation is useful for establishing how and why the system operates; however, it provides no assistance to the user who is confused as to what the system means by some statements.

PRINCIPLE 7.9: ESs that focus on clarification explain the meanings of *terms* and *concepts*.

For example, a diagnostic ES for electronic equipment might ask: "Has the breaker for the direct major power bus tripped?" A user of this system might be confused as to the intended meaning of the term "direct major power bus" or the concept "tripped." A clarification system should be able to explain either the term or the concept.

It would be possible to provide clarification of terms by compiling canned explanation text directly with each term. This process is undesirable, however, because it requires excessive storage space, requires that a system maintainer manually modify code when the system changes, and fails to reflect how the system is using the term or concept at any given time.

One of the most common causes of confusion is the overlapping of similar terms or concepts. The user may understand the general idea but may not be able to determine which of several possible interpretations was intended. For example, a large piece of electrical equipment frequently includes many different types of breakers. For the example rule given above, the user may simply be unsure as to which of the many possibilities is intended in the rule. There can also be confusion regarding concepts that are closely related. For example, if the user is asked "Did the operating system crash?," there may be confusion about the distinction between an operating system crash and an operating system hang.

PRINCIPLE 7.10: To establish the meaning of a term or concept, clarification systems frequently describe how the system uses the term or concept.

The Clear system

The Clear system (Computing Explanations Automatically from Rules; Rubinoff, 1985) is part of a front end for rule-based ESs that is designed to work with independently developed rule bases. It generates explanations for clarification by automatically analyzing the existing rule base. It determines which concept is to be clarified and then dynamically examines the rule base to identify rules that relate to the concept. The information contained in the selected rules is then translated into a basic form of English.

The rules contained in a rule base contain a great deal of information that could be used for clarification. The key to being able to use it is to be able to recognize which rules relate to the desired concept. That depends on recognizing that different *types* of rules encode different types of *relationships*. Clear categorizes rules based on several specific rule types. They include:

CAUSE-EFFECT (or EFFECT-CAUSE) rules are very valuable for rationalizing system reasoning but have very little value for clarification.

DEFINITIONAL (called PARAPHRASE in Clear) rules are very useful for supporting clarification because they are inherently intended to represent meaning. In one sense or another, in every definitional rule the left side means the same thing as the right side. This equivalence of meanings can occur in several different forms. For example, a rule can be a definitional by *attribute specification*. Consider, for example, the rule:

A person is a widow IF the person is a woman, and
the person's husband has died, and
the person has not remarried.

This rule is important for operational purposes because it can be used to establish the LHS by showing each of the components on the RHS. It is important from an explanation viewpoint because it provides a direct way of providing clarification by definition.

Definitional rules can also be examples of *isa* relations. Such a rule can be employed for clarification by using it to describe an object as a subset of a more general class of objects. In general, the hope with such clarification is that the user already has some understanding of the alternative definition.

PROBLEM-ACTION rules, which prescribe actions to be taken under specified conditions, are useful only to the extent that the user already understands the need for the specified action under the specified conditions; clarification simply consists in describing this relationship.

Concepts in the premise

Besides classifying rules by type, it can also be useful to observe where a concept is used in a rule. Clear categorizes concept use by dividing uses into those that occur in the premise of a rule and those that occur in the conclusion.

Concepts can occur in the premise of a rule as SOURCE, PREMISE PROPERTY, or TRIGGER, which correspond generally to object, attribute, and value. A rule in which the desired concept occurs in the role of SOURCE has little value for clarification because it simply indicates that something is true about the SOURCE. For example, the rule

IF tank-12   ^level full THEN start-emergency-pump

does little to clarify the concept of tank-12. Conversely, a rule that includes a concept that acts as TRIGGER or PREMISE PROPERTY can be very valuable for clarifying purposes because it indicates that something specific follows from the associated attribute and value. For example, in the above rule, "full" can be clarified by describing it as the value of the level of the tank at which the emergency pump kicks in.

A rule is somewhat useful for clarifying a concept that appears as the RESULT of the rule because it shows one way that the RESULT can be established. If, however, the concept appears in both premise and conclusion (a PASSED-FORWARD concept), then the rule has little value for clarification.

Generation of clarification in Clear

Clear provides clarifications by collecting and then translating appropriate rules into English. It selects appropriate rules by ranking all of the rules according to how relevant they are to the concept being explained. This selection process uses an algorithm that assigns specific weighting factors to the concept roles described above; it is based on the following order from most to least useful:

TRIGGER, PREMISE PROPERTY

SOURCE, INFERRED PROPERTY

RESULTS, DEDUCED VALUES

SUBJECTS

More complex weighting factors are defined for various ways of combining individual rules. Clear also includes facilities for *generalization* of rules: drawing general principles from a set of related rules. When a concept appears in the same role in several rules, Clear summarizes the general role rather than show the details of each occurrence.

7.5   Xplain—Explanation Focus on Rationalization

Explanation focusing on rationalization is intended to convince the user of the validity of the system's reasoning process. One of the advantages of explicitly storing justifications for each step in the reasoning process (as is done in dependency-directed backtracking) is that these same justifications can be used directly for explanation focusing on justification [Petrie, 1985].

It is also possible to contribute to the goal of acceptance through *rationalization* of the system's actions.

PRINCIPLE 7.11: The key to rationalization is to explain why the system is following a given path of reasoning.

Optimally, rather than simply provide some level of description of the goals on the system's goal stack, this type of explanation should address the same type of questions that would occur in a conversation between human experts. These questions might include such things as:

- Why was a particular reasoning strategy followed?
- What possible strategies were considered before one was selected?
- What factors were considered in the selection?
- What factors were considered when a given outcome was developed?
- Which factors were ignored and why?

Most ESs do little in this regard. They can provide explanation only in terms of the processing that has occurred *internal to the system*. This situation exists because the explanation systems are simply paraphrasing, in one form or another, the internal system code. They have visibility only to the code—the results of the development process— and not into the system development process.

PRINCIPLE 7.12: To provide in-depth explanation, a system must have access to the domain-related reasoning that went into developing the system.

Unfortunately, most of the domain-related reasoning has been *compiled out* of most ESs. That occurs because considerable time and system resources are required to include visibility in domain-related principles and reasoning.

PRINCIPLE 7.13: Low-level domain knowledge is not included in a compiled-knowledge ES because it is not needed for the system to execute adequately.

Thus, much like the ignoring of documentation in traditional software development, domain-related reasoning is not preserved because it is not absolutely required to achieve the primary goal of the system.

PRINCIPLE 7.14: Powerful explanation must be a primary design objective if it is to be actually realized in the system.

Xplain overview

Xplain [Swartout, 1983] is an example of a system that was specifically designed to support powerful rationalization of the system's reasoning process. Xplain is based on Digitalis Therapy Advisor [Gorry, 1978], a previously implemented ES that deals with the task of administering certain drugs. The approach used in Xplain is based on the following principle:

PRINCIPLE 7.15: One technique for developing the information required for rationalization is to specifically track the rationale used in each step leading from the domain principles to the final executing system.

Xplain accomplishes this goal by using an *automatic program development module* that accepts abstract definitions of domain principles and produces the actual executable code for the ES. The automatic programmer traps the rationale that was used in developing the system and makes it available to the explanation module during execution. The basic components of the Xplain system are shown in Fig. 7.3. The following sections describe each of these components in greater detail.

Descriptive domain knowledge.   The descriptive domain knowledge component (which is actually called the domain model in Xplain) contains descriptive facts and relations from the domain. They are represented by using a modified semantic network in which the links represent causal relations (similar to the network shown in Fig. 7.3). These facts are purely declarative and are not used to formulate the problem-solving process.

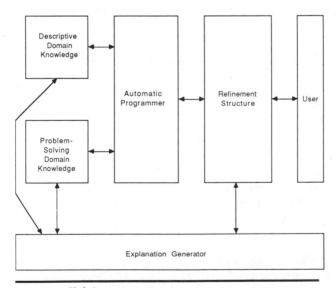

Figure 7.3 Xplain system structure.

Problem-solving domain knowledge. This component (called domain principles in Xplain) contains the knowledge that tells the automatic programmer how to accomplish some goal. Knowledge in this section is procedural. It is represented as procedural templates, each of which contains:

- *Goal.* A statement of the goal that the procedure will accomplish if executed.
- *Domain rationale.* This describes the items that should be considered when deciding whether to apply the procedure.
- *Skeleton script.* This section contains general skeleton scripts that are instantiated with facts from the descriptive domain knowledge to form specific procedures.

The procedural templates are arranged in a hierarchical goal structure based on the specificity of their goals. The proper template is selected by pattern matching of goals and domain rationale. When the pattern matcher locates a match, it saves (as well as returns) the matched structure and variable bindings for explanation purposes.

Refinement structure. The refinement structure is essentially a trace that is left behind by the automatic programmer. It is created by the programmer starting from the top-level goal (e.g., "fix the car"). It is expanded as a goal tree that reflects the actions taken by the programmer to refine the top goal into system primitives. The primary purpose of the refinement structure is to be a repository of information to support explanation.

Explanation generator. The explanation generator uses the refinement structure, the descriptive domain knowledge, and problem-solving domain knowledge to produce explanations. The generator is composed of two parts. One, the *phrase generator,* converts the basic knowledge elements into English; another, the *answer generator,* selects the elements of the knowledge base that are to be included in the explanation. One of the primary roles of the answer generator is to select the *level* at which the explanations are to be given.

PRINCIPLE 7.16: Actions that are actually part of the domain-related problem-solving process should be separated from *computer artifacts,* steps that are required to implement the problem-solving process.

One of the primary purposes of this separation is to support the ability to provide different levels of explanation to different types of users. Xplain accomplishes this specialization of explanation by identifying several user *viewpoints* (e.g., expert user and system developer) and then attaching viewpoint information to each procedural prototype. This information indicates whether the explanation for the associated prototype should be included for a given viewpoint. (For more information on tailoring explanation to specific users, see McKeown, 1985.)

Xplain also provides more useful explanation by being aware of the overall context of the dialog. It does this in several ways, including:

- Moving up and down in levels of abstraction based on the levels used in the previous parts of the explanation dialog
- Omitting parts of explanations to avoid repeating information that was previously reported in prior parts of the dialog
- Drawing analogies to elements of the previous explanation output

The concepts of Xplain have been extended in the Explainable Expert System (EES), a structure and technique for building an explainable ES. EES follows the same basic approach as Xplain, but it includes several additional types of knowledge. For example, the descriptive domain knowledge has been expanded to explicitly recognize:

- *Trade-offs.*   Knowledge of which things must be traded off to achieve desired goals. This section also identifies what is gained and what is lost during the trade-off process.
- *Preferences.*   Knowledge in this section indicates how an expert ranks and selects between multiple applicable objectives and procedures.
- *Terminology.*   This section includes knowledge of how various domain terms are defined and related.

The problem-solving domain knowledge section has also been expanded to include further refinements. For example, in EES this section includes knowledge of implementation considerations, integration techniques, and cost optimization factors. For more information on Xplain, see Swartout, 1981; and for more information on EES, see Neches, 1984.

7.6   Explanation for Training

Any explanation system can be used, at least to some extent, as a training vehicle. Some degree of domain knowledge rubs off on the user through extensive use. To provide for more disciplined use of explanation for training, techniques developed for explanation systems have been combined with techniques from computer-aided instruction (CAI) to develop intelligent computer-aided instruction (ICAI) systems.

These include *computer-based tutors,* systems that are specifically designed to tutor students in a given domain.

Early CAI systems were often simply page turners—electronic display of information regarding the domain—or electronic versions of traditional programmed textbooks. One of the primary reasons for developing ICAI was to create systems that could provide specialized teaching assistance to individual students. In an ICAI system the student takes an active role and the system plays a role similar to that of a human tutor. It customizes the tutoring session, on the basis of the student's interest, capability, and mistakes. The principal parts of a typical computer-based tutor are shown in Fig. 7.4 and are described in the following discussion.

A good teacher requires dual expertise: knowledge of the domain and knowledge of how to teach. The fact that these two forms of expertise are represented separately is characteristic of ICAI systems. The *domain expertise* is stored in a module that is similar to a typical ES knowledge base. It represents the knowledge that the student is ι. .ended to learn. Any form of knowledge representation can be used in this module, given that it meets the following constraints:

- The knowledge must directly model the techniques that a human would use to solve problems in the domain. This is necessary—even if it results in a less powerful knowledge base—because it is the human problem-solving technique that is being taught.

- Problem-solving strategies and techniques must be explicitly represented. The system must attempt to represent all likely alternate

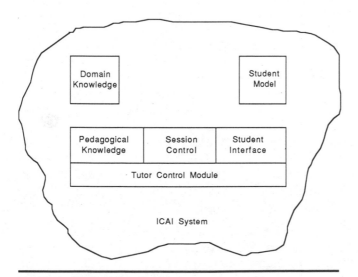

Figure 7.4 ICAI system structure.

strategies—even those that are incorrect—so that the tutor can recognize what the student is trying to do.

In some cases the knowledge base from an ES can be used directly (or with little modification) as the domain knowledge module for an intelligent tutor. For example, Guidon is a tutor that was developed from Mycin's knowledge base [Clancey, 1981, 1983a, 1984a].

The *student model* is used to represent the student's understanding of the domain at any time during a tutoring session. One common technique for structuring the student model is to develop an *overlay* model. In this model the student's responses to tutorial questions are compared to the tutor's domain knowledge for the same area. (The student's knowledge is "overlaid" on the expert's knowledge.) Each relevant skill is then marked as understood or not understood.

Other tutors rely on the concept of recording bugs in the student's understanding. Rather than represent the student's knowledge as a subset of the expert's knowledge, they record only the points at which the student's knowledge deviates from the expert's.

The third primary component of an intelligent tutor—the *tutoring control module*—includes

- *Pedagogical knowledge.*   Expertise on how to teach
- *Student interface.*   The module that actually communicates with the student
- *Tutoring session control.*   The module that integrates the activities of the other modules and organizes the overall tutoring session

The student interface normally relies on some form of natural-language processing. It accepts input and produces responses in a restricted subset of English. Optimally, the interface allows *mixed initiative* [Carbonell, 1970]: At any point in the session either the tutor or the student is free to volunteer direction or information.

The pedagogical knowledge must include a tutoring strategy that is used to structure the thrust of the tutoring process. The tutoring control module uses the tutoring strategy to make many pedagogical decisions, such as determining when to give the student a hint or to conclude that the student is headed toward a dead end. Almost all tutoring strategies rely on some form of *reactive environment* in which the system reaction is based on the responses given by the student. In addition, several specific strategies have been used:

- *Coaching.*   Assisting the student (interrupting as required) as the student engages in a game-like simulation of the domain. In this strategy, learning is an indirect consequence of acting through the simulation.

TABLE 7.1   Existing ICAI Systems

System	Domain	Expert knowledge representation	Student model	Tutorial strategy	Reference
Algebra	Math	Rules	Overlay	Coaching	Lantz, 1983
Excheck	Logic	Rules	Overlay	Adviser	Barr, 1981
Guidon	Medicine	Rules	Overlay	†	Clancey, 1983a
IDS	Diagnosis	General	*		Smith, 1985
Integrate	Math	Rules	Overlay	Adviser	Kimball, 1982
LMS	Math	Rules	Bug	†	Sleeman, 1982
Macavity	Engineering statics	Rules and frames	Overlay	Coaching	Slater, 1985
Meno	Programming	Network	Bug	Adviser	Soloway, 1983
Quadratic	Math	Rules	Overlay	Adviser	O'Shea, 1982
Spade	Programming	Rules	Overlay	Coaching	Miller, 1982
Steamer	Steamship propulsion	Funct. model	Overlay	Adviser	Williams, 1981
Wusor	Logic	Network	Overlay	Coaching	Goldstein, 1982
Why	Weather	Scripts	Bug	Socratic	Stevens, 1982
********	Math	Rules	Bug	Adviser	Anderson, 1985

*The system is intended to support many different student models.
†The system provides only a reactive environment.

- *Socratic.*   A teaching technique (frequently used in law schools) by which the tutor asks questions that are intended to encourage the student to recognize what he or she knows and then to modify his or her own understanding.
- *Adviser.*   The system is explicitly called when the student requests hints, expansions, or critiques.

Table 7.1 summarizes the characteristics of several existing tutorial systems.

7.7   Online User Aid

In several ESs, concepts similar to those used in ICAI have been applied to provide online tutorial-like assistance. Delta [Delta, 1984] (Diesel-Electric Locomotive Troubleshooting Aid) is an ES that is used to maintain diesel locomotives. A rule-based system with approximately 1500 rules, Delta is used as an alternative to flying an expert to a faulty locomotive or moving the locomotive to the expert. It functions as a diagnostic system that works by asking the user questions that are used to establish the cause of observed symptoms.

Delta includes a help system that provides the user with general information along with specific descriptions of locomotive component locations and repair procedures. In addition to this typical help system, however, Delta includes an interface to a video disk player that is used to provide online user assistance. Once Delta has identified the basic fault, it activates the video disk and shows the user how to perform the tests and observations that are required to make a final diagnosis. After the final diagnosis, Delta will provide a video description of the step-by-step procedures required to fix the problem. This capability, which relies on the use of preexisting video descriptions, provides a powerful combined capability of troubleshooting and repair.

FG502-TASP [Alexander, 1984] is an electronics troubleshooting system that shows a graphic display of the parts layout for the unit under test and a graphic display of how the waveform should appear when measured at any point on the board.

See Zissos, 1985, for an example of a system that provides on-line coaching for the use of a text-editing system.

For further information on intelligent tutors see Barr, 1981 (for a description of several early systems excluded from this text), Sleeman, 1982; Wenger, 1986; and Kearsley, 1987.

The following chapter describes the process of developing an ES.

The Expert System
Development Process

This chapter emphasizes that ES implementation is a software development process. As such, it has much in common with traditional software development: The two are more alike than they are different [Rich, 1986]. Therefore, we should take advantage of the extensive effort that has been put into the study of software engineering and its associated methodologies. There are, however, significant differences between the traditional software development process and that used for ESs. Within this chapter these differences are presented as modifications and extensions to the traditional software development model.

8.1 Expert Systems and
Software Engineering

During the late 1960s, the now-familiar term "software crisis" was coined to describe the problems associated with developing complex software systems and the term "software engineering" was used to identify an approach to solving those problems. The formulation of software engineering concepts began with the identification of two basic problems. Programming was considered a black art practiced by somewhat eccentric free spirits who carefully guarded the mystical keys to software development. Programming was difficult because of the overall complexity of the task: Any small segment of a program was fairly easy to understand, but taken as a whole, a typical program was very hard to understand.

Software engineers focused on developing *methodologies* and *tools* in response to this problem. A formal methodology, which is a detailed description of how software is to be developed, is intended to provide *visibility* to the process and to force *discipline* into it. The hope is that, with a well-understood process, it will be possible to involve more people in the activity and manage the process by using the methodology to develop a plan and the newly added visibility to check ongoing status against the plan. Tools were developed to assist the developer in managing the complexity and performing routine tasks.

The cornerstone of software engineering methodology is the concept of a software *life-cycle model*. A typical life-cycle model is shown in Fig. 8.1. This model defines the basic phases of a software development project and describes the output of each phase. Closely associated with the life-cycle model is an accompanying management technique that relies on a review at the completion of each stage to establish the true status of the development project.

The life cycle can be described ideally as follows: It begins with the expression of customer need. A systems analyst works with the customer to analyze the task and define the functional requirements of the proposed system. These requirements are formally described in a

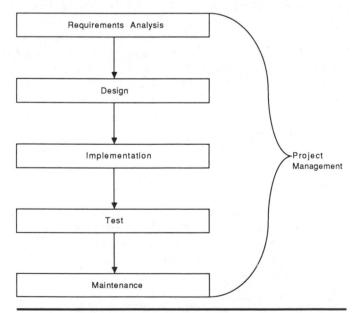

Figure 8.1 Software development life cycle model.

requirements specification. Following a review and approval of the specification, a design, which is described in a design specification, is developed to meet the requirements described in the requirements specification. Testing strategies also are outlined at this point.

The design is implemented by using a representation (i.e., programming language) that is understandable to the target machine. It is then verified by executing tests following the test plan. After the test phase, the system is released to the customer and a long period of maintenance begins.

Difficulties with the traditional life-cycle model

The use of the life-cycle model has helped to reduce the software crisis, but there are still several fundamental problems.

PRINCIPLE 8.1: The traditional life-cycle model is linear.

The use of the traditional life-cycle model assumes that each step can be completely and correctly implemented before moving onto the next. Specifically, it makes the following assumptions:

- A complete understanding of the systems requirements can be *derived* and *described* at the start of the project.
- It is possible to define discrete intermediate steps each of which can be independently realized and verified before moving on.
- The output of each stage can be exactly traced back to the original requirements.

Unfortunately, although these assumptions serve to simplify the overall problem, they are almost invariably incorrect because of the following principle:

PRINCIPLE 8.2: Iteration is inevitable in any large software development project.

Because it is difficult to control such iteration, development based on the linear model views iteration—any change in the results of a previous phase—as failure, usually resulting from a lack of discipline. In reality, there is usually no one—not even the customer—who really understands the problem at the start of the project.

In most cases the early phases of system development must be completed before anyone really understands what needs to be done. Failure to acknowledge this situation results in an elegant solution to the wrong problem. The final system meets the letter of the law (i.e., the requirements specification) but not the spirit of the law (i.e., the true expectations of the user). Software engineering experts have long recognized these weaknesses, and extensive research is being done to modify the traditional model (e.g., rapid prototyping Connell, 1984, and Keus, 1982). However, the traditional model is still widely used in industry.

8.2   Expert System Development Life Cycle

ES development generally follows a model (shown in Fig. 8.2) that is an iterative version of the traditional life-cycle model. The ES life-cycle model is based on a recognition of the evolutionary nature of software development. That is especially true of ES development be-

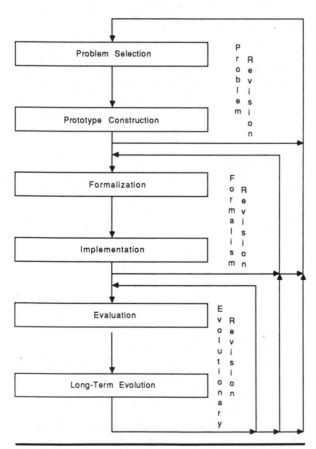

Figure 8.2 Expert system development life-cycle model.

cause, by definition, ESs deal with problem areas that initially are relatively poorly defined and not well understood. There are several unique characteristics of the ES model:

- The customer (and the domain expert) are involved throughout the entire process. This is in contrast to the traditional system, in which the user specifies the requirements and then walks away and waits for the final product.

- Frequent demonstrations of work to date are encouraged. These demonstrations allow the customer and expert to visualize the functionality of the completed system and request changes.

- Change is viewed as healthy—in fact, it is the central concept. Specifically, change is encouraged during the prototype phase. The intent is to identify the changes during the phase in which they are easiest to implement. ES development tools assist in managing the effects of change.

The following sections describe the life-cycle phases in greater detail.

8.3 Problem Selection

The problem selection process, which is one of the most critical phases of an ES development project, can be decomposed into the steps shown in Fig. 8.3.

Problem survey

The first step in the problem selection process is to hold a brainstorming session to compile a list of problems that might be considered. At this point the criteria for inclusion on the list should be very liberal. For a typical large organization, the list will have 30 to 50 items each described by a one-line entry.

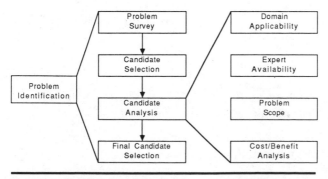

Figure 8.3 Problem identification for expert systems.

Candidate selection

The purpose of the problem selection phase is to narrow the list to the applications that will receive serious consideration. To select those candidates, each of the items on the original list is evaluated relative to a set of *screening criteria*. A yes or no answer is developed for each criterion for each candidate. Only the applications that meet virtually all of the screening criteria advance to the *candidate list*.

The following are the basic screening criteria:

- Does the task require the use of expert knowledge?
- Is the required expertise scarce (or is it likely that it will soon become scarce)?
- Are experts who know how to perform the task available?
- Is there some reason to believe that a traditional algorithmic solution would be difficult to implement?
- Does the task require a reasonable amount of judgmental knowledge or dealing with some degree of uncertainty?
- Does the task require primarily verbal (as contrasted with physical) skills?
- Is a solution to the problem very valuable to the organization; that is, is the problem definitely worth solving?
- Is a solution that is valuable today likely to stay valuable for several years to come?
- Is it acceptable for the system to occasionally fail to find a solution; is it OK to produce a suboptimum response in at least some cases?
- Is a significant amount of time available to develop the system (say, at least 6 months)?

The above questions should be answered with the benefit of the doubt going to the candidate. The purpose of this activity is to quickly filter out the problems that obviously fail to meet the criteria. Each candidate is then analyzed in more detail.

Domain applicability

This step is a more detailed analysis of the suitability of the domain for ES application. Criteria for this analysis include:

1. The task requires scarce expert reasoning; several signs point to expertise that is (or may become) scarce:

- There is a large gap between the levels of performance of the expert practitioner and the typical practitioner. It is often the case that 30 percent of the people do at least 80 percent of the work. That is due, at least in part, to the fact that the typical level of expertise is quite low. Note that, for a large workforce, even a small increase in the average level of expertise can have a large payback. It is by no means necessary to reach the expert's level of knowledge to have a large financial impact.

- There is a need to formalize a complicated set of informal procedures that are clearly understood by only a few experts.

- There is a need to preserve knowledge that may be lost (to develop an *institutional memory*).

- There is a need to distribute expertise to many locations.

- The experts are in short supply and spend a large part of their time assisting others in resolving problems.

- There are frequent occasions on which several people have to work together to solve a problem because no single person has the required expertise.

- There is a large volume of complex information that must be used to solve a problem. In this case the problem may not be conceptually difficult, but it may require a large volume of knowledge that is difficult to organize and remember.

2. The problems from the domain are solved by using primarily symbolic (e.g., verbal) knowledge. Although the solution may involve some mathematical calculation, it should not rely primarily on extensive manipulation of numeric formulas. For example, an ES for maintenance of computer storage disks might include a fairly large set of formulas for converting physical addresses to logical addresses, but the heart of the system is in knowing what to do with the converted addresses, not in the conversion process itself. This is in contrast to a storage management routine, the primary job of which is to quickly execute an extensive mathematical algorithm—which also involves conversion between logical and physical addresses—that decides where to store new information on the disk. The problem should be one that could be solved over the phone, as when a doctor advises a paramedic who is at the scene of an accident.

3. The task should be primarily cognitive and should not require extensive physical manipulation (e.g., sculpting), sensory input (e.g., radar, signal processing), or broad commonsense knowledge (e.g., a justice of the peace).

4. The problem should be similar to the problem addressed by an existing system (assuming the project is intended to use existing technology and not to perform research). This gives some general assurance that the domain is amenable to ES application.

Expert availability

The importance of this analysis is reflected in the following principle:

PRINCIPLE 8.3: It is imperative that a suitable expert be available if an ES project is to succeed.

"Suitable" in this context can be established by using the following criteria:

1. An expert who is currently actually able to solve problems in the subject domain must exist. There is a growing tendency to develop systems (as "expert systems") that attempt to solve problems that human experts—or collections of experts—are unable to solve. (They generally attempt to produce better results than humans by applying some more formal methods to the problem.) There is nothing inherently wrong with attempting to develop such a system, but there will probably be little opportunity to apply ES techniques directly.

2. The expert must be available. (Lack of expert availability is one of the most common reasons for major failures in ES development.) Typically, the expert will be required for several hours a day through the development of the prototype and for up to 10 hr/week for the remainder of the project. This is frequently one of the more difficult criteria to meet, precisely because the project is directed at a domain in which expertise is, by definition, scarce and therefore in great demand.

3. The expert must be reasonably articulate. He or she must be able to describe domain knowledge and how it is applied.

4. The expert must be willing to provide knowledge. This is frequently not the case, again, precisely because the desired knowledge is scarce and therefore valuable both to the organization and to the expert.

5. The expert must enjoy a credible reputation among the potential users of the system. If that is not the case, future users will not accept the system, even if it replicates the expert perfectly.

6. Multiple experts should agree on problem-solving techniques. This allows for final system verification by several experts. Even though not all of the experts agree with the primary expert's technique (such is rarely the case), they should at least recognize the primary expert's approach as one of several recognized, acceptable schools of thought.

PRINCIPLE 8.4: Try to get the expert that the organization doesn't want to give.

Problem scope

The most basic principle for sizing as ES project is:

PRINCIPLE 8.5: Select an ES project that appears to be too small.

1. For a small system, the expert should be able to solve a typical problem in about half an hour. It should involve the use of 50 to 300 important *chunks of knowledge* (e.g., rules or network nodes). For a large system, the problem should require from a few hours to a few days to solve and should involve the use of from a few hundred to a few thousand chunks of knowledge. The time required to resolve a typical problem is fairly easy to establish through an analysis of case records and through discussion with the expert. The number of knowledge chunks can be estimated by asking the expert to describe how many cases are considered and how much information is used to solve each case. The intent of this analysis is only to develop an order-of-magnitude level of precision (i.e., are there 100 knowledge chunks or 100,000?).

2. The proposed system should deal with a *well-bounded* problem in a *narrow domain*. If the desired domain is too broad, it may be possible to arrive at an acceptable scope by addressing only a subset of the overall problem in the first phase of a phased development. For example, an agricultural system might be designed only for giving advice regarding the choice of pesticides for winter wheat, not for giving advice about the use of pesticides in general.

3. The skill that is built into the system should be one that is (or could be) routinely taught to novices. This is, for example, actually true of many industrial diagnostic systems. The desired level of performance is similar to that presented in training classes for field service personnel. (This raises the interesting question of why the field people aren't getting the job done if they have already received the training. There are usually several reasons: The students never really understood the training; they forgot as time passed; or the domain has changed and their training was not updated.)

4. Although it is possible to build an ES that is completely embedded within another system, it is easier to develop the system if it can be used in a *stand-alone* form. It should be possible to at least test the system without requiring extensive integration with other systems (e.g., existing databases).

Cost/benefit analysis

As with any business decision, the decision to build an ES depends on an analysis of the cost of building the system compared to the expected benefit. The costs include such things as the expert's time, the knowledge engineer's time, and the costs of required hardware (possibly including delivery hardware) and software. The benefits of the system could include such things as the added revenue that results from being able to serve additional customers, the reduced cost that results from increased user efficiency, or the insurance that results from preserving critical expertise.

When it is difficult to estimate actual costs and benefits, it may be easier to concentrate on estimating a *payback point* (i.e., focusing on establishing how effective the system would have to be to just recover the cost of building it). For example, to reach the payback point, the system may have to be only 20 percent effective. If the system is designed to be 70 to 80 percent effective (a common number for an ES), then we would have a good feeling that 20 percent is very likely to be achieved. This type of analysis is especially useful for comparing different candidate systems.

8.4   Prototype Construction

Once a problem domain has been selected, the next task is to construct a prototype that represents a small part of the final system. It will typically address 5 to 10 test cases and will require from a few weeks to a few months to complete, depending on the scope and difficulty of the problem. The steps in this process are:

- Initial knowledge acquisition
- Basic problem approach
- General consultation model
- Inference paradigm selection
- Knowledge representation selection
- Tool selection
- Prototype implementation
- Prototype testing
- Prototype demonstration
- Project revisions

PRINCIPLE 8.6: The primary purpose of a *demonstration prototype* is to learn more about the domain.

The process of building a prototype is analogous to an artist producing a charcoal sketch of a painting. Before an artist begins to apply oil paint to a portrait, he or she will typically sketch the entire portrait with a charcoal pencil. This allows the artist to lay out the work, consider the details of the painting, and accurately estimate the work involved in a form that is easy to change. Prototyping, like charcoal, can be thought of as an active agent in the planning and design process.

The specific purposes of the prototype are threefold:

1. To gain a deeper understanding of the nature and scope of the problem and associated problem-solving technique.
2. To demonstrate the overall system functionality. This allows the customer to evaluate the usefulness of the system and to decide whether to continue with the development of the complete system. (In effect, it is the last stage in the problem selection process.)
3. To test the initial design decisions.

The prototype construction activity normally involves only the knowledge engineer (KE) and the domain expert. It begins with *initial knowledge acquisition.* In this phase the knowledge engineer makes an intensive overview investigation of the domain while seeking to learn as much as possible about the domain's critical aspects. This activity begins with an attempt to consume any available background information—documentation, audio tapes, video tapes, case records, training course material, etc.

After all available background knowledge has been established, the KE meets with the expert to begin to discuss specific case studies and to clarify the KE's understanding of the domain.

After the KE has developed a reasonably good understanding of the domain, the process of developing a basic problem approach, *general consultation model,* inference paradigm, and knowledge representation begins. The consultation model describes such things as the type of questions that will be asked, the type of user that will be expected to answer them, and the form in which the response will occur.

After these are defined, a tool that will effectively operate with the selected paradigm and knowledge representation is selected. As soon as one case is reasonably well understood, the implementation of the prototype is started by using the selected tool.

PRINCIPLE 8.7: The best way to implement a prototype is to put down your best understanding, even if it is wrong, and then criticize and revise it.

The sample cases that are implemented in the prototype should be instances of the major classes of problems that will be encountered. Following implementation, the knowledge engineer and expert work together to test and validate the prototype and revise it as required.

The prototype is then again analyzed to determine the validity of the selected problem and implementation techniques. This analysis and the problem understanding gained during the prototype construction activity will almost always result in some (possibly major) modification of the problem statement. It is also common for a *paradigm shift* [Hayes-Roth, 1983] to occur during the implementation. This indicates that a different paradigm appears to be more appropriate as a greater understanding of the problem develops. After the problem statement and selected paradigm have been modified, the prototype is modified (or completely reimplemented) to reflect the new situation.

Only after a satisfactory prototype has been developed is the decision made to commit to a full-scale development. By this stage the knowledge engineer should have a level of understanding about equal to that of the lower-level practitioners in the field and, similarly, the expert should have a reasonable understanding of his or her role in building the system.

Considerable debate remains as to whether the prototype should be discarded following acceptance.

PRINCIPLE 8.8: Keep only those parts of the prototype whose level of implementation quality is similar to that expected of the final system.

Even if the entire prototype is discarded, it can, at a bare minimum, serve as an immediate guide for the new implementation.

8.5   Formalization

Following the verification of the prototype, work on the final system begins in earnest. The next major task in the development process is the *formalization* phase.

Formalization is as important in ES development as it is in the development of any other large complex software system. In fact, it can be even more important because there is a need to capture an understanding of a problem that is initially not well understood and because there is always the danger of deteriorating into a kludge. The watchword in ES development is not to avoid formalism but, rather, to avoid premature formalism.

The primary purposes of the formalization phase are to:

- Capture and record the key understandings that were developed during the prototype phase
- Force planning to occur prior to the start of full implementation
- Record decisions in regard to implementation strategies
- Provide visibility to all current understandings to allow more people to contribute to the project
- Provide visibility and checkpoints to allow for management of the project and to allow the user to be involved in the project

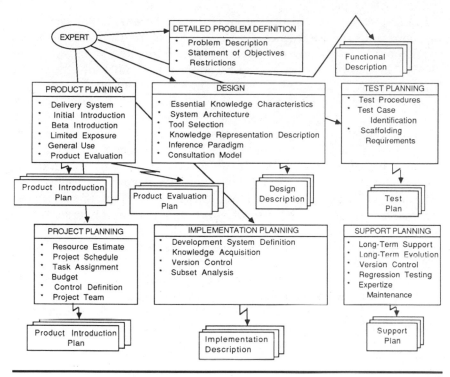

Figure 8.4 Expert system formalization process.

- Allow for concurrent development of test, deployment, and long-term support facilities

The specific steps in the formalization process, and the output of each step, are shown in Fig. 8.4.

PRINCIPLE 8.9: The larger the project the more important it is to preform a complete formalization.

Detailed problem analysis

The first step in the formalization process, *detailed problem definition,* is to develop a functional description that defines, as clearly as possible, the *problem* to be solved, the *objectives* to be met, and, most important, any *restrictions* that serve to limit the scope of the project and the customer's expectations.

Following the completion of the functional description, the processes of *design, project planning,* and *test planning* begin. The design activity culminates with the production of a *design description document* that describes a tentative design for the system.

In many cases the overall system will include considerable software in addition to the ES kernel. For example, in the Dipmeter Advisor the ES portion was only 43 percent of the completed system [Smith, 1983]. The design process for the ES portion is significantly different from that for the remaining portion. In more traditional design the software is decomposed down to a level at which specific functions are identified and allocated hierarchically to modules, interfaces are specified, control structures are developed, and data dictionaries are developed. In ES design the domain is not understood well enough to produce this level of detail (in spite of the prototyping activity). Rather, ES design focuses on identifying the correct knowledge representation, inference paradigm, and system architecture. The required system decomposition is performed (iteratively) during the implementation phase.

The design phase produces a written description for each design decision and investigates each decision in greater depth than during the prototype development. If, however, there are major discrepancies between the conclusions reached by the prototype development activity and the design activity, there should be serious reconsideration of how well the prototype actually represented typical domain problems. The prototype should be reevaluated if necessary.

Project planning

The output of the project planning phase is a *project plan* that presents an estimate of the resources that will be required to complete the project along with a *budget* that describes how the resources will be allocated. It also includes a statement of the intended project *schedule* that shows *tasks* and their *interdependencies*. Each of these tasks is *assigned* to a member of the proposed *project team*.

PRINCIPLE 8.10: The project plan should specifically state how much of the expert's time is expected during each phase of development.

Test planning

The *test planning* activity focuses on defining the elements required to verify the validity of the system after the system is developed. This includes the identification of *test cases* and the *procedures* for executing them. The selection of test cases should focus on identifying a set of *nominal cases* as well as cases that stress the system by forcing it to work on *boundary conditions*. As new cases are identified during iterative implementation, they are added to the list. Although the list will grow, the test procedures should remain substantially unchanged as test cases are added.

Product planning

Product planning deals with the activities necessary to produce a final product from the initial implementation. The *product introduction plan* describes how the product is to be introduced to the users—normally as a phased process in which each phase results in a more general exposure. The initial introduction is normally to only a few friendly and knowledgeable users. Often the only difference between test activity and the *initial product introduction* is that the system is used to address real problems (with the results being reviewed by the domain expert prior to use).

The results of the initial introduction are used to revise the system and, after a reasonable level of confidence has been developed, the system is released to a few selected (reasonably friendly) beta sites. The results of the use at beta sites are used to create a *limited exposure system* that is distributed to all users (friendly or otherwise) within a subset of final users. After an acceptable level of confidence is established, the system is released for *general use.*

The *product evaluation plan* describes how the system will be evaluated during routine use. This evaluation is intended to establish the usefulness (rather than correctness) of the system. It is used to modify the long-term direction of the project and, possibly, to influence decisions regarding future development projects.

Support planning

As soon as one user gets any version of the system, a period of long-term evolution begins. Although the system will continue to change during this period, it is necessary to provide support of functionality that is in use to solve real problems.

The *support planning* phase produces a *support plan* that identifies the elements that will be required to provide such support. This plan describes how *configuration management* will be conducted and how *long-term support* will be provided (e.g., what type of people will be required, how changes will be introduced, how users will communicate problems, and how responses will be given). Another issue is how domain expertise will be maintained. For example, will there be a hothouse for growing new experts, or is it assumed that the system will completely obviate the need for experts?

The regression testing portion of the support plan describes how regression (i.e., unintended side effects) will be detected when changes are installed. It is often very useful to collect *case histories* during development. These record the responses to system questions that are required to establish each conclusion. After changes are made, the case histories are reexecuted by a support program to check for regressions.

Implementation planning

The *implementation planning* phase produces an *implementation description* document that describes how system development will be conducted. For example, it describes what the procedures will be for knowledge acquisition (e.g., will the expert come to the knowledge engineer or vice versa?). It also describes the system that will be used for development, the process for controlling iterations, and the segmentation of the development process into subsets. Breaking the project into independent subsets makes it possible to apply the software engineering concept of *incremental development,* in which the initial build of one subset is implemented and tested before going on to the next. For additional information on formalization see Jacob, 1985.

8.6 Implementation

The steps in the implementation phase are:

- Prototype revision
- System framework development
- Core knowledge acquisition
- Ancillary software development
- Internal integration
- Internal verification

The prototype revision process consists of the following steps:

- Revision of representation and inference decisions
- Component representation level revision
- Establishment of knowledge base partitioning
- Verification

In the first step the knowledge representation scheme and the inference scheme are modified to comply with decisions made during the design phase. Following this the overall scheme for assigning knowledge primitives is reevaluated. This involves reviewing the representation level, object selection, and the attributes associated with those objects. For example, in the prototype development the knowledge engineer may have decided that several parts should be viewed as an assembly and so were represented as a single object in the system. A component evaluation might reveal that the selected representation level is too high; greater flexibility might result from representing such characteristics individually. This reevaluation is based on the clearer understanding of the domain that results from the prototype development activity and from the fundamental revisions to the representation and inference scheme that occur during the design phase.

Knowledge base partitioning makes it easier to change the knowledge base because the base is divided into logically independent segments rather than being one large blob. This principle, which is essentially important for large ESs, is essentially that established by software engineering:

PRINCIPLE 8.11: An effective technique for dealing with complexity is to decompose the system into manageable bites.

Partitioning can be approached at an architectural level—for instance, by dividing the task into independent subproblems (see Sec. 5.4) or by using completely separate knowledge bases within one system [Wright, 1984].

It is also important to consider partitioning from an implementation viewpoint. Several concepts (again, derived from established software engineering concepts) are fundamental to developing a scheme for partitioning within a knowledge base:

Cohesion.   The extent to which different knowledge chunks within a knowledge base segment are closely related (i.e., how well the parts of a segment "stick together")

Coupling.   The number of connections between segments

Partitioning base.   The characteristics that are used for grouping chunks into segments

To partition the knowledge base, the KE first selects a partitioning base and then groups chunks according to the following principle:

PRINCIPLE 8.12: Knowledge chunks should be so grouped that cohesion is maximized and coupling is minimized.

After the prototype functionality has been implemented by using the selected representation and partitioning techniques, it is verified. (For an example of an automated partitioning system see Nguyen, 1985.)

Following the revision of the prototype, the largest development phase begins. This phase includes the implementation of the *basic framework* for the system (i.e., inference engine, user interface, etc.), the *core knowledge base,* and any *ancillary software* required. These activities can generally be executed in parallel.

The core knowledge base is comprised of the knowledge required to complete the test cases identified in the test plan. It is developed by

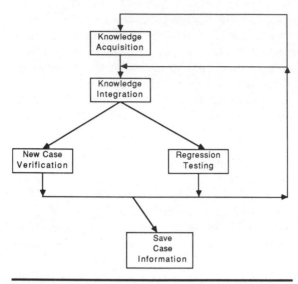

Figure 8.5 Core knowledge development.

using the process shown in Fig. 8.5. As a first step in this process, the KE acquires the knowledge from the expert. The KE then enters the new knowledge into the knowledge base. This entry follows the architectural design and the knowledge base partitioning plan and is accomplished through the use of appropriate knowledge base construction tools.

The new knowledge must be integrated with the old knowledge. The two biggest challenges in this process are determining whether the knowledge to be added is already present in the knowledge base in a slightly different or more general form (in which case it should be subsumed by the more general knowledge) and ensuring that the new knowledge is consistent with the existing knowledge.

PRINCIPLE 8.13: When knowledge is added, the existing functionality must be checked for regressions.

If regressions are discovered, the knowledge base is again modified and the test cycle restarted. Following the successful completion of these tests, the case information for the new case is saved and the knowledge acquisition process continues.

The ancillary software (i.e., communications, utilities, database connections, etc.) is developed in parallel with the system framework and by using traditional software development techniques.

Internal integration and verification

Following their completion, the main system components must be integrated into one comprehensive system. This generally requires the resolution of conflicts among various modules, generally the result of misunderstanding of interface conventions.

After the system is integrated, it is verified by the KE and the domain expert. This is a comprehensive analysis that should include representative test cases from all parts of the system. Both the KE and the expert should agree that the system is correctly implemented before sending it on to more formal verification by external people.

8.7   Evaluation

The first difficulty encountered in structuring an ES test is a result of the following:

PRINCIPLE 8.14: For many of the domains addressed by ES, it is impossible to identify an answer that is "absolutely correct" for any given problem.

As a part of the Mycin development project a now-well-known experiment (the bacterium experiment) was devised to evaluate the accuracy of Mycin's solutions. To deal with the lack of an absolute criterion of correctness, it was decided that a team of experts would be polled to establish the "correct" answer for each question.

PRINCIPLE 8.15: In ES evaluation the correct response is taken to be that given by a human expert for the same question.

When Mycin's responses were compared to this standard, the result was a somewhat disappointing accuracy of 75 percent. To analyze the results, another test (the meningitis test) was developed, this time as a *modified Turing test*. Ten randomly selected case histories of meningitis were diagnosed by Mycin and by experts from Stanford Medical School. The results were then evaluated blindly by eight experts from throughout the United States.

In this case Mycin's 69 percent accuracy was better than that of any of the acknowledged experts evaluated by the test. The following procedure for verifying ES functionality has developed as a result of such studies:

PRINCIPLE 8.16: An ES's responses should be evaluated relative to the domain expert's and then relative to the responses given by a group of experts.

It is also possible to evaluate the *structure* rather than the function of the system. This type of test, which is frequently automated, focuses on verifying the *completeness* and *consistency* of the system [Nguyen, 1985] through an evaluation of the internal implementation.

For more information on ES evaluation see Buchanan, 1984*a*, and Hayes-Roth, 1983.

8.8   Long-Term Evolution

As with any large software system, an ES continues to evolve throughout its life. Several types of evolution are involved:

1. Increase in general functionality

2. Corrections, particularly to the knowledge base

3. Additions to the knowledge base to make the base more complete

4. Expansion of the domain

5. Revisions required by external modifications (e.g., modification of the ES because the base language has been revised)

The most significant aspect of long-term evolution results from the effect that developing an ES has on an expert. The indirect benefit is that an ES forces the expert to articulate and structure knowledge. In almost all cases the presence of this large structured body of knowledge will allow the expert to revise his or her own thinking to produce better solutions. The long-term evolution process then becomes one of joint growth of the expert and the system.

In the following chapter the knowledge acquisition process, which itself is a part of the development process, is considered in greater detail.

9

Knowledge Acquisition

Knowledge acquisition (KA) has long been recognized as both an art and a bottleneck in the construction of ESs [Feigenbaum, 1977]. This chapter describes some of the root causes of the difficulty of KA and presents techniques for making it more efficient.

9.1 Expert–Knowledge Engineer Interactions

The KE plays a critical role in the construction of an ES using the expert-to-KE model of ES development. Although it is the expert's knowledge that is being modeled, it is the KE who must actually build the system. In this process the KE acts as an intermediary who hopes to catalyze the process of moving knowledge from the expert to the system. This process is particularly critical because:

PRINCIPLE 9.1: The KE's knowledge, rather than the expert's, is actually reflected in an ES.

As a result, the KE must be very careful to accurately reflect the expert's knowledge much as a human-language translator must seek to replicate the meaning of the author.

The basic process of KA is shown in Fig. 9.1. The first step in this process, *domain understanding,* is a period of general familiarization.

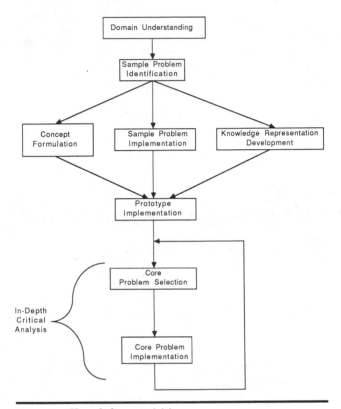

Figure 9.1 Knowledge acquisition process.

This step begins with an informal initial meeting between the KE and the expert. The purposes of this meeting are to:

- Begin establishing a rapport between the KE and the expert. Growth of this rapport should be based on mutual respect: The KE respects the expert for demonstrated expertise, and the expert respects the KE for his or her interest in the domain and willingness (and ability) to learn. The relationship often follows the analogy of the established master and apprentice. If such rapport can't be established, a new expert or KE must be found or the project should be abandoned.

- Provide the KE with a very-high-level overview of the domain.

- Acquaint the expert with the concept of an ES and with the respective roles of an expert and the KE. The KE should show the expert an example of a similar, existing system if at all possible.

PRINCIPLE 9.2: The KE must remain sensitive to the need for a continuing personal working relationship with the expert.

This is sometimes difficult because the KE, at least initially, is required to take a back seat to the expert and may also have to tolerate the expert's personal quirks (e.g., impatience with a novice). During the remainder of the familiarization period, the KE, to a large degree working alone with basic materials such as reference documents, training material, and video tapes, attempts to develop an overall view of the domain while making a conscious attempt to avoid details. In this role the KE is retracing the steps of the expert's learning process by attempting to learn about the domain in the same way that the expert did.

PRINCIPLE 9.3: Never ask the expert for basic information that could be easily acquired through background reading.

Several important items result from this study:

1. A general description of the problem.
2. A bibliography of relevant references.
3. A glossary that describes the vernacular of the domain. This includes the terms, acronyms, and symbols that are specific to the domain.

The glossary is particularly important because knowledge of vocabulary is one of the most fundamental types of knowledge in any domain:

PRINCIPLE 9.4: Whenever possible, the KE should use the domain vernacular when working with the expert.

The next step in the process is the identification of *sample problems* to be used in the initial implementation (the demonstration prototype).

PRINCIPLE 9.5: Problem identification should begin in a breadth-first way.

This breadth-first analysis identifies a list of generic problems that serve to circumscribe the overall problem space. From this overall list several specific problems, which are identified by the KE and expert working together, are selected. These should be nominal, typical of large classes of problems, important, and well understood. Following this selection process, the three most critical activities—concept formulation, sample problem implementation, and knowledge representation development—begin in parallel.

The sample problem implementation is conducted by the KE, who *interviews* the expert regarding the problem-solving activity. The knowledge structure that will be used to represent the developing concepts and problem-solving knowledge takes shape as the other processes proceed. Four basic difficulties may arise during these activities:

1. The expert may not have the required knowledge in some area.
2. The expert may not be consciously aware of required knowledge.
3. The expert may not be able to communicate the knowledge to the KE.
4. The KE may not be able to structure the knowledge for entry into a knowledge base.

9.2 Cognitive Behavior

To begin to understand the basic causes of these problems, consider that expert performance is an example of *cognitive bahavior* [Gammack, 1985]. Cognitive psychologists have studied expert problem-solving behaviors for many years and have developed extensive theories to explain them [Anderson, 1982], Several key points are significant to ES.

PRINCIPLE 9.6: Experts frequently don't follow textbook-like lines of linear reasoning [Reif, 1982].

In general, experts tend to use a more pattern-driven approach that relies on quick recognition of powerful knowledge chunks or groupings. This characteristic, which in many domains (e.g., chess) is the key aspect of expertise, results from the fact that the expert has, through many years of experience, developed an extensive repertoire of compiled knowledge. That knowledge allows the expert to respond quickly to problems while giving little thought to the detailed steps involved in the "instinctive" response.

PRINCIPLE 9.7: Expert knowledge is stored subconsciously.

Unfortunately, although this adds power to the expert's capabilities, it also makes it more difficult for the expert to explain problem-solving actions (in the same sense that a compiled-knowledge ES has difficulty explaining its actions).

PRINCIPLE 9.8: Experts often find it harder to explain their actions than novices do.

Because expertise often results from such subconscious knowledge, the expert may not be able to verbalize it [Weiser, 1983; Kolodner, 1984].

9.3   Knowledge Acquisition Techniques

Each of the three parallel KA activities is centered on the concept of some form of interaction between the KE and the expert regarding problem-solving scenarios. This, at least in part, is intended to deal with the problems described above. The interaction normally takes one of three standard forms [Johnson, 1983]:

1. *Description.*   In this form, which is most appropriate for the very early stages of the project, the expert presents a structured description of the domain. This type of presentation, which is similar to that provided in textbooks and formal lectures, is good for establishing background information. It is, however, of limited value for actual system development, primarily because it presents idealized versions of problem-solving activities and frequently omits information regarding strategies.

2. *Observation.*   In this case the KE simply (and unintrusively) watches the expert during actual problem-solving situations. This activity, which is most valuable after the KE has established a reasonable level of competence in the domain, allows the KE to observe problem-solving details in an environment that is not contrived in any sense.

3. *Introspection.*   In this mode of interaction, which normally occurs with the KE interviewing the expert, a critical assessment of problem-solving situations is conducted. This allows the KE to interactively search for required knowledge.

All three of these forms of interaction normally occur during any given project, and they progress in the order shown.

9.4   Sample Problem Implementation

As soon as the KE has developed a reasonable overall understanding of the domain, introspective analysis of specific problems begins.

PRINCIPLE 9.9: Problem analysis should be top-down and hierarchical.

The analysis should be based on top-down, hierarchical decomposition for the benefit of both the KE and the expert. The process is natural to the expert because an expert's knowledge is stored hierarchically. (This "big picture" is one of the things that the novice lacks.) It is useful for the KE because it allows the overall domain to be broken into manageable subparts.

The actual investigation process can follow one of several styles [Grover, 1983]. One style of interviewing is *goal-directed decomposi-*

tion. By using this technique, the KE focuses on identifying which goal is trying to be accomplished at each step.

The most common interviewing technique is *forward scenario simulation.* No matter how the interviews are conducted, the KE must help the expert maintain a global view and extract knowledge. That is because an expert's knowledge is *generative:* It becomes available only as it is generated (through *associative relations*) during the problem-solving process.

PRINCIPLE 9.10: It is difficult for an expert to retrieve knowledge without a problem-solving context.

To provide the necessary context, a specific type of problem is selected for investigation. (The use of case studies and review of actual problem solutions is often helpful.) The KE starts this process by asking general questions. For example, in a diagnostic domain the KE might ask the expert to describe the first thing that he or she does when a specific symptom is observed. The expert and the KE continue to walk through this example together and pause at each step for an analysis of the knowledge represented by that step.

Because the process is conducted top-down, the first explanation should be quite general. In fact, the analysis of any given problem should involve at least three passes: the first to establish general ideas, the second to begin formulating knowledge chunks, and the third (and any subsequent passes) to clarify details.

PRINCIPLE 9.11: The KE's understanding during each pass, although it may be abstracted, should be complete and accurate.

If at any point the KE does not understand the expert's statement, he or she must either ask for clarification or treat the misunderstanding as a detail and note it for resolution in a later pass. This process should continue with one problem from start to finish.

PRINCIPLE 9.12: The detailed problem investigation process should be depth-first.

This type of analysis limits complexity and allows the expert to access lower-level knowledge by serially "unwinding" successive layers of the knowledge hierarchy. Even during the later passes, the expert will omit many important problem-solving details. There are several reasons for omission. Because detailed knowledge is stored subconsciously, the expert may not even be aware that details have been omitted. In that case the KE must assist the expert in dredging up basic elements that were once valuable in developing expert skills but have now been mentally pushed below the surface.

Details may also be omitted because the expert has become accustomed to delivering explanations at a level of detail that suits the listener. A fellow expert is given an explanation that is rife with technical jargon and specific problem descriptions. Conversely, the explanation given a novice will be much more abstract and artificial. This type of explanation, which invariably understates complexities and avoids nuances, is necessary if the novice is to avoid complete confusion and develop at least a shallow understanding of the problem. This type of explanation is provided to the KE because the expert (quite correctly) views the KE as a novice. The KE must respond by reminding the expert that he or she is interested in the detailed steps required for the process rather than just the final results.

Because of these problems the KE must adopt the role of a decompiler or a forensic analyst. Each time the expert presents a piece of information the KE must dissect it to determine what critical knowledge is involved.

PRINCIPLE 9.13: The KE must ask *probing questions* until a satisfactory level of detail is established.

It is also the KE's responsibility to assist the expert in establishing consistency and completeness in the knowledge. Once the KE is satisfied that consistent knowledge, at an acceptable level of detail, has been acquired, he or she should *restate* it to the expert and ask the expert to confirm it. This will allow the KE and the expert to work together to capture the required knowledge.

PRINCIPLE 9.14: Each interview session should be tape-recorded for future use.

Recording the session allows the KE to focus on the general problem-solving process and postpone critical analysis of detailed points. After the session is complete, the KE can repeatedly listen to the tape to fill in any gaps in knowledge.

PRINCIPLE 9.15: It normally takes about four hours to do a detailed analysis of the tape from a one-hour interview session.

The tapes can also be used to introduce the domain to any additional project members who may join the project in the latter stages.

9.5   Concept Formulation

Recognition and formulation of important domain concepts occur in parallel with and as a byproduct of the sample problem implementation process.

One of the most important techniques for formulating domain concepts is to identify the subtasks that comprise the domain.

PRINCIPLE 9.16: Every subtask should have a name.

Strategies also are important conceptual components of the domain.

PRINCIPLE 9.17: Domain strategies are more difficult for the expert to articulate than factual knowledge.

As a result, the KE must be more actively involved in recognizing the strategies that are indirectly described by the expert during the interviews. Each of the significant strategies should be named and described by the KE. During the interviews, the KE should also try to determine which types of uncertainty are involved in the domain and how they are processed (e.g., identify the heuristics the expert uses to limit search).

PRINCIPLE 9.18: To tie together conceptual knowledge, the KE must discover an underlying model for the domain.

PRINCIPLE 9.19: A domain model can often be discovered by searching for analogies between the subject domain and other domains that are already thoroughly understood.

For example, a KE with a background in electrical engineering would identify an immediate analogy between water flow in pipes and electrical flow in wires when attempting to model a plumbing domain.

PRINCIPLE 9.20: A KE should have as general a background as possible to increase the probability of being able to recognize analogies.

After basic concepts are understood and the underlying model is developed, the process becomes one of infusing new concepts and recognizing when several concepts are subsumed by a more general concept.

PRINCIPLE 9.21: If several problem-solving descriptions are very similar, try to find one underlying unifying concept.

9.6   Knowledge Representation Development

The most significant problem in developing a knowledge representation is a classic dilemma: It is difficult to select an appropriate knowledge representation without having the domain knowledge, and it is difficult to elicit the knowledge without a representation defined to hold it. To resolve this dilemma an explicit action must be taken:

PRINCIPLE 9.22: Select a knowledge representation as soon as possible, even though it may not be the optimal (or final) representation.

Such an early selection is important because the KE must have some way to preserve the knowledge once it is acquired. If it is not explicitly and visibly represented, it will simply trickle down into the KE's subconscious in the same sense as the expert's. While this may be desirable when developing a new human expert, it does not help when the goal is to make knowledge generally available.

PRINCIPLE 9.23: The KE must specifically attempt to keep knowledge at a conscious level.

As a result of this desire, the KE will not become as proficient a practitioner in the domain as a trainee with an equivalent level of training because the KE seeks to hold explicit knowledge rather than develop subconscious instinctive skills. After the domain is well understood, a new "better fitting" representation is selected if necessary, and the knowledge is moved to it.

The next major problem in representation selection is the possibility of *representation mismatch* that occurs between the knowledge as contained in the expert and the knowledge as represented in the system. The extent of this mismatch will vary with the extent to which the system is based on *cognitive modeling* (i.e., mirroring the way that the expert actually performs the task) or on *functional modeling* (i.e., developing a system that produces the same result as the expert but by using a different technique). In reality, any large ES will include both types of modeling for different parts of the system.

9.7   Knowledge Acquisition
for Core Problems

The sample problems are eventually built into the system, and other necessary software is completed. This results in a complete demonstration prototype. After it has been decided to construct a complete system, the KE and expert identify the set of core problems and KA work begins again.

This time, however, it has a somewhat different flavor. By now the KE has a better understanding of the domain and should begin to delve deeper into the expert's problem-solving process in the hope of finding additional detail and more thorough justification.

PRINCIPLE 9.24: During core problem implementation, the KE takes a more assertive role in questioning the expert's statements.

This type of questioning is valuable because it gives the expert the opportunity to verify knowledge by bouncing it off an outside observer. The KE's role in this case is largely one of devil's advocate.

This type of analysis is also necessary because there are several potential pitfalls that can trap an expert—and so the corresponding ES. For example, experts, like everyone else, have biases. There may also be areas of the domain in which the expert has not remained current and so may wish to avoid.

Experts are notorious for being overconfident in their judgments and for failing to recognize or acknowledge the difference between knowing and guessing [Kahneman, 1982]. They may also fail to adequately consider boundary conditions or alternative problem approaches.

Perhaps the most insidious problem is that the expert may fail to accurately report the way that he or she actually solves problems. This may be to avoid revealing valuable tricks of the trade (to preserve image or job security). More typically, the expert is saying what he or she believes the KE wants to hear—much like the urban cowboy who wears spurs in spite of the fact that he hasn't even seen a horse for 10 years. To impress the greenhorn, the expert may describe tasks in a very textbook-like way because he or she feels that this form is generally recognized as rational and intelligent. That is especially likely if the KE comes across as highly educated or academic (i.e., the KE is trying to be what the expert expects).

9.8 Use of Multiple Experts

These problems can be mitigated through the use of multiple experts [Dym, 1985; Boose, 1985]. Gathering several viewpoints of a problem will either strengthen belief in the validity of the existing knowledge (in the event that the experts substantially agree) or identify the possibility of errors in the existing implementation (in the event that they disagree).

It should be noted that, although this use of multiple experts refers to experts in the same domain, it may also be necessary to integrate knowledge that is acquired from several experts, each representing a different part of the domain. In this case the primary problem is understanding and representing the overall system of knowledge, typically through the use of an ES architecture that is oriented toward multiple knowledge structures (for example, see Sec. 5.7).

9.9 Knowledge Acquisition without Knowledge Engineers

It has been said that the problem with parents is that by the time they are experienced they are also unemployed. Similarly, the goal of every KE should be unemployment. During the implementation of the core problems the expert becomes more familiar with the techniques used to implement the system and begins to feel more ownership of it. With any luck the expert will eventually view the KE as a necessary evil— a servant who is building the expert's system. (This implies that KEs should be people who like to explore new areas and then move on; who have curiosity about a broad range of topics. They must also be able to avoid possessive feelings.)

By the time the basic system is completed, the expert should be able to directly update and maintain the system. This is possible because the structure of the system has been established, the expert has had an extensive hands-on course in ES construction, and powerful knowledge base editing tools are available (see Chap. 10).

By far the best possible situation is when the expert can build the system directly. This is the state of the art for small, relatively simple systems and is becoming more plausible for larger systems. The long-range goal of ES research is to capture and reproduce the KE's current role—in effect, to develop an ES that represents a KE's expertise. This would allow current-performance-level ESs to be built much more cheaply and quickly and would allow KEs to move on to more challenging tasks such as tackling larger, more complex, or more judgmental domains. For more information on KA see Hayes-Roth, 1983; Kahn, 1984; Bennett, 1984; and Boose, 1986.

The following chapter describes tools that assist in all phases of developing an ES.

10

Expert System Tools

One of the main reasons for the rapid growth in the rate of ES development is the support of a rich set of powerful development tools. Selecting the correct tool, or set of tools, is a key decision in the development of an ES.

ES tools are valuable for several reasons:

1. They provide rich software development environments that would assist in the development of any software. Components of this environment include such things as structure editors, powerful debug and trace packages, multiwindowing, graphics, and pointing facilities.

2. They include specific assistance for rapid prototyping. These facilities include such things as incremental compilers, detailed change-history records, and automatic version control.

3. Much of the work of defining a consultation model, knowledge representation, and an inference paradigm can be avoided because these facilities are already built into the tools. This has several advantages. It allows someone who is less familiar with AI concepts to develop a system (e.g., in some cases the expert); it provides a solid basis for quick capture of knowledge and rapid system development; and it eliminates the labor required to build the basic software.

4. In many cases an ES tool can provide extensive assistance in some specific area of system development. For example, some ES tools are actually partially instantiated ESs (i.e., they include part of the domain

knowledge built in); others assist in KA; and still others assist in areas such as system verification.

There are many different types of ES tools with a wide variety of levels and types of functionality and hardware support requirements. In general, ES tools can be thought of as comprising a spectrum. This spectrum moves from the lowest-level general-purpose programming languages to the highest-level large hybrid development environments. The remainder of this chapter describes and gives examples of each of the types along the spectrum.

Although a general comparison of some of the most popular existing commercial tools is provided, it involves only a small subset of the total set of available tools. The primary intent of this chapter is to provide an understanding of general characteristics and evaluation criteria. No in-depth analysis is presented because existing tools are constantly being modified or discontinued and new tools are being added. Selection of a tool for building an actual system should be based on current information.

10.1 Languages for Expert System Development

The most basic ES development tool is a general-purpose programming language. Lisp has been and continues to be the most widely used language for ES development. It provides many features that ease the task of building any symbolic processing system. Moreover, Lisp is becoming more popular for conventional programming, particularly with the advent of Common Lisp (see Appendix A).

The programming language Prolog is gaining in popularity, although its use as an ES development language has been far less than that of Lisp. Prolog is also a symbolic, general-purpose programming language, because it has a built-in search method, it is somewhat more specific than Lisp.

There is also a growing trend toward the use of more conventional languages for ES development. Several important ESs have been developed by using Fortran [Weiss, 1984], and a large number have been developed by using C language. There are several disadvantages to using such languages, most notably their lack of support for symbolic processing and automatic memory management. Typically, more time is required to develop an ES by using a conventional language than by using a symbolic language.

There are, however, also several advantages. For example, C will generally run faster than Lisp on general-purpose hardware—in some cases, much faster. C is also more widely available, and it has broad general support. Another very practical consideration is that there are available many more proficient C programmers than Lisp programmers. The last major advantage is the fact that the use of C allows the final system to integrate more easily with existing external software.

To achieve the best of both worlds, many developers are applying the following principle:

PRINCIPLE 10.1: Consider developing the system by using a symbolic language and converting the final version to a conventional language for delivery.

This principle is most applicable when it is anticipated that the system will require relatively little change after delivery (e.g., a system that works with classic physics). It is less appropriate in a more typical system in which significant evolution continues indefinitely.

The following principle should also be considered when evaluating ES tools:

PRINCIPLE 10.2: Even if a higher-level ES tool is used to develop the system, it will still be necessary to write some of the system by using a general-purpose programming language.

10.2 Expert System Shells

The first major development in ES-specific tools was the introduction of the ES *shell*. The first example of such a tool was Emycin, which grew out of the Mycin project.

Mycin was developed by using Lisp rather than an ES-specific tool. After the development was completed, it was recognized that the system could be viewed as two separate components: the basic system (e.g., knowledge representation, inference engine) and the domain-specific knowledge, in this case for medical diagnosis.

From this observation, Emycin (for Empty Mycin) was born. Emycin is a shell in the sense that it is an existing ES with the domain-specific knowledge removed. This shell can then be applied to the construction of ES for different but similar domains.

Emycin is rule-based with a backward-chaining inference strategy, and it is designed for diagnostic consultation tasks. It proved to be very valuable for problems that matched this basic model, but it was not very useful for domains with a poor match (e.g., design tasks that require some form of planning).

PRINCIPLE 10.3: The value of an ES shell is directly related to the degree to which the domain's characteristics match the characteristics expected by the shell's internal model.

Table 10.1 lists several ES shells that are of historical interest.

TABLE 10.1 **Expert System Shells**

Shell	Base system	Language	Reference	Model
Age	HearsayII	Lisp	Nii, 1979	Rules, blackboard, independent knowledge sources
Emycin	Mycin	Lisp	Buchanan, 1984	Rules, backward chaining, diagnostic consultant
Expert	Casnet	Fortran	Weiss, 1984	Rules, classification, diagnostic consultant
KAS	Prospector	Lisp	Duda, 1984	Rules, semantic networks, forward and backward

10.3 Narrow Tools

The concept of a shell gives way to the concept of a *narrow* ES tool. (In this case "narrow" implies specialized, and it should not be thought of in a pejorative sense. A narrow tool is the most valuable tool for a narrow domain.) Although these tools were not developed by eviscerating an existing ES, they do have in common the characteristics that they are specialized for a particular form of processing (e.g., focus on one knowledge representation). They are also designed for the construction of systems in the colleague-expert class.

PRINCIPLE 10.4: A key to selecting an ES tool is to identify the right level of specificity.

PRINCIPLE 10.5: Choose the most specific tool that fits the problem.

Increased specificity leads to increased power and efficiency in both development and execution. In the optimum case, when a tool that exactly meets the needs of the domain is available, it can reduce the development time by an order of magnitude or more.

If, however, the tool is very specific and doesn't closely match the domain, then the developer will constantly be attempting to "bend" the domain to fit the tool and will be dropping down into the base programming language to accomplish required actions.

Also, as systems grow and additional functions are added and more problems are addressed, the demands placed on a tool will change.

PRINCIPLE 10.6: When considering the domain-to-tool match, think of the ES after it evolves, not just in its initial form.

Table 10.2 lists several examples of specialized tools and languages for building narrow ESs. In most cases these tools will execute on a

TABLE 10.2   Narrow Tools

Tool	Base language	Reference	Highlights	Commercially available?
Rule-Based				
OPS5	Lisp	Brownston, 1985	Popular basis system, Rete algorithm	Yes
OPS83	C	Forgy, 1984	User-defined control, Pascal-like procedure language	Yes
Radial	C	Michie, 1984	Built-in handling of fuzzy logic	Yes
Savior	Lisp	Savior, 1984	Demons, built-in fuzzy logic	Yes
Frame-Based				
Kandor	Lisp	Patel-Schneider, 1984	Small embedded system with simple user interface	No
Knowledge Craft	Lisp	Gilmore, 1985	Demons, object-oriented programming	Yes
KL-ONE	Lisp	Brachman, 1985a	Automatic inheritance	Yes
FRL	Lisp	Goldstein, 1979	Multiple inheritance, defaults	No
Logic-Based				
Apes	Prolog	Hammond, 1983	Explanations based on proof	Yes
Duck	Lisp	Duck, 1984	Limited built-in TMS	Yes
Mandala	Mandala	Furukawa, 1984	Object-oriented programming	No
Prolog	Various	Clocksin, 1984	Logic-based general-purpose programming language	Yes

variety of hardware platforms, including traditional mainframe systems.

10.4   Lisp Machines

ESs are developed and delivered on many different types of hardware including mainframes, minicomputers, personal computers, specialized *AI workstations* (*"Lisp machines"*) and general-purpose engineering workstations.

TABLE 10.3 Physical Characteristics of Lisp Machines

Parameter	Symbolics 3600	LMI Lambda	TI Explorer	Xerox 1100
Word size	36 bits	40 bits	32 bits	16 bits
Main memory	M–30 MB	4–32 MB	2–16 MB	2–18 MB
Cache access time	*	100 ns	*	70 ns
Memory access time	200 ns	300 ns	300 ns	480 ns
Addressable space	1 GB	128 MB	128 MB	32 MB
Maximum disk storage	3.5 GB	515 MB	280 MB	315 MB
Communications	Ethernet	Ethernet	Ethernet	Ethernet
Principal base software	Zetalisp Common Lisp Interlisp Prolog	Zetalisp Common Lisp Interlisp Prolog Unix	Zetalisp Common Lisp Prolog	Common Lisp Interlisp Small talk Prolog

In the mid-1970s a machine that was specialized to execute Lisp was developed at the MIT AI laboratory to support and expedite MIT's research. Several commercial systems have grown out of this effort, including those available from LMI, Symbolics, and Texas Instruments. At about the same time, a similar system was developed independently at Xerox Palo Alto Research Center (PARC).

The largest and most sophisticated ESs have traditionally been developed on specialized Lisp machines because of the power and capacity of the basic hardware and the software development environments that run on them.

All popular Lisp machines have in common: (1) high-speed Lisp processing, (2) large physical memory, (3) high-resolution, bit-mapped display, (4) mouse for pointing, (5) communications link, and (6) support for powerful ES development environments.

Table 10.3 shows the characteristics of several Lisp machines. For more information see Schwartz, 1986, or Mishkoff, 1985.

10.5 Large Hybrid Expert System Tools

The most generally powerful ES tools are *large hybrid* tools that combine sophisticated development environments with multiple knowledge representations and multiple inference paradigms. This integration of several basic facilities is very useful because it allows any given tool to be used with many different types of problems or on problems that involve several different types of knowledge representations and inference paradigms.

PRINCIPLE 10.7: Large complex domains are most effectively modeled by using a combination of representations and strategies.

A hybrid tool allows the use of a single tool to solve a large complex problem when different parts of the problem require different types of support. (An example of such a problem is described in Chap. 12.)

Large hybrid tools are typically used on AI workstations, although some will execute on traditional systems. They make use of high-resolution bit-mapped graphics, windowing, and mouse to provide a very powerful user interface. This interface helps the system developer build the system quickly and accurately. The same interface facilities can also be customized to provide a powerful interface for the end user (assuming the ES is delivered on a system that supports a sophisticated interface).

Table 10.4 presents a brief overview of the capabilities of some of the most popular hybrid tools, each of which corresponds to the general description given above. Boxes that are checked indicate that the corresponding tool includes the corresponding function (or the function could be easily programmed by using the tool).

TABLE 10.4 Large Hybrid Tools

	S1	KEE	Art	Loops	SRL$_+$
Inference					
Forward chaining	×	×	×	×	×
Backward chaining	×	×	×	×	×
Inheritance	×	×	×	×	×
Representation					
Rules	×	×	×	×	×
Frames	×	×	×	×	×
Logic	No	×	×	No	×
Active values	No	×	No	×	×
Built-in uncertainty					
Certainty factors	×	No	×	No	No
Dependency backtracking	No	No	×	No	No
User interface					
Graphics editor	No	×	×	×	×
Menus	×	×	×	×	×
Multiwindows	×	×	×	×	×
Trace	×	×	×	×	×
Built-in explanation	×	×	×	No	×

For more information on hybrid tools, see Waterman, 1986; Gilmore, 1985; or Beach, 1986.

10.6 PC-Based Expert System Tools

In the past it was popularly believed that it was impossible to develop "real" ESs on small computers. Although it is still likely that a larger computer will be required to support large complex developments, there are now many useful PC-based ESs [Lehner, 1985]. This is increasingly true with the advent of increasingly large and powerful general-purpose PCs.

PCs are used in several different ways in ES development. For some systems (typically in the assistant category with 50 to 200 rules) the small PC is suitable as both a development and delivery environment. In other cases the prototype development can be done on a PC; and if it is decided that a complete system is to be built, the development of the complete system can then be moved to a larger system (e.g., a Lisp machine). This process is facilitated by the use of a tool that will execute on both the PC and a workstation (e.g., Experlisp running on a Macintosh and a Symbolics workstation).

The PC can also be used in somewhat the opposite sense. The system can be built by using the rich development environment of a Lisp machine; and when such development is complete, the delivery is made by using a PC.

Table 10.5 lists several examples of the capabilities of PC-based ES tools. For more information on PC-based tools, see Karna, 1985; and for more information on the development of ES, on PCs, see PCAI, 1987.

TABLE 10.5 PC-Based Expert System Tools

	Deciding factor	Insight2	M1	Exsys	Esip Advisor
Forward chaining	×	×	×	No	No
Backward chaining	×	×	×	×	×
Representation					
Rules	×	×	×	×	×
Semantic networks	×	No	No	No	No
Built-in uncertainty	No	×	×	No	×
User interface					
Built-in editor	×	×	No	×	No
Menus	×	×	No	No	×
Softward interface					
Dbase	No	×	×	×	No
Lotus 123	No	No	No	×	No
Built-in explanation	No	No	No	×	No

10.7 Knowledge Acquisition Tools

As described in Chap. 9, because KA is a difficult and time-consuming task, it would be extremely valuable to remove the middleman by replacing the KE with a tool that allows the expert to build the system directly. Such a tool would allow an expert who is not familiar with the intricacies of ES design to build a system in much the same way that the introduction of Fortran allowed scientists to write programs without understanding computer hardware or machine language.

Meta-Dendral [Lindsay, 1980] and Teirasias [Davis, 1982a] were early attempts to construct KA tools. Teirasias was intended to help an expert extend and maintain the Mycin knowledge base. It interacts with the expert by using a restricted subset of English to add new rules and correct existing ones. One of the primary ways that an expert uses Teirasias is to execute Mycin and use the explanation facility to observe any errors, which are then corrected through the use of Teirasias.

More recently, several tools have been developed to assist experts in building ESs from scratch. Roget is the first tool intended to construct an original ES by direct interaction with an expert. Roget assists the expert from the initial design stages through the construction stage. The assistance provided includes the development of the system's conceptual structure and inference strategy and the identification of critical facts. Roget also suggests a reasonable scope for the system and recommends appropriate tools.

As the first step in this process, Roget establishes the conceptual structure. (It deals only with variations of the classification model.) To establish this structure, it provides the expert with examples of existing ESs and asks the expert to identify the closest match. Several other design decisions follow, including the selection of a mechanism for dealing with uncertainty and the enumeration of a set of sample problems.

After the overall design definition is complete, detailed KA on specific problems begins. Knowledge is elicited depth-first by proceeding through several levels of knowledge gathering called *evidence categories*. These categories include such things as distinguishing factors, reported symptoms, observed symptoms, test identification, event classification, and exception condition analysis.

As the sample problems are completed, the resulting system fragments are fed back to the expert (by using a subset of English) for review and revision. After gathering knowledge for the specific problems, Roget reviews the entire emerging ES, revises the structure as required, and suggests changes in the system's scope. The detailed knowledge is then revised—primarily by pruning the knowledge base—and the result is presented to the expert for final verification. After

TABLE 10.6 Knowledge Acquisition Tools

System	Domain type	Approach	Target language	Reference
ETS	Classification	Psychological modeling	OPS5	Boose, 1984
More	Classification	Revision of existing knowledge base	OPS5	Kahn, 1985
Roget	Classification	Revision of sample models	Emycin	Bennett, 1985
Salt	Constructive	Identification of knowledge roles	OPS5	Marcus, 1985
Salt	Constructive	Identification of knowledge roles	OPS5	Marcus, 1985

this verification, Roget translates the knowledge from its internal representation to actual executable rules (in this case, Emycin rules). The overall result of this process is a prototype ES suitable for execution and evaluation after a sufficient number of sessions.

Although the development of KA tools appears very promising, there are many potential pitfalls. For example, most of the people problems still remain, at least on the expert side (e.g., the expert will still be concerned about job security and the time commitment required to develop the system). In many cases these problems are actually exacerbated by the use of an automated tool. It is also yet to be seen how effective these tools will be when applied to large and varied domains or how efficient the resulting systems will be relative to systems constructed by human KEs. No existing systems attempt to construct a complete system in a complex domain automatically.

Other examples of KA tools are shown in Table 10.6. For more information on KA tools see Hill, 1986. Machine learning, potentially the most powerful form of automated KA, is a major current topic of AI research.

The following chapter provides a more detailed description of the internal activities in an inference process, and Chap. 12 describes the use of a large hybrid ES tool to construct an actual system.

11

Inference Based on Formal Logic

This chapter describes the techniques that are used for inference in a system based on formal logic. It is intended to serve as an example of how an inference engine functions and to provide greater insight into formal-logic-based systems. Formal logic (Chap. 4) can be used to represent facts about the world and to describe relations between those facts. We can, by applying rules of inference, derive new facts that can be very useful. However, although it is relatively easy to *confirm* that a proposed sequence of inference steps actually produces a required proof, it can be very difficult to develop such a proof originally.

PRINCIPLE 11.1: To avoid combinatorial explosion, it is imperative that we follow a specific strategy to develop inferences systematically.

The following section introduces *resolution,* a powerful technique for reducing the proof process to the execution of a simple mechanical task.

11.1 Resolution with Ground Clauses

Resolution forms the basis of many formal logic systems and is also the computational basis for Prolog (Appendix B). As an introduction to the basic concepts of resolution, consider the following situation:

Two detectives, Sally Brown and Harlow Jones, have been called to investigate a recent suspicious death. Outside the victim's apartment, the neighbors tell Brown and Jones that the victim, known to be a loner with few friends, returned home at about midnight. Upon entering the blue apartment, which they find to be completely intact, they talk with the coroner, who tells them that the cause of death was either a heart attack or poisoning by a rare and obscure drug.

Following further discussion with the neighbors—which establishes that one of the victim's few acquaintances was Jay Collins, a pharmacist—the detectives formulate the facts in Fig. 11.1.

The additional facts ~HEART and AFTER-MIDNIGHT are added following a call from the coroner that places the time of death at 2:00 A.M. and further establishes that the victim did not die of a heart attack. After these facts are added, Brown arrests Collins for suspicion of murder.

When challenged by Jones to prove her assertion regarding Collins, Brown produces the following justification based on resolution (Fig. 11.2).

The first step in this justification (i.e., resolution) process is to reduce the WFFs to *conjunctive normal form* (CNF), a standard form that allows for mechanical manipulation. This conversion process is based on the use of the equivalence expressions shown in Table 3.2. When the conversion process is applied to a set of WFFs, it produces an equivalent set of clauses, each of which is a *finite disjunction of literals* (i.e., each clause is some set of literals OR'ed together).

Each of the resulting clauses is called a *conjunct* because the entire set can be thought of as one large conjunction: All of the clauses are AND'ed together because they all must be simultaneously true.

PRINCIPLE 11.2: The use of CNF is completely general because there is an algorithm for converting any set of WFFs into CNF [Davis, 1960].

```
HEART ∨ POISON
(POISON ∧ FRIEND) → COLLINS
BLUE
(INTACT ∨ AFTER-MIDNIGHT) → FRIEND
INTACT

where:
HEART ::= The victim died of a heart attack.
FRIEND ::= The killer was a friend of the victim.
BLUE ::= The apartment was blue.
INTACT ::= The apartment was intact (i.e., no signs of struggle).
AFTER-MIDNIGHT ::= The murder occurred after midnight.
COLLINS ::= There is reason to suspect that Collins murdered the
            victim.
```

Figure 11.1 Example facts.

```
        Original Form                  Conjunctive Normal Form

 POISON V HEART                   POISON V HEART
 (POISON ^ FRIEND) → COLLINS      ~POISON V ~FRIEND V COLLINS
 (INTACT V AFTER-MIDNIGHT) →      ~INTACT V FRIEND
    FRIEND                        ~AFTER-MIDNIGHT V FRIEND
 BLUE                             BLUE
 INTACT                           INTACT
 AFTER-MIDNIGHT                   AFTER-MIDNIGHT
 ~HEART                           ~HEART
```

Figure 11.2 Example WFFs in CNF.

The following are examples of this conversion process:

(POISON ∧ FRIEND) → COLLINS	Original Form
~(POISON ∧ FRIEND) ∨ COLLINS	Expression 3.1
~POISON ∨ ~FRIEND ∨ COLLINS	Expression 3.11

(INTACT ∨ AFTER-MIDNIGHT) → FRIEND	Original Form
~(INTACT ∨ AFTER-MIDNIGHT) ∨ FRIEND	Expression 3.1
(~INTACT ∨ FRIEND)	Expression 3.4
∧ (AFTER-MIDNIGHT ∨ FRIEND)	

The final expression is then divided into the separate conjuncts (~IN-TACT ∨ FRIEND) and (AFTER-MIDNIGHT ∨ FRIEND).

Figure 11.2 shows the example set of WFFs in original and corresponding CNF. (See Rich, 1983 for a complete description of the conversion algorithm.)

Because all the clauses in Fig. 11.2 are conjoined (implicitly AND'ed together), we can select and operate on any combination at will. We could, for example, consider the following clauses:

$$\sim \text{POISON} \lor \sim \text{FRIEND} \lor \text{COLLINS}$$
$$\text{POISON} \lor \text{HEART}$$

In this case the literal POISON occurs in both clauses, once in a positive form and once in a negative form. We can infer a new clause by recognizing that:

1. Only one form of POISON (the positive or the negative) can be true.

2. Both clauses must be simultaneously true.

Therefore, if POISON is true, then ~FRIEND ∨ COLLINS must be true to preserve the truth of the first clause. Conversely, if POISON is not true, then HEART must be true to preserve the truth of the second clause. The result can be restated as, "HEART is true or (~FRIEND ∨ COLLINS) is true." This can be shown more formally as HEART ∨ ~FRIEND ∨ COLLINS.

This process, which is called *resolving* clauses, can be generalized as follows:

1. Select two parent clauses that contain the same literal, once in the positive form and once in the negative form.
2. Form a new clause (the *resolvent*) by OR'ing together all of the literals from the parent clauses except for the *canceled pair*.

This technique, when applied iteratively, is the foundation of resolution [Robinson, 1965.]

Returning to the detective example, it is possible to prove the COLLINS assertion by repeatedly resolving clauses as shown in Fig. 11.3. Unfortunately, although this form of resolution is straightforward and intuitively appealing, it is limited by the following:

PRINCIPLE 11.3: There is no guarantee that applying simple resolution will produce a desired WFF from the given clauses even if it does, in fact, follow from them.

There is, however, a modified form of resolution that overcomes this problem. As an example of this form of resolution, suppose that Brown (in the detective example) was challenged by Jones to prove her as-

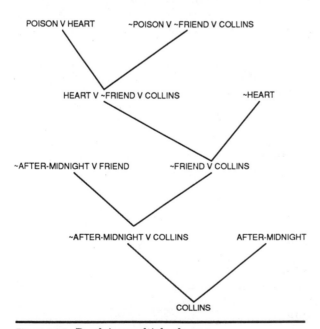

Figure 11.3 Resolving multiple clauses.

sertion and was unable to do so directly. As an alternative approach, she might suggest to Jones that he attempt to show that Collins should not be a suspect. If it is true that Collins should not be a suspect, then we should be able to add ~COLLINS to the set of clauses shown in Fig. 11.2 without damaging the consistency of the clauses. That is, prior to the addition, there was some set of truth values that would satisfy the requirement that all the clauses be simultaneously true. The addition of an added piece of truth should not invalidate this.)

Figure 11.4 shows a series of resolution steps that results in a clause consisting only of NIL. Recall that a set of clauses is unsatisfiable if there is no possible interpretation (i.e., set of truth values) for the symbols in the clauses that will make all of the clauses simultaneously true.

Because there is, by definition, no way that NIL could possibly be true, it has been shown that the clauses are unsatisfiable. We must conclude that the unsatisfiability in the set of previously satisfiable clauses has been introduced by the inclusion of ~COLLINS. Therefore,

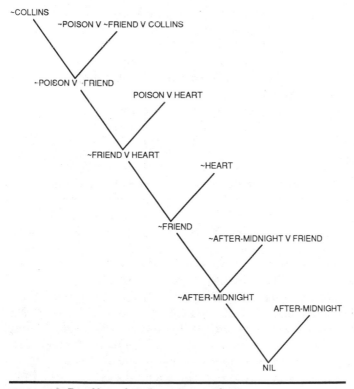

Figure 11.4 Proof by refutation using resolution.

~COLLINS cannot possibly be true, and because ~COLLINS is false, ~(~COLLINS), or more simply stated, COLLINS, must be true.

The reasoning process described above is an informal description of *resolution refutation,* which is the typical form of resolution.

PRINCIPLE 11.4: Resolution refutation is guaranteed to produce a desired clause from a set of clauses if the desired clause does in fact follow from them.

The usefulness of this procedure is based on the fact that resolution is *refutation complete* [Chang, 1973]; that is, resolution refutation is guaranteed to eventually *demonstrate unsatisfiability* (detect an inconsistency) if one actually exists.

The resolution process for a given set of WFFs (expressed by using propositional logic only) can be described more formally as:

1. Negate the desired proposition (called the *goal*) and add it to the set of WFFs to form a new set.

2. Convert the set of WFFs to a set of clauses in CNF.

3. Repeat until NIL is produced, or until no more progress is possible:
   a. Select two parent clauses.
   b. Resolve the parent clauses.
   c. IF   the resolvent is NIL,
      THEN   conclude that a contradiction has been found and the goal proved,
      ELSE   add the resolvent to the set of clauses.

11.2   Unification

The resolution process, as described so far, is based on the finding and canceling of two offsetting literals. We have no trouble determining whether two candidate literals should actually cancel as long as they involve only simple predicates as shown in Fig. 11.4. However, the process becomes more complicated when we consider the general case (i.e., expressions in predicate logic) in which we must decide if literals with predicates, functions, and variables can be canceled.

Consider, for example, Fig. 11.5. P1 and ~P1 cancel immediately, but what should we do with ~WOMAN(LINDA) and WOMAN(x)? We would certainly give up if one of the predicate symbols were, for example, ARDVARK; but because in this case the predicate symbols are identical and opposite, we are tempted to try to cancel them.

Certainly these two literals could not be thought of as identical for all, or even most, interpretations, but in the resolution process we are

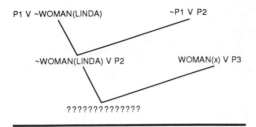

Figure 11.5 Resolution with variables.

looking for a pair of literals that have at least *one* interpretation for which they cannot be simultaneously true. If the clause set is to remain consistent, it can't include both WOMAN(x) and ~WOMAN(LINDA) because there is one case, namely that in which x = LINDA, that is inconsistent.

Unification is the formal process of determining whether two literals can be made to match identically. The unification process focuses on the substitution of terms—variables, constants, or function expressions (a function symbol and associated terms)—for variables in literals.

A *substitution instance* of a literal results from such substitution. A specific *substitution set* is a set of ordered pairs such that the first element is the new item and the second element is the variable for which it is substituted. For example, the set s1 = {A/x, y/z, f(h)/k} includes substitutions of A for x, y for z, and f(h) for k. When this substitution is applied to the expression PRED1(x,g(k),f2(z)), it produces PRED1(A,g(f(h)),f2(y)).

The unification procedure can be thought of informally as a process for matching the elements in two lists to determine whether there is some substitution set that would make the lists identical. The procedure is as follows:

1. Represent each predicate as a list in which the predicate symbol is the first element, which is followed by the predicate's arguments in order.

2. Give up if the two lists are not the same length.

3. Do a pairwise comparison of the elements in the list by using the following rules:
   - Predicate symbols, function symbols, and constants must match exactly.
   - For variables, create a match through substitution. Specifically, when a variable is encountered, replace it, *and all subsequent occurrences of it in the list,* with the corresponding element from the other list. The only restriction on this matching is that a

variable can't be replaced by a term that contains the same variable (to prevent infinite loops).

4. The two predicates can be unified if all elements match. Note that it may be necessary to call the routine recursively to evaluate list elements that are nested lists.

This procedure is described more formally in Wos, 1984.

We can, for example, use this procedure to show that the predicates SHORTED(voltage, run_id, node_name(run_id)) and SHORTED(VEE, 14, node_name(14)) are *unifiable* by using the substitution set (*unifier*) {VEE/voltage, 14/run_id}.

As a counterexample, the literals SHORTED(voltage, run_id, node_name(run_id)) and SHORTED(VEE, 3, node_name(4)) can't be unified.

11.3 Resolution in Predicate Logic

By using unification, it is possible to extend resolution to operate on expressions in predicate logic (rather than simply propositional logic). Resolution for predicate logic is the same as that described previously except that:

1. Two literals must be unified before they can be canceled.

2. Substitutions made to accomplish unification within a clause must be made throughout the entire clause, not just the literal being unified.

As an example of resolution in predicate logic, consider the clauses and predicate interpretations shown in Fig. 11.6, which is a fragment

```
~LOADED(module,location) ∨ STEPPED_ON(module)
~NO_MEM(modsiz) ∨ LOADED(module, locl) ∨ WAIT_IO(module)
ABORTED(process) ∨ HUNG(process)
NO_MEM(size(progl)) ∨ LOADED(progl,location)

where:
WAIT_IO(x) ::= Module x is waiting for I/O to complete.
LOADED(x,y) ::= Module x is loaded starting at location y.
STEPPED_ON(x) ::= At least some of the code from module x has been
                  unintentionally overwritten.
NO_MEM(x) ::= No memory block, of at least size x, is available.
ABORTED(x) ::= Module x aborted during execution.
HUNG(x) ::= Module x is hung.
size(x) ::= Function that calculates the size required to load
            module x.
```

Figure 11.6 Example of predicate logic clauses.

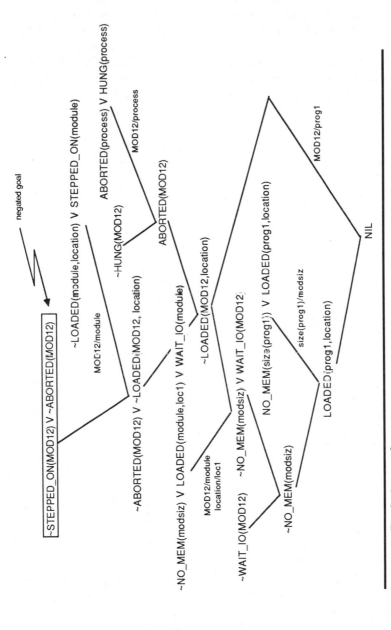

Figure 11.7 Resolution proof.

187

of a system that might be used to assist in the diagnosis of problems in a large software system.

Figure 11.7 gives a resolution proof for the following:

Given the information from Fig. 11.6, and also given the facts that a module MOD12 is not hung and is not waiting on I/O, show that it has been unintentionally overwritten and aborted. For additional examples of resolution, including a detailed solution of the classic monkeys and bananas problem, see Chang, 1973, and Wos, 1984.

The following chapter describes an actual ES that includes formal logic-based processing.

12

An Example of a Multiparadigm Expert System

This chapter describes Permaid, a large, multiparadigm ES that is in actual commercial use. It is intended to demonstrate how the concepts described in the preceding chapters are applied in real systems (including the compromises that must be made to fit the theory to reality). The use of rule-based and network/frame-based reasoning is emphasized in this discussion.

Permaid [Rolston, 1987] is a multiparadigm ES that is used for diagnosis and maintenance of approximately 10,000 large fixed-head disk subsystems that are components of Honeywell mainframe computers. It is used to support several thousand field service engineers (FSE) with excellent results. Its use has increased the target system's availability and decreased the mean time to repair. In its lifetime, it is expected to result in a savings of several million dollars.

Permaid performs three primary functions:

- Troubleshooting of observed problems
- Predictive maintenance
- Media and file recovery

It also provides training as an important secondary function.

The troubleshooting function is used by an FSE to identify and repair faults in a large fixed-head disk subsystem (i.e., the disk drive, disk controller, and the associated operating system software). The media and file recovery function is used by the FSE in collaboration with the customer's site representative to perform file recovery and to repair any media that is damaged by a fault (e.g., removing a disk track from service by declaring it to be faulty and restoring its data to a spare track). The predictive maintenance function is normally used to direct an FSE through a routine check-up procedure that determines whether any preemptive maintenance action should be taken to prevent serious solid faults from occurring. It is also used when there is a general suspicion that a problem is developing but no specific symptoms are externally visible.

12.1 User Interface

Permaid can be used in a graphics mode (which assumes that the user has a Xerox 1185 workstation) or in a tty mode (which is provided to users who dial in remotely by using an unintelligent tty terminal).

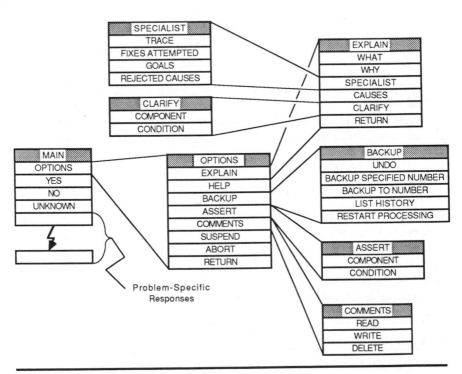

Figure 12.1 Overview of user interface.

Although the same information is provided in either case, the tty version uses textual menus because tty terminals lack graphics. Figure 12.1 provides an overview of the graphics version of the menus that comprise the Permaid user interface.

The troubleshooting portion of Permaid operates by using a question-and-answer consultation model. After the user has indicated which initial symptoms are present (by selection from symptom menus), the troubleshooting process asks the user to run tests and make observations that are required to identify the problem. The following is an example of a small part of a Permaid troubleshooting session (presented in the tty mode):

```
Welcome to Permaid (B.2 12/2/86 09:44)
Please enter your site ID: CN0013
Please enter your employee number: 12345
Please choose one of the following:
1) Troubleshooting
2) Predictive Maintenance
3) File and Media Recovery
4) Resume Previously Suspended Session
5) Fault Dictionary
6) Utilities
7) General Information
8) Help
  1

Please choose one of the following:
1) Error Message    2) Observed Error    3) Both
  1

Please indicate which error messages have been reported. The
items that you enter must be separated by blanks.
  0/2    2/10

Is bit 5 of detailed status word 4 (''spindle speed lost'' bit)
set?
1) options    2) yes    3) no    4) unknown
  2

Use the zero to two inch water gauge (pressure gauge to
measure the air pressure at the access hole of the magnetic
assembly. The correct pressure is 2.2 - 3.7* inches of
water. Is the pressure correct according to the gauge?
1) options    2) yes    3) no    4) unknown
  2

Is the spindle stopped?
1) options    2) yes    3) no    4) unknown
  1

Please select one of the following:
1) explain    2) help    3) backup    4) assert    5) comments
6) suspend    7) abort    8) return
  1
```

---

*Actual values for illustration purposes only.

```
Please select one of the following:
1) why    2) what    3) specialist    4) causes    5) clarify
6) return
  1

We are trying to determine if ''spindle stopped'' is the cause
of ''spindle speed lost bit set.''

Please select one of the following:
1) why    2) what    3) specialist    4) causes    5) clarify
6) return
  6

Is the spindle stopped?
1) options    2) yes    3) no    4) unknown
  2

Is the ''motor thermal breaker'' tripped?
1) options    2) yes    3) no    4) unknown
  2

Wait 5 minutes and then reset the breaker and restart the
spindle. Did this action fix the problem?
1) yes    2) no    3) comments
  1

The cause/effect chain was:
  * ''motor thermal breaker'' tripped
  * spindle stopped
  * ''spindle speed lost'' bit set
  * 2/10 error
```

12.2   Internal Design Overview

An overview of the internal structure of Permaid is shown in Fig. 12.2. The heart of the system is the "fault-resolution kernel," which is used to identify faults on the basis of symptom observations and specific test results. The knowledge representation for this kernel is based on the use of frames and networks (Sec. 4.2), and inference for this section is based on abduction [Pople, 1982] (as described later in this chapter). The kernel can be entered in several different ways. When specific problem symptoms are reported, the kernel is entered in a "locate fault" mode which is used to locate and correct faults which are known to exist.

The kernel is entered in an "identity suspected fault" mode when predictive maintenance processing suggests that there is probably a fault in the subsystem. When processing in this mode, Permaid will recommend a repair action if it can specifically determine that a fault exists; but it will not recommend actions based solely on suspicions or the process of elimination.

The kernel can also be entered in a "find secondary fault" mode, which is used to determine whether any permanent secondary ("ripple effect") faults have been caused by the occurrence of a "primary" fault

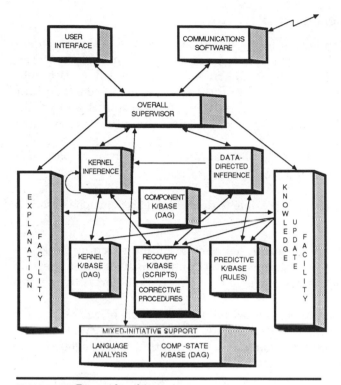

Figure 12.2 Permaid architecture.

[e.g., a faulty circuit breaker (a primary fault) can cause a motor to fail (a secondary fault)].

The predictive maintenance section uses rules and forward-directed reasoning based on pattern recognition. The mixed-initiative section relies on a very basic natural-language analysis system and uses frames, networks, and formal logic (Sec. 3.5) for knowledge representation along with *active values* ("when filled" procedures, Sec. 3.5) for processing. It allows the user to seize the initiative and supply information that was not requested by Permaid. When such information is supplied, it can result in a major change in the strategy being used in the session.

Permaid supplies explanation information (Chap. 7) that is tailored for four different types of user: expert, knowledge engineer, specialist user, and FSE (the typical end user). At the end of each session, a complete trace of the session is written to a long-term history file that is used to analyze and modify Permaid's performance.

The development and maintenance of Permaid is supported by a powerful graphic knowledge base editor and automated correctness and validation software.

12.3 Fault Resolution Kernel

The fault resolution kernel is based on the concept of *abductive inference* and follows in large part from work done in Internist [Pople, 1977]. Unlike deduction (where given the rule A → B, we deduce B by observing A), by using abduction, we (quite dangerously) conclude that A is true by observing B. Given A → B, upon observing B we hypothesize that A is true as a way of explaining the situation we have observed.

Unfortunately, unlike deduction, abduction is a form of *plausible inference* and is not sound:

PRINCIPLE 12.1: It is quite possible to draw invalid conclusions based on abduction.

For example, if we see an armed person running from a bank, we may conclude that we have seen a bank robber. Although it is possible that such a person is indeed a bank robber, it is certainly not an absolute fact.

Tied into the concept of abduction is the notion of causality. We believe that A is true because we know that A causes B. This concept is applied operationally by using an approach that is analogous to the scientific method [Jackson, 1986]:

> A hypothesis is formed on the basis of observations and a knowledge of causality relationships. Tests are then conducted and additional evidence is gathered, and the results serve to strengthen belief or disbelief in the conclusion.

If, for example, we observe that an armed person running from a bank is also carrying a large bag trailing money, we begin to strongly believe that we have seen a bank robber. (Note that this may still be incorrect; the person could be an actor involved in filming a scene for a movie.) Given sufficient evidence, we conclude that it is reasonable to believe that the hypothesis is true. This decision, even when final, is based on some degree of uncertainty:

PRINCIPLE 12.2: Reasoning based on abduction is most useful when satisficing solutions are sought (Sec. 2.3).

The fault resolution kernel applies this concept in the form of cause-effect reasoning in which specific causes are hypothesized to explain observed events. For example, Fig. 12.3 shows three different faults that can cause a 2/10 console error message (a user-visible effect):

A characteristic of most diagnostic domains is the occurrence of "cascading errors" [Pau, 1986]: The effect of the primary fault is to cause

```
Spindle problem → 2/10
Loss of air pressure → 2/10
Electric power failure → 2/10
```

Figure 12.3 Causes of a 2/10 error.

some intermediate problem which in turn causes another intermediate problem until visible symptoms are eventually produced. For example, a 2/10 error message is reported if there is a problem with the main spindle in the drive unit (as shown in Fig. 12.3). A spindle problem is the effect of an intermittent loss of spindle speed or the fact that the spindle has stopped turning. The spindle can stop turning for many different reasons, including the failure of the spindle drive motor.

PRINCIPLE 12.3: Knowledge representations should be selected to take advantage of any natural structure that is present in the knowledge.

The use of networks to represent cascading errors is an example of this principle.

The kernel knowledge base is a semantic (or *associate*) *network* (Sec.

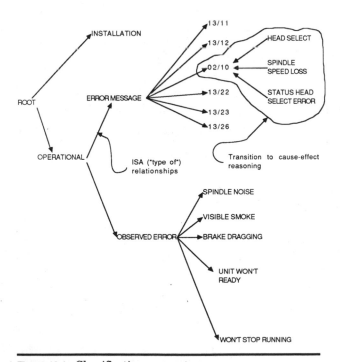

Figure 12.4 Classification segment.

4.1) that is composed of two segments: the *classification segment* that breaks down general error classes (e.g., "error message") into specific symptoms and the cause-effect segment which is based on the cause-effect analysis described above.

Figure 12.4 shows a portion of the classification segment. This portion of the network is used to collect the initial problem symptoms. No form of search is conducted for this part of the graph; the user is simply asked to identify the symptoms by using the menus described in Sec. 12.1.

The remainder of the kernel knowledge base is implemented by using cause-effect analysis to form an associative network made up of cause-of relationships. The network takes the form of a *directed acyclic graph* (DAG) (a graph in which the arcs are connected by directed arcs) that represents the cause-effect relationships between the nodes on the graph. (The graph for Permaid includes approximately 2500 nodes.) The portion of the kernel knowledge base that represents the causes of a 2/10 error is shown in Fig. 12.5 in the form that it is displayed by the knowledge base editor. Note that the structure is a graph (and not a tree) because any given cause can have many effects and any given effect can have many causes.

Kernel knowledge base implementation

The kernel knowledge base implementation consists of the following components:

1. A collection of network nodes. Associated with each node is:
   - A test procedure for establishing the truth value of the node
   - A script-like fix structure (Sec. 4.3) that is used to direct repair actions for the node
   - An attribute frame (Sec. 4.2)
2. Links among the nodes.
3. An inheritance hierarchy for the overall network.

The network is implemented as a Loops (Sec. 10.5) class-lattice structure by using object-oriented programming. Each node is represented physically as a class in the lattice.

PRINCIPLE 12.4: Using a powerful tool that is matched to the task frequently means the difference between success and failure in an ES development project.

In the case of Permaid the powerful graphics editors in Loops pro-

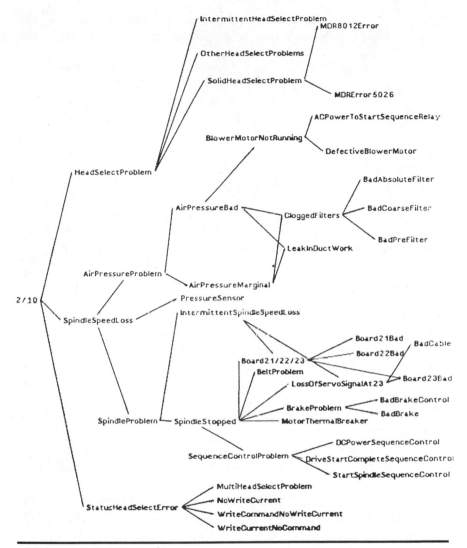

Figure 12.5 Cause-effect segment.

vided the structure that makes it possible to understand a complex problem and to quickly change the implementation in response to revisions in understanding.

The following sections describe the network components in greater detail:

Test procedure.   A Lisp function that describes the actions to be taken to establish the truth value of the corresponding node. This procedure requests the user to take various actions and enter the results. The actions may include such things as executing tests, contacting the customer, and making observations.

There are nodes that have no test function (either because the node is an "organizational node" that is used to structure the network and has no physical significance or because no test for a given condition is available).

Attribute frame. Each frame includes a number of slots that contain information that is either local to the particular frame or inherited from a higher frame. Each frame has the following slots:

Name of creator
Date and time of creation
Date and time of last modification

Local state description. Formal logic representation of the state represented by the node. (More details are presented later in this section.)

Local state value. The value for the state represented by this node is established through the execution of test procedures that evaluate the values of the predicates in the formulas contained in the local state description. Values can be either true, false, or not yet determined. They can also be established by inference from other formulas [e.g., Spindle Stopped can be inferred from ~(Spindle Turning)]. The initial inherited default value is "not yet determined."

PRINCIPLE 12.5: Never ask for the same information more than once.

For example, without the inference noted above, the question "Is the spindle moving?" would be followed by the question, "Is the spindle stopped?"—the same information in a different form.

Test impact factor (TIF). An integer value, with a range of 0–10, that describes the potential negative impact of the testing required to establish the truth value of this node. Impact in this sense can include such things as the time required to run the test, the cost of materials consumed by the test (i.e., replacing parts), and the requirement that the customer's system be released prior to test. A value of 10 corresponds to severe impact. This slot inherits a default value of 5 at the time of the node's creation. The expert assigns an actual value based on experience if there is reason to believe that the default value is not appropriate.

Likeliness factor (LF). A likeliness factor is a value with a range of 0–10 that describes the likeliness (pseudo-probability) that this node is actually the cause of the observed effect. A value of 10 corresponds to "highly likely." The value for this slot is a list of likeliness factors, one for each effect associated with this cause. Each LF is assigned by the expert based on experience.

Local decision factor (LDF). A heuristic selection factor that represents how desirable the node is for selection during the search of the cause-effect graph. This value is calculated by a heuristic evaluation function (Sec. 2.4) that combines LF and LDF. (Desirable nodes are those with high likeliness and low impact.)

Collapsed decision factor (CDF). A selection factor that is used to estimate the desirability of a node when an LDF is not available. This value is calculated by combining and "averaging" the LDFs for all the offspring nodes by using a collapsing technique similar to that used to develop cutoff factors in alpha/beta pruning [Barr, 1981]—a classic AI search technique.

Name of test procedure. This slot contains the name of the test procedure (a Lisp function) that describes the actions to be taken to establish the local state value [e.g., an attached "when required" function (Sec. 4.2)]. When no test is available, the value of this slot is "none" (the default value).

Name of fix procedure. This slot contains the name of the script-like structure that contains the procedures that are required to repair the fault associated with this node. (Scripts are used rather than direct procedures because of their use in inference of unspecified actions for mixed-initiative processing as described in a later section.) The default value is the name of a script that simply directs the user to swap all components associated with the node.

Fix-attempted flag. A flag that indicates that the fix procedure associated with this node has already been executed during this session.

Verification information. Date and time the expert verified this node.

Comments. Free-form comments inserted by the developer that relate in any way to the node.

Secondary action pointer. A list of secondary effects associated with this node. The inherited default value is nil.

Prerequisites. List of all nodes that must be tested prior to this node. (For example, it is possible to damage the media if the read/write hardware is not verified before the media tests are executed.) Any values inserted in this slot are inherited to all frames lower in the network.

Organizational node flag. A flag that indicates that the associated node is an organization node. Such nodes are used only to structure the network; they have no direct physical significance.

Node explanation. The explanation of the semantics of the node that is provided at the user's request.

PRINCIPLE 12.6: The use of frames and defaults for representation provides economy in space requirements and development time.

PRINCIPLE 12.7: Inheritance is never complete; it must be tuned to match reality.

For example, in some special cases the inheritance of prerequisite values must be manually blocked.

Software configuration management

An important secondary use of frames and inheritance is to provide software configuration management (version control) for Permaid. Version control is a classic problem in software engineering [Bersoff, 1980] and more particularly in software systems that address hardware as a target application [Rolston, 1983]. In the case of Permaid, the functionality of the system—the specific tests and repair actions that are recommended—vary with the version of the hardware, version of the test and diagnostic software, and version of the operating system software that are configured at the target site.

PRINCIPLE 12.8: Software configuration management issues must be addressed early in the project when changes in the domain knowledge are likely.

Version control in Permaid is accomplished by using different instances of cause-effect nodes to represent the knowledge associated with different configuration combinations. An example is shown in Fig. 12.6.

The class nodes represent the test-and-repair knowledge that applies to the "base version configuration" (the collection of hardware, test,

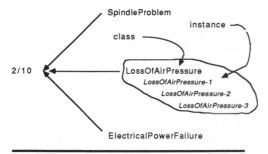

Figure 12.6 Use of instances to support version control.

and diagnostics software, and system software versions that occurs most commonly in the field). Instances of a given node are created whenever the value of any slot in the node depends on the version configuration that is being used at the subject site. Default values for the slots in the instance frame are inherited from the class frame and exception conditions for the particular version-configuration are stored in the instance.

Kernel inference

A simplified version of the inference activity for the problem resolution kernel is shown in Fig. 12.7. This process begins with the collection of initial symptoms. These symptoms can be either error messages or observed problems. The user selects any number of symptoms from the two categories by using symptom menus.

The initial symptoms are then evaluated to select one primary symptom that will be the starting node for the search process. The selection process operates by first identifying the most probable cause of all the observed symptoms. The symptom that is selected as the start symptom is any symptom that is an effect of the most probable cause. The remaining symptoms are placed on a symptom list ordered by their CDFs. Ties that occur anywhere in this process are broken by arbitrary selection.

Once the primary symptom has been identified, the process is based on the systematic selection and test of possible causes for a given effect. Once the cause of a given effect is identified, the process moves to the new cause and is recursively restarted with the newly identified cause being treated as an effect. Multiple original symptoms are used in only two ways during this search process: (1) During the selection of the best candidate node for expansion, the nodes that relate to multiple observed symptoms are preferred. (2) When the search process that

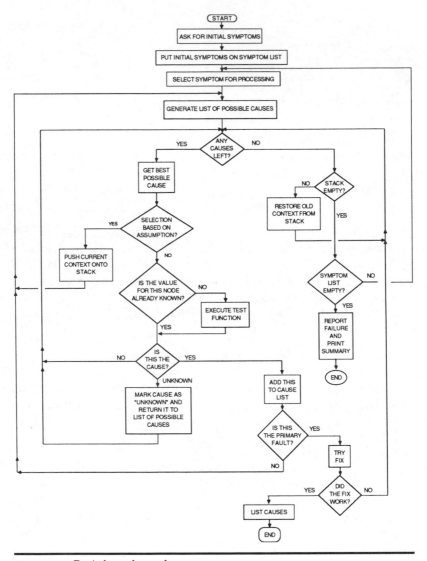

Figure 12.7 Basic kernel search.

emanated from the original primary symptom fails, a new primary symptom is selected from the symptom list (without further user interaction).

PRINCIPLE 12.9: Use as simple an inference process as possible, even though it may not be the most "powerful" available.

This form of search, which focuses on one primary starting symptom, is in contrast to the more sophisticated techniques used in some diagnostic systems such as Internist (which continuously quantitatively updates belief based on evidence accumulated from multiple symptoms) and similar techniques described in Shenoy, 1986, and Gordon, 1985. This contrast can best be understood by considering each of these search processes as being versions of heuristic generate and test (Sec. 5.4) in a very general sense. The issue is the extent to which the process will emphasize the generater vs. the tester. In the case of Internist, the generation process considers the accumulating weight of the evidence that supports any given cause by continuously referring to all available symptom information. This approach emphasizes the generater and attempts to avoid generating invalid solutions. In the case of Permaid, the emphasis moves toward the tester. This results from two primary factors:

1. It is much easier to test electronic equipment than humans (e.g., test results tend to be more definitive, and it is possible to shotgun problems by systematically replacing parts [Breuer, 1976]).

2. Multiple independent faults in electronic equipment are relatively infrequent (as contrasted with the human situation where the possibility of multiple diseases is very important [Buchanan, 1984b]).

Multiple symptoms are accepted in Permaid; however, Permaid is not specifically intended to address *multiple independent faults* [Maletz, 1985]. (In many cases, multiple independent faults will be corrected, but in other cases they will not be.)

The selection process that is conducted after the primary symptom is identified is based on depth-first search (Sec. 2.5) of the cause-effect graph. In the selection of the best node to analyze at any given point, the causes that connect to multiple symptoms are preferred. When multiple-symptom causes are not present (or to choose between several multiple-symptom causes), selection is based on a comparison of the decision factors described previously.

In this selection process LDFs are used to represent nodes when possible. CDFs are used to estimate the desirability of collection nodes, nodes that have no test procedure, and nodes that are marked as unknown because a previous execution of the test procedure (during the current session) produced a response of unknown.

An unknown response results from the fact that the user is unable to gather test results for some reason. The unknown option allows Permaid to continue processing in the face of uncertain or incomplete information. That is an important feature of Permaid because it allows the users to provide honest answers to the questions. It is typically used at least once during a Permaid session.

PRINCIPLE 12.10: The presence of the "unknown" response allows users to answer questions honestly.

It is very important to realize that the presence of this option implies that, even if the system is perfectly implemented, it may produce advice that is incorrect (Sec. 2.4). For example, Permaid may recommend the replacement of a board that is not actually bad. This advice is "incorrect" in the sense that it does not fix the problem, but "correct" in the sense that it is the best possible advice given the situation and information available; it is the same advice that a human expert would have given under identical circumstances.

After the best candidate cause is processed, it is either accepted, in which case the search process moves to the new node and recursively restarts itself, or rejected, in which case the next candidate cause is investigated. Nodes are accepted on the basis of a positive definitive test result or on the basis of an unsupported assumption. (For example, the system may decide that the best move is to "guess" when no test is available or the user answers "unknown" in response to a test query.)

Any number of assumptions are accepted until a node at which all possible causes are tested and rejected (i.e., a dead end) is reached. Chronological backtracking (Sec. 2.4) is used to recover from bad assumptions. It is adequate in this case, in spite of the fact that it is relatively inefficient, because the typical causal chains are relatively short (i.e., typically no more than five links).

In theory it would be most efficient to base Permaid inference on best-first search, in which a given branch may be abandoned in favor of expanding a higher-level node that was previously rejected. Permaid is actually based on depth-first search primarily because people tend to do depth-first troubleshooting and find it difficult to understand why the system "jumps around" while doing best-first search.

PRINCIPLE 12.11: The design of an inference engine should take into consideration a human's ability to understand it.

12.4 Component Knowledge Base

The component knowledge base is implemented as a DAG that is similar to the kernel knowledge base. A fragment of the component knowledge base is shown in Fig. 12.8.

The component knowledge base consists of the following components:

- A collection of network nodes
- An attribute frame associated with each node
- Partof links between the nodes

The component base is used to support mixed-initiative processing (Sec. 7.6) and clarification (Sec. 7.4).

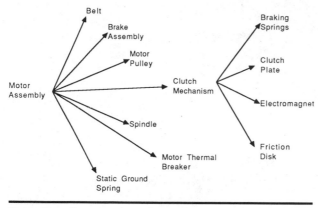

Figure 12.8 Component graph segment.

The attribute frame includes the following slots:

Name of component

Aliases. A list of aliases (i.e., common names) that are used to refer to the component

References. Names of the nodes in the troubleshooting DAG that make reference to the component

Number of occurrences. The number of this type of component that occur in a complete device

Organizational node flag. A flag to indicate that this node is used to organize the network and does not represent a physical component

12.5 Representation of State

Representation of state in Permaid relies on the use of an empirically derived subset of predicate logic (Sec. 3.5). The expression of the global state can be viewed as the conjunction of the currently known local states that are stored in the frames in the kernel graph.

The objects in the local description are components of the disk subsystem and the states of those components viewed as predicates [e.g., STOPPED(spindle), OFF(check_light)].

The maintenance of truth values for the global description depends on the use of the three-dimensional graph structure shown in Fig. 12.9. One side of the structure is the cause-effect graph; a second side is the component graph; and the third side is formed by adding new relations between the already existing nodes from the other two sides. The added arcs are "referenced in" relationships that tie system components to

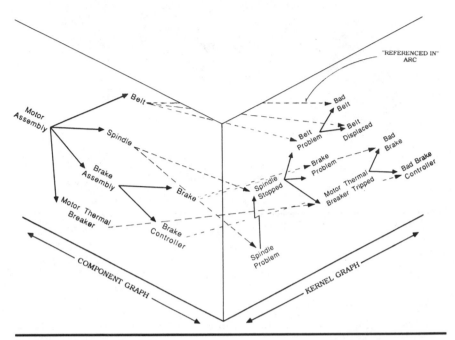

Figure 12.9 3-D graph relations.

the kernel nodes in which they are referenced (e.g., the arc Spindle →
Spindle Stopped).

The actual propagation process is implemented by using demons that
are based on Loops *active values* (i.e., values that have "when added"
functions as attached procedures, Sec. 4.3). The truth value of a local
state expression is modified [e.g., STOPPED(spindle) is assigned a value
of true]. The Lisp function associated with the active value traverses
its "referenced in" arc back to the component nodes for all components
involved in its state description and then develops a list of the nodes
that reference the affected components. The state truth value for each
affected node is first modified to "recalculate." The demon process associated with each target node's active value then recalculates its truth
value by using the change information passed by the calling function
along with any applicable rules of inference for the state expression.

12.6 Mixed-Initiative Processing

The mixed-initiative function relies on the fact that most discourse in
a maintenance and troubleshooting system focuses on two types of
statements:

- An assertion that some component is in some faulty state (e.g., "The
main bearing is smoking.")

- A declaration that some fix action has been attempted (e.g., "I changed the main spindle bearing.")

Mixed-initiative processing, a heavily used function, is one of the most difficult functions to implement and formally evaluate. (One of the chief reasons for the selection of the structure in Mycin was to avoid the need for mixed-initiative processing [Buchanan, 1984c].) The mixed-initiative function is important because many FSEs call Permaid only after they have worked on a problem for some time and have ceased to make progress. When that occurs, the FSE will ask Permaid for assistance starting at the point in the troubleshooting process where he or she is stuck. (Mixed-initiative processing is limited to the troubleshooting function.)

The FSE uses the "assert" option to gain the initiative in Permaid. In response to the selection of this option, Permaid saves the current context on the backtracking stack and then performs the following steps:

1. Accept the assertion in a limited natural-language format. This input is accepted in two parts: component-state descriptions and fixes attempted.

2. Develop the formal logic representation of the state description and fixes-attempted information represented by the assertion.

3. Mark the fixes attempted in the cause-effect graph.

4. Detect and resolve conflicts introduced by the asserted information. There is limited detection of direct conflicts (e.g., assertion of states that conflict with previously established states).

5. Determine the best state at which to start processing (by using the same procedure as that which is used to select the best initial starting symptoms). Note that this may or may not alter the search process (i.e., the node that was being processed prior to the assertion may still be the best node).

6. Restart processing by using the newly acquired information. Because the backtracking stack still contains the information that was previously added in the session, the process will return to the state that was being processed before the assertion was made in the case of a dead end.

The language analysis function evaluates on a single-sentence basis. There is no discourse analysis (i.e., analysis of an overall conversation). When the analysis function cannot establish the required information, it will revert to menu-based processing.

When it can identify a component description that "almost" matches a known description (as contained in the component graph), the user is given a menu of possible matches and is asked to select the intended item. This is similar to the spelling correction routines used in many word processing systems [Dreger, 1984]). If none of the menu items represents the intended object, then the analysis function walks down the component graph interactively while listing increasingly detailed components and asking the user to select an option until the desired component is identified. Component states and fix actions are treated similarly.

This analysis allows for rapid recognition when possible but still allows for user initiative even if the natural-language analysis is a complete failure. The result of the analysis (however it is developed) is reflected back to the user for confirmation prior to use and is then passed back to the kernel routine.

The following is an example of a simple mixed-initiative exchange (assuming that the user is operating in tty mode from an unintelligent terminal):

```
Is the coarse filter clogged?

1) Options  2) yes  3) No  4) Unknown
   1

Please select an option:
1) Explain  2) Help  3) Backup  4) Assert  5) Comments
6) Suspend  7) Return
   4

Do you want to describe:
1) The condition of system components
2) Repair actions that you have done
3) Both
   2

Please enter single—sentence descriptions of repair
actions that you have tried. Enter ''help'' for help and
''done'' when you are done.
I swapped the PLO board.
I trimmed the cabinet clock.
done

It is my understanding that you have:
    Replaced the PLO board.
    Adjusted the CLO clock.
Is this correct?
1) Yes  2) No  3) Help
   1

Is the coarse filter clogged?
```

In the above example the only effect of the user's assertion is to mark the repair actions in the cause-effect graph. Components are recognized by their official names (as shown in the component diagrams in the maintenance manuals) or by common aliases (which are stored in the frames that comprise the component network).

In this example the user's input has no immediate effect on the cause-effect analysis because the user did not make any assertion regarding the state of system components.

12.7 Predictive Maintenance

As an example of the predictive maintenance process, consider the effect of a simple media "bad spot" on a fixed-head disk drive. Many times the presence of a bad spot will result in a 13/26 error. When called in response to this error message, the troubleshooting portion of Permaid will initiate a cause-effect analysis starting at 13/26. This process will eventually test for "media problem" as one of the causes of 13/26. It will identify the bad spot as the cause of the media problem, will advise the user to run procedures to correct the problem, and will provide instructions regarding any required file recovery.

It is possible, however, for a bad spot to result in many retriable errors. In this case no explicit error message is printed, but information is logged on the site error log. This situation can be detected by the user of the predictive maintenance function. The process would determine that it is probable that a media problem exists. It would then enter the kernel routine at the point of "media problem." Processing from that point would continue as if it had been entered from the troubleshooting function and would eventually detect the bad spot.

The predictive maintenance section is generally based on the classification model (Sec. 5.7), and it contains approximately 400 Loops rules. An overview of processing in this section is shown in Fig. 12.10. It initially focuses on the interpretation of general information (e.g., error summary logs) in an attempt to isolate potential problems to specific devices. The remainder of the processing classifies possible problems within a device.

Once a list of possible problems has been developed, this "possible problem" information is converted into a format similar to that used for mixed-initiative processing (i.e., component-state descriptions) and switches to the kernel analysis.

The following are examples of typical simple rules (expressed in English format):

IF   an abnormally high number of errors exist on this device and
        the errors are confined to one surface,
THEN suspect a media flaw.

IF   an abnormally high number of errors exist on this device,
        the errors are on multiple tracks, and
        the errors are on one head,
THEN suspect head shift.

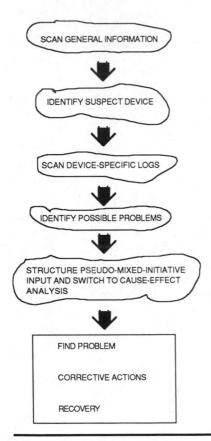

Figure 12.10 Overview of predictive maintenance.

IF   an abnormally high number of errors exist on this device,
       the errors are on multiple heads, and
       the errors are on the same cylinder,
THEN   suspect a servo problem.

The following is an example of the use of the predictive maintenance function based on the tty mode of execution. (Note that the unknown option for some predictive maintenance questions is not included.)

```
Welcome to PERMAID (B.2 12/2/86 09:44)
Please enter your site ID: NC1075
Please enter your clock number: 12345

Please choose one of the following:
1) Troubleshooting
2) Predictive Maintenance
```

```
3) File and Media Recovery
4) Resume Previously Suspended Session
5) Fault Dictionary
6) Utilities
7) General Information
8) Help
2
```

Do you need general information regarding the use of ELAN?
1) Options 2) Yes 3) No
3

Attempt to obtain an MPC statistical report for the disk
subsystem.
Were you able to obtain this report?
1) Options 2) Yes 3) No
1

Please select one of the following:
  1) explain 2) help 3) backup 4) assert 5) comments
  6) suspend 7) abort 8) return
2

Help is available for:
  1) Format and description of Summary Report
  2) Format and description of Detailed Peripheral Report
  3) Format and description of Raw Report
  4) The procedure required to gather the requested
     information

Enter the menu number for the type of help required.
4

Execute the following command on the main system console:
  DE_-DV_MPCDSK

Were you able to obtain this report?
1) Options 2) Yes 3) No
2

Scan the report for disk devices with an abnormal number of
errors (when compared with the other drives). Are there any
devices with an abnormal number of errors?
1) Options 2) Yes 3) No

12.8 File and Media Recovery

The file and media recovery function is implemented by using an associated network in which the nodes represent script-like structures. The use of such scripts is intended to allow the representation of the procedural knowledge required for recovery actions, to assist in establishing structure in the recovery process, to allow for inheritance between scripts, and to allow for the inference of implied actions when mixed-initiative input describes several actions attempted. The use of a network with explicit nodes also allows for consistent implementation of the node-oriented help system. The scripts are also used for mixed-initiative processing. (If the user indicates that two actions have been taken, then intermediate actions are inferred from the scripts.)

12.9   Explanation

Explanation for the knowledge engineer makes use of the high-resolution, bit-mapped, window-oriented graphics and mouse on the workstation and is intended to assist in debugging the system. It is based on the display shown in Fig. 12.11. This explanation system provides an interactive view of the knowledge bases during execution. As the search process proceeds, nodes in the graph are colored to indicate various search statuses. (For example, nodes flash as they are being considered, accepted nodes are darkened, rejected nodes are shaded, and the current node is boxed.) The display is an active version of the knowledge base editor, and it allows complete dynamic access to all aspects of the knowledge bases.

The clarify option provides more detailed descriptions of component names or conditions than are used in Permaid questions. This form of explanation is provided to help overcome any difficulty that might arise from the lack of a common vocabulary. There are two suboptions for clarify. The component suboption attempts to clarify the meaning of

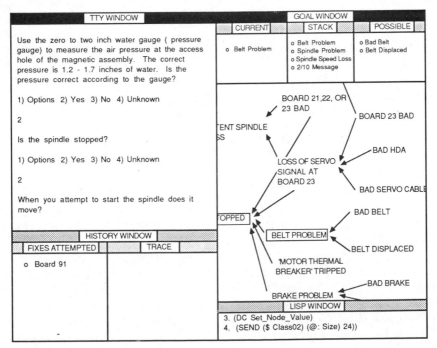

Figure 12.11   Explanation display.

component names. The condition suboption attempts to clarify the meaning of state descriptions.

The implementation of the component suboption is based on the use of the component graph. The explanation output consists of a description of:

1. The higher-level component that includes the component in question

2. The lower-level components that make up the component in question

3. Any aliases for the component in question (i.e., from the associated frame in the component knowledge base)

12.10 Support Tools

The development of Permaid is supported by powerful development and verification aids. A graphics editor is used to construct and review the knowledge bases. The editor includes various functions that guide the user through the process of expanding or modifying the knowledge base. For example, when the user indicates that a new cause (for a given effect) is to be added, the editor queries the user for each piece of information that is associated with a cause (e.g., the test function and likeliness factors). It then integrates the Lisp and Loops code in the format required by Permaid.

The verification system is used to perform a variety of consistency and completeness checks as well as utility functions. Most of these functions are based on the application of a Lisp program that accepts the name of a function as an argument and then systematically visits each node in the graph and applies the specified function.

The capability of Lisp to address recursion, symbolic processing, and higher-order functions makes it possible to use the above-described search in a variety of ways (depending on which function is passed as an argument). For example, if the function "printframe" is passed as an argument, it will systematically print all of the information from all of the frames in the knowledge base. Another function, "checkexplain," verifies that explanation information has been entered for each node. An overall completeness checker is provided by calling a series of these simple check functions.

12.11 Analysis of Results

Each time Permaid is used, a history record is written to a history-tracking file that is periodically analyzed to develop statistics regarding Permaid's performance. This analysis indicates that approximately 87 percent of Permaid's diagnosis and fix prescriptions are "correct."

Many interesting questions arise when this result is considered. For example, can a software system that is wrong 13 percent of the time be considered a high-quality product? If the system is wrong 13 percent of the time, how do you know when to believe it? Shouldn't the effort be invested to produce a system that is correct 100 percent (or nearly 100 percent) of the time?

Formulating a response to these questions begins with an understanding of the following (as introduced in Sec. 2.3):

PRINCIPLE 12.12: ESs often work in domains in which there is no absolute agreement as to whether a given result is "correct."

The initiation of many young engineers to the real world comes at the completion of their first task assignment when they discover that there is no "answer in the back of the book" that can be used to verify their results. In the case of equipment diagnosis it is not immediately obvious whether a fault has been fixed (e.g., faults often come and go intermittently), and it is certainly not clear whether any given fix procedure is the most efficient one possible.

PRINCIPLE 12.13: "Correct" is defined as the opinion of a recognized expert or team of experts.

The definition of "correct" for Permaid is based on the opinion of such a team.

In the final analysis it is actually the effectiveness of the system that is most important, where "effectiveness" is defined as the extent to which it solves the customer's problem. (Certainly maximum effectiveness requires correctness.)

The practical effectiveness of a system is established according to the following:

PRINCIPLE 12.14: The effectiveness of an ES should be measured relative to the performance of the humans who would otherwise do the job.

This is further qualified by the following:

PRINCIPLE 12.15: One of the primary applications of ES is to distribute an expert's knowledge to a group of nonexpert users.

In this case the ES is acting in the role of a guru to less-knowledgeable people. Thus it is important to realize:

PRINCIPLE 12.16: Although an ES models an expert's knowledge, the people "replaced" by it are not necessarily experts.

The typical user of Permaid accepts its recommendation and acts on it. This acceptance is not because the recommendation is guaranteed to be correct, but rather because it is the best information available—normally much better than the typical user could generate (and would act on) without Permaid.

The effectiveness of Permaid when measured in this sense—relative to the typical practitioner rather than relative to an expert or some theoretical measure of absolute correctness—is very high. This is the bottom line effectiveness that is of concern to the customer; the misdiagnosis rate for FSEs using Permaid is approximately 50 percent less than the misdiagnosis rate for FSEs without Permaid. This translates to an overall savings of several million dollars and to a significant reduction in customer downtime.

12.12   Future Directions for Expert Systems

Although, as described above, Permaid is successful when viewed from a cost/benefit analysis viewpoint, it falls significantly short of the theoretical ideal of duplicating an expert's performance. In Permaid this shortfall occurs in several areas:

1. *Analysis of new problems.*   The expert's performance is marked by the ability to respond to new, unforeseen problems. For example, in one case a fatal problem that was occurring once every few months resisted resolution by any means. After extensive and innovative analysis, a human expert determined that the device's operation was being disrupted by the main radar on an aircraft carrier when it passed a certain point in a harbor. Permaid would never have solved such a problem.

2. *Problems that must be resolved through recognition of past site history.*   Permaid does not match an expert's ability to resolve intermittent problems by applying knowledge that is based on remembering past events at the subject site.

3. *Ability to respond to calls for help on partially solved problems.*   Although, as described earlier, Permaid provides useful mixed-initiative capabilities, it does not approximate the expert's ability to listen to an extended freeform description of the problem-solving activity to date and then decide which steps should be taken next.

4. *Detecting misinformation.*   Permaid does not match the expert's ability to detect misinformation (e.g., an oversight on the part of the FSE).

5. *Customer relations.*   The expert's ability to deal with human relations problems (a nontrivial part of the task) is not addressed by Permaid.

PRINCIPLE 12.17: Current ESs, although they are very powerful and economically valuable, do not reproduce expert performance.

The ES community appears to be moving in three general directions in response to this situation:

1. The use of ES techniques to develop PC-based systems that address the lower-end segment of "expert" problems (economically, a very valuable segment)

2. The integration of ESs with existing software systems (e.g., to use existing databases)

3. The development of more generally intelligent systems that will more faithfully provide true expert performance

The development of more generally intelligent systems is required to address the needs of the high-end segment of expert problems: to expand the set of problems that can be addressed by using AI technology and to deal with domains in which the expert must be completely replaced to achieve the desired goal. (An example is a domain in which the primary goal is to remove the expert from a dangerous environment.)

The key to such development is continued research in AI techniques. The CYC project [Lenat, 1986] at Microelectronics and Computer Technology Corporation in Austin, Texas, is an example of such research. CYC is attempting to capture general commonsense knowledge by developing a very large general knowledge base that includes all of the knowledge (represented as frames and networks) contained in a desktop encyclopedia. Representation of this knowledge is intended to reduce the "brittleness" of current ESs (their tendency to fail precipitously at boundary conditions) and to greatly reduce the difficulty of the knowledge acquisition process.

The results of research such as this may allow the development of systems that faithfully duplicate behaviors which are currently considered "expert" and will allow humans to move on to even more creative and useful activities.

Lisp Programming

This appendix provides enough detail for the reader to get a general understanding of the Lisp programming language and to follow basic programming examples. Lisp was introduced in the late 1950s by John McCarthy; since then it has grown to be the most commonly used language for AI and ES development. During that time the language, along with the terminology used to describe it, has evolved significantly and many different versions have developed. All versions share certain core ideas but differ significantly in exact syntax and functionality. This section is based on Common Lisp, which, by the mid-1980s, had begun to emerge as an industry standard.

A.1 Lisp Theory

One of the differences between Lisp and more conventional programming languages, such as Fortran, Pascal, and Ada, is that Lisp provides specific facilities for *symbolic* processing. In symbolic processing the basic elements being manipulated are *symbols* that represent *arbitrary* objects from the domain of interest.

Symbols—which are frequently called *atoms* because of the physics analogy to the smallest indivisible units—are the most important data types in Lisp. A symbol is composed of an arbitrary sequence of characters.

The name "Lisp" was taken from *LIS*t *P*rocessing. Historically, list processing was the conceptual core of Lisp, and even in modern usage list-processing activities are very important. Lists in Lisp are represented in two basic forms. The printable, programmer-visible, form is composed of an opening parenthesis followed by any number of blank-separated *symbolic expressions* followed by a closing parenthesis. A symbolic expression can be a symbol or another list. (Symbolic expressions are sometimes referred to simply as *expressions;* historically, they were known as *s-expressions*.)

Examples of Lisp lists include:

```
(A B2 BOZO TIME-OF-DAY)
(Z B (A LIST WITHIN A LIST) D (E F))
```

Internally, a list is represented as a chain of *cons cells*. Each cons cell is composed of a CAR (the upper half) and a CDR (pronounced coo-dr) (the lower half). (The names CAR and CDR are historic and have no mnemonic significance.)

Lists are represented *internally* by linking cons cells into chains by using the CDR of each cons cell to point to the CAR of the next cell.

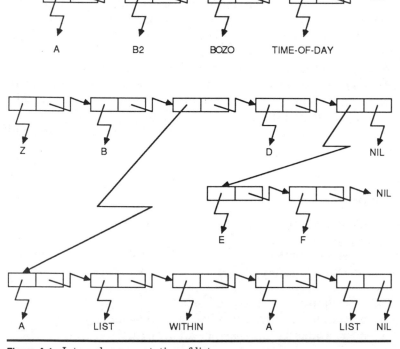

Figure A.1 Internal representation of lists.

Internal representations for the above example lists are shown in
Fig. A.1.

NIL is the Lisp symbol for an "empty list" and it is also used to
represent the Boolean value "false."

A.2 Functional Programming

Historically, Lisp has been classified as a *functional* programming language in which simple *functions* are defined and then combined to
compose more complex functions.

In mathematics a function defines a specific *mapping* between its
arguments and its output. The Lisp use of the term "function" does
not correspond directly to the mathematical concept; Lisp functions
are used to define *procedures* that describe the action to be taken when
it is executed.

A *form* is an expression that is intended for *evaluation,* the Lisp
terminology for executing a procedure and *returning* the result of the
execution. Because Lisp uses *prefix notation,* a form is generally composed of a *function name* followed by the arguments to be used during
evaluation.

When a form is presented to Lisp at the *top level* (i.e., command
level), the Lisp interpreter will evaluate the form, return the result,
and wait for another form to evaluate. (Although many years ago
almost all Lisp implementations relied on interpreters, modern Lisps
include efficient compliers as well as interpreters.)

Lisp provides many built-in functions, called *primitives,* that perform
commonly required actions. For example, when the form (+ 2 3) is
evaluated, a primitive will calculate and return the sum of 2 and 3.
Primitives fall into several categories such as functions to support
numerical calculations, list manipulation, and I/O. Functions from
each of the major categories will be introduced as part of the discussion
in the following sections.

A.3 Variable Assignment and
Function Definition

As part of the evaluation of a function, it may become necessary to
evaluate yet another function. To do so, the *higher-level* function calls
for evaluation of the *lower-level* function, passing it the appropriate
arguments, and awaiting a *return value.* This return value can then
be used by the higher-level function.

The value returned by a function is simply a transient result that
is presented back to the higher-level function. However, in addition to
accepting arguments and calculating a return value, the evaluation of

a function may cause *side effects,* actions that are taken as part of the evaluation process but are done "on the side" in the sense that they have no effect on the return value. Side effects are important because they produce changes in the state of the system that *persist* after the evaluation of the function is complete. This process is diagrammed in Fig. A.2.

In some cases the higher-level function wants to produce a specific side effect and also wants the returned value. In other cases a function is evaluated only because it performs a desired side effect. In such a case the return value is discarded. One of the most commonly used side effects is the *assignment of a value* to a symbol. The SETQ primitive can be used to accomplish such an assignment. For example, if during the evaluation of a function, the expression (SETQ A 2) is executed, a value of 2 will be assigned to the symbol A.

DEFUN is another commonly used primitive that is executed for its side effects. DEFUN is a function for *defining new functions.* DEFUN has the following syntax:

⟨DEFUN ⟨function name⟩

((parameter 1) ⟨parameter 2⟩ . . . ⟨parameter N⟩)
⟨procedure body⟩)

where ⟨function name⟩ is a symbol that identifies the new function and ⟨parameter⟩ is a symbol that can be used in the body of the procedure. When a form containing the new function name as its first element is evaluated, the form will include actual arguments to be substituted for each of the parameters. ⟨procedure body⟩ is composed of a series of

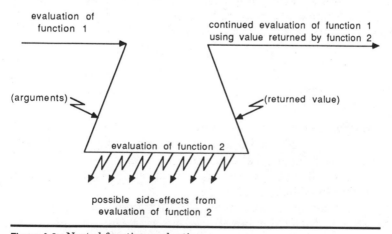

Figure A.2 Nested function evaluation.

forms that define the procedure to be executed when the function is evaluated.

When a DEFUN is evaluated, Lisp "remembers" the forms in the procedure body as the procedure to be executed when it needs to evaluate the newly defined function. DEFUN returns the new function name, but this return value is typically discarded.

As an example of the use of DEFUN, consider the following definition of a function called ADD-EM:

```
    (DEFUN ADD-EM (first second third)
 ; a simple function to add up three numbers
 ; the sum of the numbers is returned
        (SETQ sum 0) ; init the sum
        (SETQ sum (+ sum first)) ; add the first
        (SETQ sum (+ sum second)) ; add the next
        (SETQ sum (+ sum third)) ) ; add the last
```

Note that Lisp is freeform in the sense that expressions are separated by white space (i.e., one or more blanks) and can appear on an arbitrary number of separate source lines. (Of course, although the placement of the various components is not significant to Lisp, it may be very important to the readability and so the maintainability of the program.) The semicolon is the comment character in Lisp. It is ignored along with the remainder of the source line on which it occurs.

When the form (ADD-EM 98.6 2.54 3.14) is encountered, Lisp will rely on its stored definition of ADD-EM to evaluate the form and a value of 104.28 will be returned.

This same result could be achieved by evaluating the following sequence of expressions:

```
(SETQ normal-temp 98.6)
(SETQ cm-per-inch 2.54)
(SETQ pi 3.14)
(ADD-EM normal-temp cm-per-inch pi).
```

Lisp will proceed in one of two different ways when evaluating a form:

If the expression to be evaluated is a symbol, Lisp will simply return its current *binding* (i.e., the value currently assigned to it). An error message is printed if no such binding exists.

If the expression to be evaluated is a list, Lisp treats the first element as the name of a function to be evaluated. All of the remaining elements are evaluated to find the values to be passed as the arguments of the function. For the form shown above, the evaluation of the arguments consists of simply returning the binding for each of the symbols. In the form (ADD-EM normal-temp cm-per-inch (+ 3 0.14)), the first two arguments are simply symbols, but the last argument is itself a form that must be evaluated. When the interpreter encounters the new form, it will "suspend" the evaluation of the ADD-EM form. The + form will then be evaluated; and when the value of 3.14 is returned, the suspended evaluation of ADD-EM is restarted and completed. In this way the interpreter may move down into many levels of form evaluation to complete the evaluation of a given form.

In some cases the program developer may wish to *suppress evaluation,* that is, to tell Lisp to accept a given element as is without any further evaluation. This desire is indicated by preceding the element with a single quote symbol. For example, evaluation of:

```
(SETQ Louise 1)
(SETQ Lenny Louise)
Lenny
```

would return a value of 1, whereas the evaluation of:

```
(SETQ Louise 1)
;   assign the literal ''Louise'' rather than the value
;   of the symbol ''Louise''
(SETQ Lenny 'Louise)
Lenny
```

would return a value of "Louise."

A.4   List Manipulation

The functions described in the following subsections are used to perform basic list manipulations.

List definition

Lists can be defined explicitly in two ways. The most simple way is to use a quote followed by the literal list. For example, to define a list containing the literal A, B, and C, the expression '(A B C) could be used.

The LIST function is also used to define lists. LIST makes a list of its arguments. For example, the above list could also be defined by evaluating (LIST 'A 'B 'C) or the sequence:

```
(SETQ x 'B)
(LIST 'A x 'C).
```

List construction

It is also possible to *construct* a list by building it during execution. The basic list *construction* function is CONS. CONS accepts two arguments. It returns a list which is constructed by inserting the first argument as the head of the list specified by the second argument.

For example, evaluating the following forms produces the corresponding results:

```
(CONS 'a '(b c)) ———→ (a b c)

(SETQ x '(c d))
(CONS x '(b c)) ———→ ( (c d) (b c) )

(CONS 'a NIL) ———→ (a)
```

Note also that evaluating:

```
(SETQ list-1 '(a b))
(CONS 'c list-1)
list-1
```

will return (a b) and not (c a b). To assign a new value to list-1, we must evaluate:

```
(SETQ list-1 '(a b))
(SETQ list-1 (CONS 'c list-1)).
```

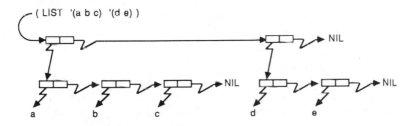

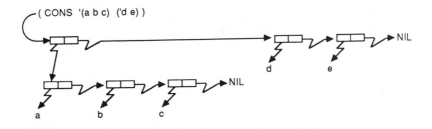

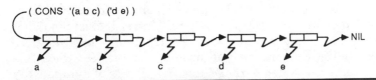

Figure A.3 Examples of list construction.

The APPEND function can also be used to construct lists. APPEND accepts two (or more) lists and produces a new list that is formed by combining all of the elements of the component lists.

For example, (APPEND '(a b c) '(d e)) produces (a b c d e). Figure A.3 presents several examples and the associated internal cons cell actions.

Functions for decomposing lists

The CAR function returns the first element of the list provided as its argument. Evaluation of (CAR '(a b c)) returns a, and the evaluation of (CAR (LIST '(a b) c d)) returns (a b).

The function CDR returns the portion of its argument (which must be a list) that follows the first element. Thus the result returned by CDR is always a list. (CDR '(a b c)) returns (b c) and CDR '(b)) returns NIL. From an internal viewpoint, to find the CAR of a list, we simply use the pointer associated with the CAR half of the first cons cell in the chain that represents the list. CDR simply returns the portion of the chain pointed to by the CDR half of the same cell.

Lisp also provides many more sophisticated list-processing functions including functions for reversing lists, finding lengths of lists, and replacing specific elements of lists.

A.5   Dynamic Memory Management

Another distinguishing characteristic of Lisp is its provision for automatic dynamic memory management. Lisp maintains a free storage list that keeps track of available memory. As new values are created, memory is taken from this list.

It is possible, however, that memory once assigned may become unusable. For example, consider the sequence:

```
(SETQ x (list 'a 'b 'c))
         .
         .
         .
(SETQ x (CONS 'g '(e f)).
```

The original action will construct a cons cell chain by removing cells from the free storage list. When the second assignment occurs, the original pointer to the a cell is changed to point to the new chain starting at g. Unfortunately, the old a→b→c chain still exists in memory even though it is now a vestige; it is inaccessible and therefore worthless (assuming that no other form is pointing to it.) Such "orphaned" structures are called *garbage,* and the process of dynamically reclaiming them is called *garbage collection.*

Garbage collection in Lisp is performed when free storage becomes exhausted. Such collection is typically a two-stage process. In the first step, called the *marking phase,* the garbage collector goes through memory and marks locations that could potentially still be in use. In the second step, called the *sweep* phase, the collector again passes through memory, returning all unmarked locations to the free storage list. This process limits the need for static allocation of memory and frees the program developer from memory management concerns.

A.6   Control

As noted previously, Lisp program construction is based primarily on function application. Small functions are defined to perform each desired individual action. Programs are then constructed by combining a large number of these component functions. Programs are essentially an extension of the language itself.

As noted previously, function application in Lisp is not a simple application of a function to its arguments (as it would be in a "pure" functional language that did not allow side effects [Henderson, 1980] and applied the term "functional" in its mathematical sense). The need for side effects and explicit sequencing of expression evaluation requires that a *control* structure be established. The following sections describe the most common structures.

Conditional execution

Lisp provides several simple functions for conditional execution. WHEN, which is defined as WHEN (⟨test⟩) (⟨body⟩), evaluates ⟨test⟩. If ⟨test⟩ is non-NIL, it then sequentially evaluates the expressions in ⟨body⟩. If ⟨test⟩ is NIL, no action is taken. UNLESS is the opposite of WHEN. Action is taken only if ⟨test⟩ returns NIL.

IF provides for "two-way" conditional execution.

$$(IF (⟨test⟩) (⟨then⟩) (⟨else⟩))$$

defines the IF primitive. IF evaluates ⟨test⟩. If a non-NIL value is returned, the forms in ⟨then⟩ will be evaluated. If a NIL value is returned, the forms (if any) in ⟨else⟩ will be evaluated.

Repetitive execution

The basic primitive for explicit iteration in Lisp is the special form DO. The syntax and operation of DO can be understood by considering a syntax definition in conjunction with a specific example. The following is a definition of the syntax of DO:

    (DO (⟨parameter set 1⟩ ⟨parameter set 2⟩ . . . ⟨parameter set n⟩)
        ((⟨termination forms⟩) (body)))

The following section informally explains this syntax by using the following example:

EXAMPLE A.1 Develop a function that will sum the first five elements of the following three series:
1 2 3 4 5 6 . . .
2 4 6 8 10 12 . . .
3 6 9 12 15 18 . . .

```
(SETQ sum 0) ; init sum to zero
(DO
; parameters
(series1 1 1) ; start at 1 and bump by 1
(series2 2 2) ; start by 2 and bump by 2
(series3 3 3) ; start by 3 and bump by 3
; termination test
((eq loop_counter 6) sum) ; return the sum after 5 reps
; body
(setq sum (+ sum series1))
(setq sum (+ sum series2))
(setq sum (+ sum series3)) )
```

DO has the following operation:

1. Each ⟨parameter set⟩ consists of:

⟨parameter symbol⟩ ⟨initial value⟩ ⟨update expression⟩

Upon entry, each of the parameter sets is evaluated. For each set the ⟨parameter symbol⟩ is bound to the associated ⟨initialize value⟩. The value of the parameter symbol will be assigned a new value based on the ⟨update expression⟩ each time the loop is executed. In the example above, loop_counter is initialized to 1 and stepped by 1 for each loop. Series1 is treated similarly. Series2 is initialized to 2 and incremented by 2, and series3 is initialized to 3 and incremented by 3.

The symbols used in the parameter sets are returned to their previous values (if any) after termination of the loop.

2. The ⟨termination form⟩ consists of a ⟨test condition⟩ and one or more ⟨return forms⟩. The ⟨test condition⟩ is a form that is evaluated before each execution of the loop (including the first pass). If the test condition evaluates to true, the loop terminates and all of the ⟨return forms⟩ are evaluated. The value returned by the last return form is returned as the value of the DO.

In the above example, as soon as loop_counter reaches 6, the value of sum will be returned. Note that a nonterminating loop will result if NIL is entered as the test condition.

3. If the termination test fails, each of the forms in the body is executed in sequence. In the above example the three argument forms would be evaluated. There are, however, special cases in which this does not occur. If, during evaluation of a DO, a RETURN function is

encountered, the evaluation will immediately terminate and the value associated with the return will be returned as the value of the DO. Consider, for example, the following function to compute the value of $1/x^2$:

```
(DEFUN divide-it (x)
   (DO () (index 1) ( (eq index 3) div)
          (IF (eq x 0) (return 'error))
             (SETQ div (/ 1 (* x x)))))
```

Recursion

A *recursive* function is a function that calls itself, either directly or indirectly. Lisp provides for recursive as well as iterative function definition.

To understand recursive programming in Lisp, consider how we might go about computing the factorial of a given number. If we were asked to calculate the value of the factorial of 6, we might observe that, although we don't know what the value of (FACTORIAL 5) is, we do know (from our understanding of the definition of factorial) that (FACTORIAL 5) = 5 * (FACTORIAL 4), whatever (FACTORIAL 4) is. At this point, we could find (FACTORIAL 5) if only we knew what (FACTORIAL 4) was. Therefore we "remember" the need to find (FACTORIAL 5) and then temporarily suspend the effort in favor of attacking the problem of finding the value of (FACTORIAL 4).

Finding the value of (FACTORIAL 4) is simply a very slightly revised version of the above problem. (FACTORIAL 4) is equal to 4 times whatever (FACTORIAL 3) is. After we suspend this activity, we will have remembered the need to find:

(FACTORIAL 5), which is equal to 5 * (FACTORIAL 4)

(FACTORIAL 4), which is equal to 4 * (FACTORIAL 3)

We then begin to look for a value for (FACTORIAL 3). This process continues until we reach the following point:

(FACTORIAL 5) = 5 * (FACTORIAL 4)

.

.

.

(FACTORIAL 1) = 1 * (FACTORIAL 0)

However, when attempting to find the value of (FACTORIAL 1), the situation changes somewhat. We observe that, by definition, we know directly that (FACTORIAL 0) = 1.

Because (FACTORIAL 0) is defined, we can find the value of (FAC-TORIAL 1). Recalling our previously suspended activities, we find that the attempt to evaluate (FACTORIAL 2) was suspended because of the lack of a value for (FACTORIAL 1). It is therefore now possible to find (FACTORIAL 2). This process continues to "roll up" by using each newly defined value to calculate its higher-level neighbor. A Lisp function to describe this process is:

(DEFUN FACTORIAL (n)

   (TIMES n (FACTORIAL (− n 1))))   ; recursive call

The process described above can be generalized as:

1. Solve a small piece of the problem.
2. Express the remainder of the problem in terms of a more limited version of the original problem. [It is "more limited" in the sense that the "small piece" identified in (1) has been removed.]
3. Define the conditions under which some version of the problem can be directly solved. This *bottoming out* condition is used to terminate the recursion.

A.7 Additional Lisp Functions

Lisp provides several other powerful capabilities including facilities for processing *higher-order functions,* a function that takes another function as input or returns a function as output. The most commonly used higher-order functions are MAP functions. For example, the primitive MAPCAR accepts a function name as an argument and operates by applying it to a list of elements that also are accepted as arguments.

Another powerful function is the APPLY primitive, which allows for *dynamic program construction*—a process in which the executing program actually constructs another program dynamically and then executes APPLY with the new program as an argument in order to execute the new program.

For more information regarding LISP see Steele, 1984, and Winston, 1984.

Prolog Programming

This appendix consists of a limited presentation of background theory followed by a discussion of Prolog programming specifics. The level of detail is sufficient to develop a general understanding of the language and follow basic programming examples. Prolog has been growing in popularity since it was originally introduced in Europe in the early 1970s. The following section presents a brief introduction to the foundational theory of Prolog.

B.1 Theoretical Concepts

Almost any system of mathematics, given certain restrictions, can, in theory, be used as a programming language. Languages based on set theory and lambda calculus have actually been implemented [Danforth, 1985]. Prolog, which is the first practical and widely available *logic programming* language, is based on the basic mathematical theory of relations.

Conceptually, Prolog is a *declarative programming* language in which the programmer simply specifies (i.e., declares) *what* is required rather than indicate *how* it is to be computed, as would be done in a more traditional imperative, sequential programming language such as C, Pascal, or Ada. This frees the programmer from worrying about the underlying implementation details (i.e., from thinking like a computer and concentrating on the operations of sequencing and replacement) and allows more concentration on the details of the application task.

This declaration is essentially a description of *objects* (i.e., elements) from the domain and *relations* between those objects. A subset of formal logic (Chap. 4) called *Horn clause logic* is used to specify the desired conditions.

The most common examples come from human relationships. To refer to a person named Antonio (using the syntax described in Chap. 4), simply select a constant, say TONY, that represents him. Function descriptions, for example, weight(TONY), can then be added along with formal logic implications that describe relationships, for example, FE-MALE(person1) ^ PARENT(person1,person2) → MOTHER(person2).

Logical specifications such as these are added as required to describe the application environment (i.e., the domain) to whatever level of detail is required.

In Prolog, the description of the domain is called a *database*. (For purposes of this book, "knowledge base" would be more appropriate, but "database" is the accepted Prolog term.) To get useful work from a Prolog program, the user poses *questions* that ask Prolog's *application-independent inference system* to draw *conclusions* based on *inferences* developed from the database.

Prolog is frequently presented as a declarative language [Genesereth, 1984], and it is useful to understand the conceptual basis. However, as described later in this section, Prolog deviates from this basis in several important ways that must be understood by anyone who is actually developing Prolog programs.

B.2 Basic Programming Elements and Syntax

The most basic component of a Prolog database is a *fact*, which makes a statement about some set of objects and the relations between them.

Facts

Formal logic predicates are used to represent facts; but in Prolog syntax (as described in Clocksin, 1981), predicate symbols and constant symbols must begin with a *lowercase letter*, whereas variables must begin with an *uppercase letter*.

To represent the fact "Juan owns Ruben (his pet Cockateil)" in Prolog, we could enter:

```
owns(juan,ruben).
```

in the database.

As in any formal logic system, there is one arbitrary but fixed interpretation associated with each symbol. It is very important that the programmer clearly understand these interpretations to avoid inconsistencies in the database (e.g., interpreting the predicate symbol "long" to refer to length in one usage and time duration in another).

Rules

In addition to facts, a Prolog database can include *rules* (i.e., implications) that describe *dependency relationships* among objects in the domain. For example, the rule:

> The water will flow if the valve is open.

could be expressed in Prolog as:

```
flow(water) :- open(valve).
```

Note that the above rule could be stated as a forward implication: "If the valve is open, then the water will flow." (It would normally be stated in the "forward" form for a rule-based programming system.) Prolog uses the equally valid "reverse implication" style because of the way that it goes about proving facts (as described later in this section). Thus a Prolog programmer thinks of the statement, "Walk to the exit if the fire alarm sounds," rather than the equivalent, "If the fire alarm sounds, then walk to the exit."

Conjunctions can be used to express more complicated relationships such as:

```
flow(water) :- open(valve), running(pump).
```

which is used to represent:

> The water will flow if the valve is open and the pump is running.

Note that in this type of Prolog expression, the :- is read as "if" and the comma is read as "and."

In general, a Prolog rule states a conclusion or action followed by the facts on which its truth depends. The conclusion (the part of the rule to the left of the :-) is called the *head* of the rule and the set of facts on which its truth depends (the part of the rule to the right of the :-) is called the *body*.

Variables

Variables in Prolog are used to represent unspecified domain elements. A variable that, at a particular point during execution, stands for a specific domain object is said to be *instantiated* (i.e., it is a specific *instance* from a general *class* of similar things). Variables that do not stand for specific objects are *uninstantiated*.

The *scope* of a variable in Prolog is the entire rule in which the variable occurs. Therefore, whatever a variable stands for in one part of a rule, it must also stand for that in the remainder of the rule. For example, in the rule:

```
bigger(mary,Y) :- bigger(mary,X), bigger(X,Y).
```

we are free to select any object for X, but it must be the same in both cases. Once a variable is instantiated for any part of a rule, it is instantiated for the entire rule. Remember, however, that the scope of a variable is limited to the containing rule. There is no inconsistency in the set of rules:

```
bigger(X,Z) :- bigger(X,Y), bigger(Y,Z).
smaller(X,Z) :- smaller(X,Y), smaller(Y,Z).
```

because there is no connection between the variables in the two rules.

Questions

In Prolog we can ask questions about objects and relationships from the domain. For example, consider the database, shown in Fig. B.1, that describes commonly recognized relationships.

```
 (1)  parent(fred,steve).
 (2)  female(jill).
 (3)  male(jack).
 (4)  male(igor).
 (5)  parent(igor,jack).
 (6)  female(regiena).
 (7)  parent(regiena,jack).
 (8)  parent(regiena,jill).
 (9)  parent(igor,seth).
(10)  parent(fred,regiena).
(11)  male(seth).
(13)  female(ellen).

(14)  grandparent(X,Z) :- parent(X,Y), parent(Y,Z).
(15)  grandmother(X,Y) :- grandparent(X,Y), female(X).
(16)  grandfather(X,Y) :- grandparent(X,Y), male(X).
(17)  mother(X,Y) :- parent(X,Y), female(X).
(18)  father(X,Y) :- parent(X,Y), male(X).
(19)  brother(X,Y) :- parent(P,X), parent(P,Y), male(X).
(20)  sister(X,Y) :- parent(P,X), parent(P,Y), female(X).
(21)  niece(X,Y) :- parent(P,X), brother(P,Y), female(X).
(22)  niece(X,Y) :- parent(P,X), sister(P,Y), female(X).
(23)  sibling(X,Y) :- parent(P,X), parent(P,Y).
```

Figure B.1 Example of Prolog database.

The most straightforward question is one that asks a simple fact. For example, the user might ask the question, "Is Igor the parent of Jack?," which would be presented to the Prolog system as:

```
?- parent(igor,jack).
```

where the characters ?- are used to signify a question.

When presented with a question, Prolog will answer it on the basis of information from the database. In this case, Prolog will find the fact directly in the database without doing any inferring. After finding the fact, Prolog will respond with yes.

If the question

```
?- grandparent(fred,jill).
```

were presented, Prolog would respond with yes after performing some straightforward inference.

If, however, we presented the question

```
?- male(fred).
```

Prolog would respond with a no. We might be tempted to believe that this response is probably incorrect because we suspect that Fred is, in reality, a male. To interpret this response correctly, we need to recognize that "no" actually means, "It can't be shown to be true, given the current information in the database."

This type of response is very similar to a verdict in a criminal trial. In such a trial a defendant may be found guilty—within the limits of reasonable doubt. This is intended to be a definite conclusion based on the evidence. In other cases, however, a defendant may be found "not guilty." This verdict is not an equally definite conclusion. It does not state that the defendant is definitely innocent (although such may actually be the case). It simply says that there was not sufficient evidence to prove the defendant guilty. When working with Prolog, it is sometimes easy to lose sight of that distinction.

Prolog also accepts "fill in the blank" questions such as "Who is the grandfather of Jill?" Given the question:

```
?- grandfather(X,jill).
```

Prolog would respond with X = fred.

In the discussion to this point the examples have been fully *deterministic;* each question has had only one possible correct response. That is typically the case with conventional and also with functional programming languages (see Appendix A). Following the mathematical concept of "function," which has a 1-to-1 mapping from input to output, every unique input will produce a unique output.

Prolog, however, is based on the theory of *relations* rather than functions. Relations are *nondeterministic* in that there can be many different correct outputs from any given input. For example, suppose we give Prolog the following question based on the database of Fig. B.1:

```
?- female(X).
```

The "correct" response could be `jill, regiena,` or `ellen.` In this case Prolog will respond with X = `jill`. The next section describes how Prolog generates this response.

B.3   Inference in Prolog

When Prolog receives the question ?- `female(X)`, it views the question as a *goal* to be *satisfied.* This is essentially a way of looking for some instantiation of X that will make the statement `female(X)` true. X is uninstantiated at the start of the search process. Prolog looks through the database while searching for a fact that *matches* the question. [This search process is a modification of *unification* (Chap. 11).] During the search, uninstantiated variables act simply as "place holders." An uninstantiated variable will match *any* argument that happens to be in its position in the fact. This means that any fact whose predicate is "female" will match. Prolog responds with X = `jill` because the search is conducted *starting at the top of the database.*

If, after receiving the response, the user enters a carriage return, Prolog will go back to its "idle" state and wait for a question or for additional facts to be entered. If, however, the user enters a semicolon, Prolog will respond with a different way of satisfying the goal if one exists; in this case X = `regiena`.

This ordering is an important distinction between theory and practice. As noted previously, Prolog is conceptually a declarative, nonprocedural programming language. However, rules in Prolog can be thought of in two distinctly different ways. For example, rule 14 (from Fig. B.2) can be thought of as a simple definition (the *declarative reading*):

> X is the grandparent of Z if X is the parent of Y and Y is the parent of Z.

or as a description of a procedure for how to calculate "grandparent" when it is needed. Thought of in this way (the *procedural reading* [Kowalski, 1974]), rule 14 could be stated as

> To prove that X is the grandparent of Z, first find a Y such that X is the parent of Y and then prove that Y is the parent of Z.

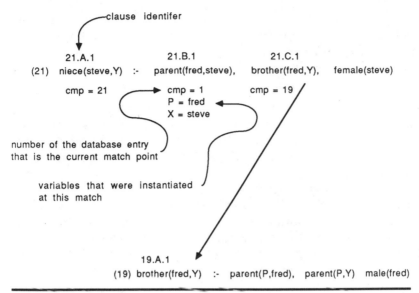

Figure B.2 Recursive processing of subgoals.

Prolog is, in fact, sometimes directly presented as a procedural language [Wos, 1984], where the term "procedure" is used rather than "rule." This view is certainly computationally accurate and needs to be recognized, but a Prolog programmer should not lose sight of the declarative intent and development paradigm of Prolog.

In practice, the order of database entries can be very important. It is significant in three ways:

1. The efficiency of a program can depend heavily on the order because of the amount of search required to satisfy a goal.

2. When there are many possible ways to satisfy a goal, the order in which answers are produced depends directly on the order of the database.

3. Because of the exact nature of the search process, there are some cases in which Prolog will not find a solution even when one can logically be inferred from the given information. The ordering of the entries in the database and the order of the component subgoals in each rule determine whether Prolog will actually find a solution.

Because of those restrictions (which were imposed primarily to allow Prolog the efficiency required for a practical programming language) a Prolog programmer can't simply make declarative statements and ignore the underlying implementation. To understand and predict the details of a program's performance, the programmer must have a good understanding of the inference process that is used by Prolog.

This inference process can be described as follows:

1. Given a goal, Prolog searches the database, starting at the top, for a fact that matches the goal. Uninstantiated variables in the goal will match whatever argument is in their position in the fact. Instantiated variables must match the associated fact argument for the overall fact to match.

For example, given the goal ?- parent(X,Y), Prolog would match parent(fred,steve). X would be instantiated to fred, Y to steve, and both values would be printed. If instead the goal ?- parent(regiena, X) had been entered, Prolog would bypass the first occurrence of parent (because regiena will not match fred) and would match parent(regiena, jack) with X instantiated to jack and printed.

2. When Prolog finds a match and instantiates the appropriate variables, it leaves a pointer where the match occurred (the *current match point*).

If, after asking a question and receiving Prolog's response, the user responds with a semicolon, Prolog will again start the match process in an attempt to resatisfy the goal, this time starting from the *current match point* rather than from the top. If a match is found, Prolog will print the new instantiations for the variables; otherwise, Prolog will return to wait for another question. Thus, if a semicolon were entered in response to the X = jack answer, Prolog would resatisfy the goal and return with X = jill.

At the start of the attempt to resatisfy the goal, Prolog retracts any instantiations that occurred at the current match point (e.g., Prolog "forgets" that X was instantiated to jack when it begins the attempt to resatisfy the parent(regiena,X) goal.

3. When a goal matches the head of a rule rather than a fact, the atoms within the body of the rule are treated as *subgoals* that must all be satisfied to prove that the head is satisfied.

As an example of this process, consider the action that would occur in response to the question

```
?- niece(A,B).
```

The goal would match with the head of rule 21. Even though a match has been located, it is impossible to instantiate A or B because each is matched to a variable and the variables are themselves uninstantiated. In this case, the variable A is *shared* with the variable X and B is shared with Y. Because the variables are shared (and are, in effect, *partially instantiated*) as soon as X is instantiated to some value, A will be immediately instantiated to the same value.

Prolog will then attempt to satisfy the subgoals, *starting from the left side of the body*. For this example, the first subgoal to be satisfied would be parent(P,X). This matches rule 1. P is instantiated to fred and X is instantiated to steve. The current match point for this subgoal is set to 1.

After it has satisfied this subgoal, Prolog moves to the right and then attempts to satisfy brother(fred,Y). (Note that P has been replaced by fred because when P was instantiated, it applied to the entire rule.)

```
brother (fred,Y) matches with the head of rule 19.
```

The X from rule 19 is instantiated to fred and the Y from the subgoal brother(fred,Y) shares with the Y from rule 19. (Recall that the scope of a variable is limited to a rule and therefore the two Y's are different variables.) Prolog maintains separate current match points for each subgoal. The current match point for this subgoal points to rule 19. Because brother(fred,Y) is itself the head of a rule, the inference process must be, in effect, called recursively to attempt to satisfy the body of brother(fred,Y). Note also that, from the viewpoint of this satisfaction process, the variable X from rule 19 was instantiated to fred at creation.

The current situation in the inference process is shown in Fig. B.2. The next step in the process is an attempt to satisfy the subgoal parent(P,fred). Unfortunately, parent(P,fred) is unsatisfiable and, therefore, the attempt to satisfy clause 19.A.1 fails.

Given this failure, the inference process, which has now returned to focus on rule 21, will try to satisfy 21.C.1 in some other way. In this case there is no other way because there are no "brother" facts and rule 19 is the only rule with "brother" as a head.

Because 21.C.1 is unsatisfiable, the inference process *backtracks* and *reenters* 21.B.1 from the *right side* and attempts to find another way to satisfy 21.B.1, starting from 21.B.1's current match point. As part of this backtracking, the cmp for 21.C.1 is reset and any instantiations made at this point (in this case, none) are dropped. Any later attempt to satisfy 21.C.1 will start again from the top of the database.

The attempt to resatisfy 21.B.1 will succeed at fact 5. The inference

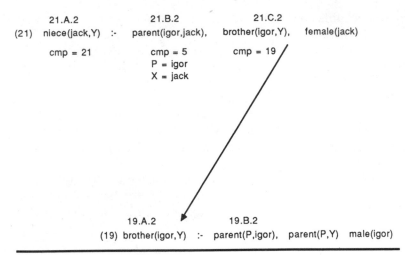

Figure B.3 Subgoal processing.

process will then attempt to satisfy the right-hand neighbor, brother(igor,Y), resulting in the situation shown in Fig. B.3. Clause 19.B.2 fails, and the inference process is forced to again attempt to resatisfy 21.B.2. Rule 7 matches.

Processing continues as before with an attempt to satisfy parent(P,regiena) as part of satisfying brother(regiena,Y). In this case, however, parent(P,regiena) will match with fact 10 and P will be instantiated to fred. The inference process will then enter parent(fred,Y) from the left side. This will match with rule 1 and the result will be the situation shown in Fig. B.4.

Processing will then continue as shown in Fig. B.5 until the failure of brother(regiena,Y) is detected. It will then resatisfy parent(X,Y) from rule 21 by matching it with fact 8 and instantiating P to regiena and X to jill. It will then attempt to satisfy brother(regiena,Y) and eventually fail.

The attempt to satisfy rule 21 will continue by matching the parent(P,X) clause to fact 9, which will result in failure, and then to fact 10, which also will fail.

The inference process will then abandon the attempt to find a proof for niece by using rule 21 and will look for another match for niece. Rule 22 will match, and the inference process, after detecting failures based on the matching of parent(P,X) with facts 1, 5, and 7, will succeed as shown in Fig. B.6. Prolog will return X=jill and Y=steve.

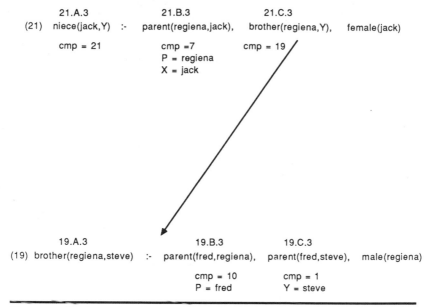

Figure B.4 Further subgoal processing.

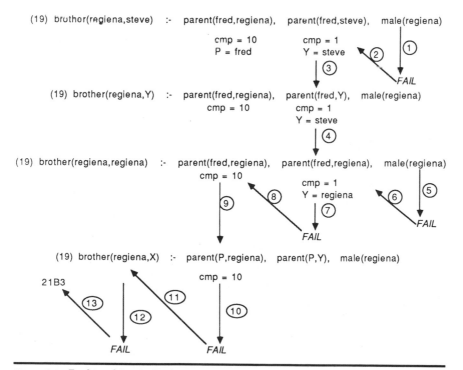

Figure B.5 Backtracking in Prolog.

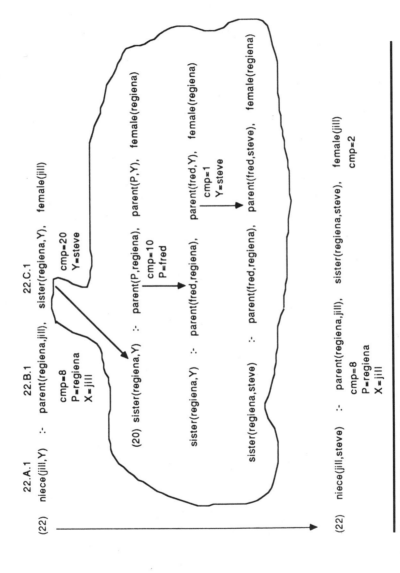

Figure B.6 Goal satisfaction.

240

B.4   Explicit Control in Prolog

Several interesting observations can be drawn from the above example. For instance, we can observe that efficiency could be improved by placing the female(X) clause at the beginning of the body of rule 21 rather than at the end. This would significantly reduce the search required when failure occurs.

Consider also what would happen when attempting to satisfy sibling(X,Y) from rule 23:

> parent(P,X) would match with parent(fred, steve) with P instantiated to fred and X to steve. There would then be an attempt to satisfy parent(fred, Y) which would match with parent(fred, steve). This instantiates Y to steve and, as an unfortunate side effect, also proves that steve is his own sibling!

This anomaly can be corrected through the use of an *explicit control directive*. Such a directive allows the user to explicitly control the operation of the inference process.

One such directive is ! (called a cut), which is used to modify the search within a given clause. Cut is a special subgoal that, by definition, always succeeds. Once the cut is reached, no backtracking is permitted for any goals or subgoals that are to the left of it. There can be no attempt to resatisfy any of the previous subgoals or the predicate from the head of the rule. The instantiations that have been established up to the point of the cut are "frozen," and any attempt to satisfy subgoals to the right of the cut must be carried out in light of the constraints imposed by the frozen instantiations.

To eliminate the possibility of finding that steve is his own sibling, we could modify rule 23 (from Fig. B.1) and add clauses 24 and 25 to produce:

```
(23)  sibling(X,Y)  :- not-equal(X,Y), parent(P,X), parent(P,Y).
(24)  not-equal(X,Y) :- -X=Y,!,fail.
(25)  not-equal(X,Y).
```

When attempting to satisfy sibling(X,Y), Prolog first tries to satisfy not-equal(X,Y). Rule 24 will match, and Prolog will attempt to satisfy X=Y. This subgoal is an example of an *equality predicate*. It will be satisfied only if X can be matched with Y. If X and Y are equal, the equality predicate will be satisfied and Prolog will move to the cut subgoal, which will automatically be satisfied, and then undo the *fail* subgoal. "Fail" is a special predicate that indicates unconditional failure.

In this case, because the cut prevents attempts to backtrack, the attempt to satisfy the head of rule 24 would fail and therefore, so will the attempt to satisfy sibling(steve, steve).

When X and Y are not equal, the equality predicate in rule 24 will

fail; therefore, the cut will not be reached. Rule 25 will then immediately succeed because it has no body that must be satisfied.

The control directives described in this section, although they detract
from the declarative "purity" of the language, greatly enhance the
programmer's capability to control and direct the inference process
when developing practical applications.

Other examples of *extra-logical* features in Prolog include the "read,"
"write," and "is" predicates.

Read and write are used to perform traditional input and output.
The *built-in predicate* nl is used to issue a carriage return and line
feed.

"Is" is, in effect, an assignment statement. It has the effect of assigning the value represented by the right side of the statement to the
variable on the left side.

B.5 Prolog Program Example

The following is an example of part of a Prolog program to solve the
two-pail problem in Sec. 2.2. The overall control information that
selects the next move is omitted. The program fragment shown is
used to determine which moves are possible from any given state
(where state is represented as s(⟨content of large pail⟩,
⟨content of small pail⟩)—similar to the representation used in Sec.
2.2). The arguments to the predicate move represent states before and
after the move is executed.

```
move(s(X,Y), s(0,Y))  :-
write('empty the small pail'),
nl.

move(s(X,Y), s(X,0))  :-
write('empty the large pail'),
nl.

move(s(X,Y), s(6,Y))  :-
write('fill the small pail'),
nl.

move(s(X,Y), s(X,8))  :-
write('fill the large pail'),
nl.

move(s(X,Y), s(0,S))  :-
S is X + Y,
S <= 8,
write('empty the small pail into the large pail'),
nl.

move(s(X,Y), s(E,0))  :-
E is X + Y,
E <= 6,
write('empty the large pail into the small pail'),
nl.
```

```
move(s(X,Y), s(6, S)) :-
S is X + Y - 6,
S )= 0,
write('fill the small pail from the large pail'),
nl.

move(s(X,Y, s(E,8)) :-
E is X + Y - 8,
E )= 0,
write('fill the large pail from the small pail'),
nl.
```

Coelho, 1980, includes a large set of example Prolog programs; Ceri, 1986, presents a program for building schema for relational databases; and Wos, 1984, includes a description of a Prolog-based controller for a power plant.

For more information on Prolog see Clocksin, 1981, and Conlon, 1985; and for more information on the theory of Prolog see Lloyd, 1984.

Bibliography

Adams, J.: "Probabilistic Reasoning and Certainty Factors," in B. Buchanan and E. Shortliffe (eds.), *Rule-Based Expert Systems,* Addison-Wesley, Menlo Park, Calif., 1984.

Aikins, J.: "Prototypical Knowledge for Expert Systems," *Artificial Intelligence,* **20:**163– 210 (1983).

Alexander, J., and M. Freiling: "Troubleshooting with the Help of an Expert System," *Tech. Rept. CR-85-05,* Artificial Intelligence Department, Computer Research Laboratory, Tektronix, Inc., November 1984.

Allen, E.: *YAPS: Yet Another Production System, Pub. TR-1146,* Department of Computer Science, University of Maryland, College Park, Md., 1983.

Anderson, B., N. Cramer, M. Lineberry, G. Lystad, and R. Stern: "Intelligent Automation of Emergency Procedures for Advanced Fighter Aircraft," *Proceedings of the First Conference on Artificial Intelligence Applications,* IEEE Press, 1984.

Anderson, J.: *The Architecture of Cognition,* Harvard University Press, Cambridge, Mass., 1982.

——— and B. Reiser: "The LISP Tutor," *Byte,* **10**(4) (1985).

Bandler, W.: "Representation and Manipulation of Knowledge in Fuzzy Expert Systems," *Proceedings of the Workshop on Fuzzy Sets and Knowledge-Based Systems,* Queen Mary College, University of London, 1983.

Barr, A., and E. A. Feigenbaum: *The Handbook of Artificial Intelligence,* Vol. I, Kaufman, Los Altos, Calif., 1981.

Beach, S.: "A Comparison of Large Expert System Building Tools," *Sprang-Robinson Report-2,* **2**(10) (October 1986).

Bennett, J.: "ROGET: Acquiring the Conceptual Structure of a Diagnostic Expert System," *Proceedings of the First Conference on Artificial Intelligence Applications,* IEEE Press, 1984.

———: "ROGET: A Knowledge-Based System for Acquiring the Conceptual Structure of a Diagnostic Expert System," *Journal of Automated Reasoning,* **1**(1) (1985).

Bersoff, E., V. Henderson, and S. Siegel: *Software Configuration Management,* Prentice-Hall Englewood-Cliffs, N.J., 1980.

Boose, J.: "A Knowledge Acquisition Program for Expert Systems based on Personal Construct Psychology," *AAAI84,* 1984.

———: "Rapid Acquisition and Combination of Knowledge from Multiple Experts in the Same Domain," *Proceedings of the Second Conference on Artificial Intelligence Applications,* 1985.

——— (ed.): *Proceedings of Knowledge Acquisition for Knowledge-Based Systems Workshop,* AAAI, Banff, Canada, November 1986.

Brachman, R., and J. Schmolze: "An Overview of KL-ONE Knowledge Representation System," *Cognitive Science,* **9**(2) (April 1985*a*).

———: "I Lied About the Trees," *AI Magazine,* **6**(3): 80–93 (Fall 1985*b*).

——— and H. Levesque (eds.): *Readings in Knowledge Representation,* Morgan Kaufmann, Los Altos, Calif., 1985*c*.

Breuer, M., and A. Friedman: *Diagnosis and Reliable Design of Digital Systems,* Computer Science Press, Rockville, N.Y., 1976.

Brownston, L., R. Farrell, E. Kant, and N. Martin: *Programming Expert Systems in OPS5*, Addison-Wesley, Reading, Mass., 1985.

Buchanan, B., and R. Duda: "Principles of Rule-Based Expert Systems," in M. Yovits (ed.), *Advances in Computers*, Vol. 22, Academic Press, New York, 1983.

———— and E. Shortliffe (eds.): *Rule-Based Expert Systems*, Addison-Wesley, Menlo Park, Calif., 1984a.

———— and ————: "Human Engineering of Medical Expert Systems," in B. Buchanan and E. Shortliffe (eds.), *Rule-Based Expert Systems*, Addison-Wesley, Menlo Park, Calif., 1984b.

———— and ————: "Explanation as a Topic of AI Research," in B. Buchanan and E. Shortliffe (eds.), *Rule-Based Expert Systems*, Addison-Wesley, Menlo Park, Calif., 1984c.

————: "Expert Systems: Working Systems and the Research Literature," *Expert Systems*, 3(1):32–51 (January 1986).

Carbonell, J.: "AI in CAI: An Artificial Intelligence Approach to Computer-Assisted Instruction," *IEEE Transactions on Man-Machine Systems*, 11 (1970).

Ceri, S., and G. Gottlob: "Normalization of Relations and Prolog," *CACM*, 29(6):524–544 (June 1986).

Chang, C., and R. Lee: *Symbolic Logic and Mechanical Theorem Proving*, Academic Press, New York, 1973.

Charniak, E., C. Riesbeck, and D. McDermott: "Data Dependencies," in E. Charniak, C. Riesbeck, and D. McDermott, *Artificial Intelligence Programming*, Erlbaum, Hilldale, N.J., 1979.

———— and D. McDermott: *Artificial Intelligence*, Addison-Wesley, Reading, Mass., 1985.

Clancey, W., and R. Letsinger: "NEOMYCIN: Reconfiguring a Rule Based Expert System for Application to Teaching," *LJCAI81*, 1981.

————, D. Warner, D. Wilkins, D. Slemman, and B. Buchanan: "The NEOMYCIN/GUIDON2 Project," *AI Magazine*, Fall 1983a.

————: "The Epistemology of a Rule-Based Expert System—A Framework for Explanation," *Artificial Intelligence*, 20(3) (1983b).

————: "Use of MYCIN's Rules for Tutoring," in B. Buchanan and E. Shortliffe (eds.), *Rule-Based Expert Systems*, Addison-Wesley, Menlo Park, Calif. 1984a.

————: "Classification Problem Solving," *AAAI84*, 1984b.

Clocksin, W., and C. Mellish: *Programming in Prolog*, Springer-Verlag, New York, 1981.

Coelho, H., J. Cotta, and L. Pereira: *How to Solve it With PROLOG*, Laboratorio Nacional de Engenharia Civil, Lisbon, 1980.

Conlon, T.: *Learning Micro-Prolog: A Problem Solving Approach*, Addison-Wesley, Reading, Mass., 1985.

Connell, J., and L. Brice: "Rapid Prototyping," *Datamation*, 30(13) (August 1984).

D'Ambrosio, B., and M. Fehling: "Selection and Construction of Qualitative Constraint-Based Models," *SIGART Newsletter*, July 1985.

Danforth, S., S. Tighe, and S. Redfield: "Novel Languages: Features and Applications," MCC, Inc., Austin, Tex., March 20, 1985.

Davis, M., and H. Putnam: "A Computing Procedure for Quantification Theory," *JACM*, 7 (1960).

————: "The Mathematics of Non-Monotonic Reasoning," *Artificial Intelligence*, 13(1) (1980).

Davis, R., H. Shrobe, W. Hamscher, K. Weickert, M. Shirley, and S. Polit: "Diagnosis Based on Description of Structure and Function," *AAAI82*, August 1982a.

———— and D. Lenat: *Knowledge-Based Systems in Artificial Intelligence*, McGraw-Hill, New York, 1982b.

————: "Problem Solutions with Expert Systems," *Proceedings of the TI Artificial Intelligence Symposium*, Texas Instruments, Dallas, Tex., 1985.

DELTA, "DELTA/CATS-1," The Artificial Intelligence Report, 1(1) (January 1984).

Dijkstra, E.: Presentation at *Fifth Annual Phoenix Conference on Computers and Communications*, IEEE, Phoenix, Ariz., 1986.

Doyle, J.: "A Glimpse of Truth Maintenance," in P. Winston and R. Brown (eds.), *AI: An MIT Perspective*, Vol. 1, MIT Press, Cambridge, Mass., 1979.

———: "A Truth Maintenance System," *Artificial Intelligence,* 12(3) (1979).

——— and P. London: "A Selected Descriptor-Indexed Bibliography to the Literature on Belief Revision," *AI Memo 568,* MIT AI Lab, MIT, Cambridge, Mass., 1980.

———: "Expert Systems without Computers, or Theory and Trust in Artificial Intelligence," *AI Magazine,* 1984.

Dreger, C.: *The Complete Guide to Multimate,* Sybex, Berkeley, Calif., 1984.

DUCK: "DUCK Builds Intelligent Systems," *Applied Artificial Intelligence Reporter,* 2(2) (November 1984).

Duda, R., J. Gaschnig, and P. Hart: "Model Design in the Prospector Consultant System for Mineral Exploration," in D. Michie, (ed.), *Expert Systems in the Microelectronic Age,* Edinburgh University Press, Edinburgh, 1980.

——— and R. Reboh: "AI and Decision Making: The Prospector Experience," in W. Reitman (ed.), *Artificial Intelligence Applications for Business,* Ablex, Norwood, N.J., 1984.

Dym, C. and S. Mittal: "Knowledge Acquisition from Multiple Experts," *AI Magazine,* 7(2) (Summer 1985).

Erman, L.: "The HEARSAY-II Speech-Understanding System: Integrating Knowledge to Resolve Uncertainties," *Computing Surveys,* 2(12): 213–253 (June, 1980).

Feigenbaum, E.: "The Art of Artificial Intelligence: Themes and Case Studies of Knowledge Engineering," *IJCAI5,* 1977.

Fikes, R. and N. Nilsson: "STRIPS: A New Approach to the Application of Theorem Proving to Problem Solving," *Artificial Intelligence,* 2(3,4) (1971).

Findler, N., (ed.): *Associative Networks: Representation and Use of Knowledge by Computer,* Academic Press, New York, 1979.

———, W. Horn, and R. Trappl (eds.), *Progress in Cybernetics and Systems Research,* Vol. XI, McGraw-Hill, New York, 1982.

Fink, P., J. Lusth, and J. Duran: "A General Expert System Design for Diagnostic Problem Solving," *Proceedings of the First Conference on Artificial Intelligence Applications,* IEEE, 1984.

Fletcher, J.: "Intelligent Instructional Systems in Training," in S. Andriole (ed.), *Applications in Artificial Intelligence,* Princeton, N.J., 1985.

Forgy, C.: "Rete: A Fast Algorithm for the Many Pattern Many Object Pattern Match Problem," *Artificial Intelligence,* 19(1) (September 1982).

———: *The OPS83 Report,* Production Systems Technologies, Pittsburgh, Pa., 1984.

Fox, M., B. Allen, and G. Strohm: "Job-Shop Scheduling: An Investigation in Constraint Directed Reasoning," *Proceedings of the Second Annual National Conference on Artificial Intelligence,* Carnegie-Mellon University, August 1982.

Froscher, J., and R. Jacob: "Designing Expert Systems for Ease of Change, Proceedings of Conference on Expert Systems in Government, IEEE *1985.*

Furukawa, K., A. Takeuchi, S. Kunifuji, H. Yasukawa, M. Ohki, and K. Ueda: "MANDALA: A Logic Based Knowledge Programming System," *Proceedings of the International Conference on Fifth Genereation Computer Systems,* 1984.

Gammack, J., and R. Young: "Psychological Techniques for Eliciting Expert Knowledge," in M. Bramer (ed.), *Research and Development in Expert Systems,* Cambridge University Press, Cambridge, 1985.

Genesereth, M.: "The Role of Design Description in Automated Diagnosis," *Artificial Intelligence,* 24 (December, 1984).

Gilmore, J., and K. Pulaski: "A Survey of Expert System Tools," *Proceedings of the Second Conference on Artificial Intelligence Applications,* IEEE *1985.*

Ginsberg, A., and S. Weiss: "SEEK2: A Generalized Approach to Automatic Knowledge Base Refinement," *IJCAI85,* 1985.

Goldstein, I., and R. Roberts: "Using Frames in Scheduling," in P. Winston and R. Brown (eds.), *AI: An MIT Perspective,* Vol. 1, MIT Press, Cambridge, Mass., 1979.

———: "The Genetic Graph: A Representation for the Evolution of Procedural Knowledge," in D. Sleeman and J. Brown (eds.), *Intelligent Tutoring Systems,* Academic Press, New York, 1982.

Gordon, J., and E. Shortliffe: "A Method for Managing Evidential Reasoning in Hierarchal Hypothesis Spaces," *Artificial Intelligence,* 26:323–358 (1985).

Gorry, G., H. Silverman, and S. Pauker: "Capturing Clinical Expertise: A Computer Program That Considers Clinical Responses to Digitalis," *American Journal of Medicine,* **64** (1978).

Grover, M.: "A Pragmatic Knowledge Acquisition Methodology," *IJCAI83,* 1983.

Gupta, M., and E. Sanchez (eds.): *Approximate Reasoning in Decision Analysis,* North-Holland, Amsterdam, 1982.

Hammond, P.: "APES: A User Manual," *Rept. 82/9,* Imperial College, London, May 1983.

Hankins, G., J. Jordan, J. Dumoulin, J. Katz, A. Mulvehill, and J. Requsa: "Expert Mission Planning and Replanning Scheduling System," *Proceedings of the Conference on Expert Systems in Government,* IEEE, 1985.

Hart, P., N. Nilsson, and B. Raphael: "A Formal Basis of the Heuristic Determination of Minimum Cost Paths," *SIGART Newsletter,* **37** (1972).

Hayes-Roth, F., D. Lenat, and D. Waterman: *Building Expert Systems,* Addison-Wesley, Reading, Mass., 1983.

Henderson, P.: *Functional Programming: Application and Implementation,* Prentice-Hall, Englewood Cliffs, N.J., 1980.

Hill, R.: "Automating Knowledge Acquisition from Experts," *Tech. Rept. AI-082-86,* Microelectronics and Computer Technology Corporation, Austin, Tex., March 1986.

Jackson, P.: *Introduction to Expert Systems,* Addison-Wesley, Reading, Mass., 1986, pp. 117–118.

Jacob, R., and J. Froscher: "Developing a Software Engineering Methodology for Rule-Based Systems," *Proceedings of 1985 Conference on Intelligent Systems and Machines,* Oakland University, 1985.

Johnson, P.: "What Kind of Expert Should a System Be?," *Journal of Medicine and Philosophy,* **8** (1983).

Johnson, R.: "Bell Mints First Artificial Intelligence Chip; Engine Uses Fuzzy Logic," *Electronic Engineering Times,* Dec. 16, 1985.

Kahn, G., S. Nowlan, and J. McDermott: "A Foundation for Knowledge Acquisition," *Proceedings of the First Conference on Artificial Intelligence Applications,* IEEE, 1984.

——, ——, and ——: "Strategies for Knowledge Acquisition," *IEEE Transactions on Pattern Analysis and Machine Intelligence,* September 1985*a.*

——, ——, and ——: "MORE: An Intelligent Knowledge Acquisition Tool," *IJCAI85,* 1985*b.*

Kahneman, D., P. Slovic, and A. Tversky: *Judgement Under Uncertainty: Heuristics and Biases,* Cambridge University Press, Cambridge, 1982.

Kandel, A.: *Fuzzy Mathematical Techniques with Applications,* Addison-Wesley, Reading, Mass., 1986.

Karna, A.: "Evaluating Existing Tools for Developing Expert Systems in PC Environment," *Proceedings of the Conference on Expert Systems in Government,* IEEE Press, 1985.

Kearsley, G.: *Artificial Intelligence and Instruction,* Addison-Wesley, Reading, Mass., 1987.

Kelly-Bootle, S.: *The Devil's DP Dictionary,* McGraw-Hill, New York, N.Y., 1981.

Keus, H.: "Prototyping: A More Reasonable Approach to System Development," ACM SIGSOFT, *Software Engineering Notes,* **7**(5) (December 1982).

Kimball, R.: "A Self-Improving Tutor for Symbolic Integration," In D. Sleeman and J. Brown (eds.), *Intelligent Tutoring Systems,* Academic Press, New York, 1982.

Klenk, V.: *Understanding Symbolic Logic,* Prentice-Hall, Englewood Cliffs, N.J., 1983.

Kolodner, J.: *Retrieval and Organizational Strategies in Conceptual Memory: A Computer Model,* Erlbaum, Norwood, N.J., 1984.

Kowalski, R.: "Predicate Logic as a Programming Language," *IFIP74,* pp. 569–574, 1974.

Kuipers, B. J.: "A Frame for Frames," in D. G. Bobrow and A. Collins (eds.), *Representation and Understanding,* Academic Press, New York, 1975.

Lantz, B., W. Bregar, and A. Farley: "An Intelligent CAI System for Teaching Equation Solving," *Journal of Computer-Based Instruction,* **10** (1983).

Lehner, P., and S. Barth: "Expert Systems on Microcomputers," in S. Andriole (ed.), *Applications in Artificial Intelligence*, Petrocelli, Princeton, N.J., 1985.

Lenat, D.: "AM: An Artificial Intelligence Approach to Discovery in Mathematics as Heuristic Search," in R. Davis and D. Lenat, *Knowledge Based Systems in Artificial Intelligence*, McGraw-Hill, New York, 1982.

———, M. Prakash, and M. Shepherd: "CYC: Using Common Sense Knowledge to Overcome Brittleness and Knowledge Acquisition Bottlenecks," *AI Magazine*, 6(4):65–85 (Winter 1986).

Lindsay, R., B. Buchanan, E. Feigenbaum, and J. Lederberg: *Applications of Artificial Intelligence for Organic Chemistry: The Dendral Project*, McGraw-Hill, New York, 1980.

Lipkis, T., and W. Malk: "Knowledge Base Explainer Design Document—CONSUL Project," USC Information Science Institute, 1984.

Lloyd, J.: *Foundations of Logic Programming*, Springer-Verlag, New York, 1984.

Mackworth, A., and E. Freuder: "The Complexity of Some Polynomial Network Consistency Algorithms for Constraint Satisfaction Problems," *Artificial Intelligence*, 25(1) (January 1985).

Maletz, M.: "An Architecture for Consideration of Multiple Faults," *Proceedings of the Second Conference on Artificial Intelligence Applications*, IEEE, 1985.

Marcus, S., J. McDermott, and T. Wang: "Knowledge Acquisition for Constructive Systems," *IJCAI85*, 1985.

Martins, J., and S. Shapiro: "A Model of Belief Revision," *Proceedings of AAAI Workshop on Non-Monotonic Reasoning*, pp. 241–294, *AAAI84*, 1984.

McCarthy, J., and P. J. Hayes: "Some Philosophical Problems From the Standpoint of Artificial Intelligence," in D. Michie and B. Meltzer (eds.), *Machine Intelligence 4*, Edinburgh University Press, Edinburgh, 1969.

McDermott, D., and J. Doyle: "Non-Monotonic Logic I," *Artificial Intelligence*, 13 (April 1980).

McDermott, J.: "R1: An Expert in the Computer System Domain," *AAAI80*, 1980.

———: "RI: A Rule-Based Configurer of Computer Systems," *Artificial Intelligence*, 19:39–88 (1982).

McKeown, K., M. Wish, and K. Mathews: "Tailoring Explanations for the User," *Rept. CUCS-172-85*, Columbia University, 1985.

Mendelson, E.: *Introduction to Mathematical Logic*, 2d ed., Van Nostrand, New York, 1979.

Michie, D., (ed.): *Introductory Readings in Expert Systems*, Gordon and Breach, New York, 1984a.

———, S. Muggleton, C. Riese, and S. Zubrick: "Rulemaster: A Second-Generation Knowledge Engineering Facility," *Proceedings of the First Conference on Artificial Intelligence Applications*, IEEE Press, 1984b.

Miller, M.: "A Structural Planning and Debugging Environment for Elementary Programming," in D. Sleeman and J. Brown (eds.), *Intelligent Tutoring Systems*, Academic Press, New York, 1982.

Minsky, M.: "A Framework for Representing Knowledge," in P. Winston (ed.), *The Psychology of Computer Vision*, McGraw-Hill, New York, 1975.

Mishkoff, H.: *Understanding Artificial Intelligence*, Texas Instruments Publishing, Dallas, Tex., 1985.

Mulsant, B., and D. Servan-Schreier: "Knowledge Engineering: A Daily Activity on a Hospital Ward," *Computers and Biomedical Research*, 17:71–91 (1984).

Neches, R., W. Swarthout, and J. Moore: "Enhanced Maintenance and Explanation of Expert Systems through Explicit Models of Their Development," *Proceedings of the Workshop on Principles of Knowledge-Based Systems*, IEEE Press, 1984.

Newell, A., and H. Simon: "GPS, a Program that Simulates Human Thought," in E. Feigenbaum and J. Feldman (eds.), *Computers and Thought*, McGraw-Hill, New York, 1963.

Nguyen, T., A. Perkins, T. Laffey, and D. Pecora: "Checking an Expert System Knowledge Base for Consistency and Completeness," *IJCAI85*, 1985.

Nii, P., and N. Aiello: "AGE (Attempt to Generalize): A Knowledge-Based Program for Building Knowledge-Based Programs," *IJCAI79*, 1979.

———, E. Feigenbaum, J. Anton, and A. Rockmore: "Signal-to-Signal Transformation: HASP/SIAP Case Study," *AI Magazine*, pp. 23–35, Spring 1982.

———: "The Blackboard Model of Problem Solving," *AI Magazine*, **7**(2):38–53, Summer 1986*a*.

———: "Blackboard Systems Part Two: Blackboard Application Systems," *AI Magazine*, **7**(3):82–104 (1986*b*).

Nilsson, N.: *Problem-Solving Methods in Artificial Intelligence*, McGraw-Hill, New York, 1971.

———: *Principles of Artificial Intelligence*, Tioga, Palo Alto, Calif., 1980.

O'Shea, T.: "A Self-Improving Quadratic Tutor," in D. Sleeman and J. Brown (eds.), *Intelligent Tutoring Systems*, Academic Press, New York, 1982.

Patel-Schneider, P.: "Small Can Be Beautiful in Knowledge Representation," *Proceedings of the Workshop on Principles of Knowledge-Based Systems*, IEEE Press, 1984.

Pau, L.: "Survey of Expert Systems for Fault Detection, Test Generation, and Maintenance," *Expert Systems*, **3**(2):100–111 (April, 1986).

PCAI: *PCAI*, **1**(1) (Spring, 1987).

Pearl, J.: "The Solution for the Branching Factor of the Alpha-Beta Pruning Algorithm and Its Optimality," *CACM*, **25**(8):559–564 (August 1982).

Petrie, C.: "Using Explicit Contradictions to Provide Explanations in a TMS," *MCC Tech. Rept. AI-0100-05*, Microelectronics and Computer Technology Corporation, Austin, Tex., November 1985.

Pople, H.: "The Formulation of Composite Hypotheses in Diagnostic Problem Solving: An Excercise in Synthetic Reasoning," *IJCAI77*, pp. 1030–1037, 1977.

———: "On the Mechanization of Abductive Logic," *IJCAI82*, pp. 147–152, 1982.

Reif, F., and J. Heller: "Knowledge Structure and Problem Solving in Physics," in *Educational Psychology*, **17**(2) (1982).

Rich, E.: *Artificial Intelligence*, McGraw-Hill, New York, 1983.

Rich, C., and R. Waters (eds.): *Readings in Artificial Intelligence and Software Engineering*, Morgan Kaufmann, Los Altos, Calif. 1986.

Robinson, J.: "A Machine-Oriented Logic Based on the Resolution Principle," *JCAM*, **12**(1), 1965.

Rolston, D.: "Maintenance Support Software for a Mainframe-Support Computer," *Proceedings of the Second Annual Phoenix Conference on Computers and Communications*, IEEE Press, March 1983.

———: "DPS90 Configuration through Expert System Application," *Proceedings of Fifth Annual Phoenix Conference on Computers and Communications*, IEEE, March 1986*a*.

———: "An Expert System for Reducing Software Maintenance Costs," *Proceedings of the Second Conference on Expert Systems in Government*, IEEE, 1986*b*.

———: "A Multiparadigm Knowledge-Based System for Diagnosis of Large Mainframe Peripherals," *Proceedings of the Third Conference on Artificial Intelligence Applications*, IEEE Press, February 1987.

Rubinoff, R.: "Explaining Concepts in Expert Systems: The CLEAR System," *Proceedings of the Second Conference on Artificial Intelligence Applications*, IEEE, 1985.

Sacerdoti, E.: "Planning in a Hierarchy of Abstraction Spaces," *Artificial Intelligence*, **5**(2) (Summer, 1974).

———: *A Structure for Plans and Behavior*, Elsevier, New York, 1977.

SAVIOR: "SAVIOR: Expert Systems Meet the Videotex Mass-Market," Expert Systems, **1**(2) (1984).

Schank, R. and R. Abelson: *Scripts, Plans, Goals, and Understanding*, Lawrence Erlbaum, Hillsdale, N.J., 1977.

Schwartz, T.: "AI Hardware and Chips for the Future," *Sprang Robinson Report*, **2**(2) (February 1986).

Shenory, P., and G. Shafer: "Propagating Belief Functions with Local Computations," *IEEE Expert*, **1**(2):43–52 (Fall 1986).

Simon, H.: *The Sciences of the Artificial*, 2d ed., MIT Press, Cambridge, Mass., 1981.

Slater, J., R. Petrossian, and S. Shyam-Sunder: "An Expert Tutor for Rigid Body Mechanics, ATHENA CATS—MACAVITY," *Proceedings of the conference on Expert Systems in Government,* IEEE, 1985.

Sleeman, D., and J. Brown (eds.): *Intelligent Tutoring Systems,* Academic Press, New York, 1982.

Smith, H., P. Fink, and J. Lusth: "Intelligent Tutoring Using the Integrated Diagnostic Model: An Expert System for Diagnostics and Repair," *Proceedings of the Conference on Expert Systems in Government,* IEEE Press, 1985.

Smith, R., and J. Baker: "The Dipmeter Advisor System: A Case Study in Commercial Expert Systems Development," *IJCAI83,* 1983.

Soloway, E., E. Rubin, B. Woolf, J. Bonar, and W. Johnson: "MENO-II: An AI-Based Programming Tutor," *Journal of Computer-Based Instruction,* **10** (1983).

Spiegel, M.: *Probability and Statistics,* McGraw-Hill, New York, 1975.

Steele, G.: *COMMON LISP: Reference Manual,* Digital Press, Billerica, Mass., 1984.

Stefik, M.: "Inferring DNA Structures from Segmentation Data," *Artificial Intelligence,* **11**:85–114 (1978).

———: "Planning with Constraints, MOLGEN: Part 1," *Artificial Intelligence,* **16** (1981).

———, J. Aikins, R. Balzer, J. Benoit, L. Birnbaum, F. Hayes-Roth, and E. Sacerdoti: "The Organization of Expert Systems: A Tutorial," *Artificial Intelligence,* **18**(2) (March 1982).

———, D. Bobrow, and K. Kahn: "Integrating Access-Oriented Programming into a Multiparadigm Environment," *IEEE Software,* **3**(1):10–18 (January 1986).

Stevens, A., A. Collins, and S. Goldin: "Misconceptions in Students' Understanding," in D. Sleeman and J. Brown (eds.), *Intelligent Tutoring Systems,* Academic Press, New York, 1982.

Strandberg, C., D. Abramovich, D. Mitchell, and K. Prill: "PAGE1: A Troubleshooting Aid for Nonimpact Page Printing Systems," *Proceedings of the Second Conference on Artificial Intelligence Applications,* IEEE Press, 1985.

Sussman, G.: *A Computer Model of Skill Acquisition,* Elsevier, New York, 1975.

Suwa, M., A. Scott, and E. Shortliffe: "An Approach to Verifying Completeness and Consistency in a Rule-Based Expert System," *AI Magazine,* Fall 1982.

Swartout, W.: "Explaining and Justifying Expert Consulting Programs," *IJCAI81,* 1981.

——— "XPLAIN: A System for Creating and Explaining Expert Consulting Systems," *Artificial Intelligence,* **21**(3) (September 1983).

Tate, A.: "Interacting Goals and Their Use, *IJCAI75,* 1975.

Turing, A.: "Computing Machinery and Intelligence," in E. Fiegenbaum and J. Feldman (eds.), *Computers and Thought,* McGraw-Hill, New York, 1963.

Wallis, J., and E. Shortliffe: "Customizing Explanation Using Causal Knowledge," in B. Buchanan and E. Shortliffe (eds.), *Rule-Based Expert Systems,* Addison-Wesley, Menlo Park, Calif., 1984.

Waterman, D.: *A Guide to Expert Systems,* Addison-Wesley, Reading, Mass., 1986.

Weiser, M., and J. Shertz: "Programming Problem Representation in Novice and Expert Programmers," *International Journal of Man-Machine Studies,* **19** (1983).

Weiss, S. M., and C. Kulikowski: *A Practical Guide to Designing Expert Systems,* Rowman and Allanheld, Totowa, N.J., 1984.

Wenger, E.: *Artificial Intelligence and Tutoring Systems: Computational Approaches to the Communication of Knowledge,* Morgan Kaufmann, Los Altos, Calif., 1986.

Wiener, J.: "BLAH: A System Which Explains Its Reasoning," *Artificial Intelligence,* **15** (1980).

Wilkins, D.: "Domain-Independent Planning: Representation and Plan Generation," *Artificial Intelligence,* **22**(3) (April 1984).

Williams, M., J. Hollan, and A. Stevens: "An Overview of STEAMER: An Advanced Computer-assisted Instruction System for Propulsion Engineering," *Behavior Research Methods and Instrumentation,* **13** (1981).

Winograd, T.: "Extended Inference Modes in Reasoning by Computer Systems," *Artificial Intelligence,* **13**(1) (1980).

Winston, H. W.: *Artificial Intelligence,* 2d ed., Addison-Wesley, Menlo Park, Calif., 1984.

Winston, P., and B. Horn: *Lisp,* 2d ed., Addison-Wesley, Reading, Mass., 1984.

Wos, L., R. Overbeek, E. Luck, and J. Boyle: *Automated Reasoning,* Prentice-Hall, Englewood-Cliffs, N.J., 1984.

Wright, J., F. Miller, G. Otto, E. Siegfried, G. Vesonder, and J. Zielinski: "ACE: Going from Prototype of Product with an Expert System," *Proceedings of 1984 ACM Annual Conference on the Fifth Generation Challenge,* 1984.

Zadeh L.: "Fuzzy Sets," *Information and Control,* **8:**338–353 (1965).

Zissos, A., and I. Witten: "User Modelling for a Computer Coach: A Case Study," *International Journal of Man-Machine Studies,* **23**(6):729–750 (December 1985).

Index

ABOUT THE AUTHOR

David Rolston is an engineer at ESL, Inc., a subsidiary of TRW, Inc., in Sunnyvale, California. He has been employed in the computer industry for the past twelve years in various capacities, including hardware design, systems and application software development, and technical management. Involved with artificial intelligence since 1981, he has developed several large commercial artificial intelligence systems and served as a consultant for several others.

In addition, Mr. Rolston has created and presented formal courses on artificial intelligence and expert systems as well as published several technical articles. He has also served as a member of the advisory committee on excellence in engineering for artificial intelligence at Arizona State University, where he is presently completing his doctoral dissertation on time-oriented logic.